RENEWALS 45
DATE D

D0405141

DISSIDENT WOMEN

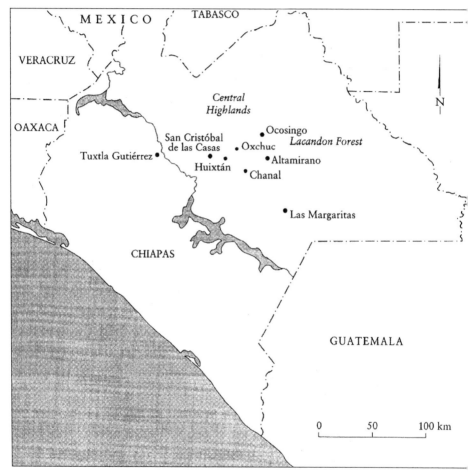

Area of the Zapatista rebellion and the location of Chiapas in Mexico.

BOOK FOURTEEN
Louann Atkins Temple Women & Culture Series
Books about women and families, and their changing role in society

DISSIDENT WOMEN

Gender and Cultural Politics in Chiapas

EDITED BY SHANNON SPEED,
R. AÍDA HERNÁNDEZ CASTILLO,
AND LYNN M. STEPHEN

UNIVERSITY OF TEXAS PRESS

AUSTIN

Copyright © 2006 by the University of Texas Press
All rights reserved
Printed in the United States of America
First edition, 2006

The Louann Atkins Temple Women & Culture Series is supported by
Allison, Doug, Taylor, and Andy Bacon; Margaret, Lawrence, Will,
John, and Annie Temple; Larry Temple; the Temple-Inland Foundation;
and the National Endowment for the Humanities.

The authors gratefully acknowledge a
University Cooperative Society Subvention Grant
awarded by the University of Texas at Austin.

Photographs by Jutta Meier-Wiedenbach

Map on page ii reproduced with permission from:
Lynn Stephen/*Zapata Lives!: Histories and Cultural Politics in Southern
Mexico*/© 2002/The Regents of the University of California

Requests for permission to reproduce material from this work
should be sent to:
Permissions
University of Texas Press
P.O. Box 7819
Austin, TX 78713-7819
www.utexas.edu/utpress/about/bpermission.html

♾ The paper used in this book meets the minimum requirements of ANSI/
NISO Z39.48-1992 (R1997) (Permanence of Paper).

Library of Congress Cataloging-in-Publication Data to come

Dissident women : gender and cultural politics in Chiapas / edited by
Shannon Speed, R. Aída Hernández Castillo, and Lynn M. Stephen.
— 1st. ed.
p.   cm. — (Louann Atkins Temple women & culture series ; bk. 14)
Includes bibliographical references and index.
ISBN-13: 978-0-292-71417-5 (cloth : alk. paper)
ISBN-10: 0-292-71417-3 (cloth : alk. paper)
ISBN-13 978-0-292-71440-3 (pbk. : alk. paper)
ISBN-10: 0-292-71440-8 (pbk. : alk. paper)
1. Maya women—Mexico—Chiapas—Social conditions.
2. Maya women—Mexico—Chiapas—Politics and government.
3. Chiapas (Mexico)—Social conditions. I. Speed, Shannon, 1964–
II. Castillo, R. Aída Hernández. III. Stephen, Lynn.
F1435.3.W55S64 2006
305.800972'75—dc22
2006003689

Library
University of Texas
at San Antonio

Dedicated to the courage, creativity, and vision of the dissident women of Chiapas

~

En memoria de la Comandanta Ramona,
Mujer disidente, que trastocó muchos mundos

WITHDRAWN
UTSA LIBRARIES

CONTENTS

Photo section follows page 114

ACRONYMS AND ABBREVIATIONS

ANCIEZ   Alianza Nacional Campesina Independiente Emiliano Zapata (National Independent Emiliano Zapata Peasant Alliance)

ANIPA   Asamblea Nacional Indígena Plural por la Autonomía (Pluralistic Indigenous National Assembly in Support of Autonomy)

ARIC-UU   Asociación Rural de Interés Colectivo-Union de Uniones (Rural Association of Collective Interest-Union of Unions)

CCRI   Comité Clandestino Revolucionario Indígena (Clandestine Indigenous Revolutionary Committee)

CEB   Comunidades Eclesiales de Base (Ecclesiastical Base Communities)

CEOIC   Consejo Estatal de Organizaciones Indígenas y Campesinas (State Council of Indigenous and Campesino Organizations)

CIAM   Centro de Investigación y Acción para la Mujer (Center for Women's Research and Action)

CIOAC   Central Independiente de Obreros Agrícolas y Campesinos (Independent Center of Agricultural Workers and Peasants)

CNI   Congreso Nacional Indígena (National Indigenous Congress)

CNMI   Congreso Nacional de Mujeres Indígenas (National Congress of Indigenous Women)

COCOPA   Comisión de Concordia y Pacificación (National Commission of Concord and Pacification)

CODIMUJ   Coodinadora Diocesana de Mujeres (Diocesan Council of Women)

CONAMI   Congreso Nacional de Mujeres Indígenas [formerly CNMI] (National Congress of Indigenous Women)

DIF   Sistema para el Desarrollo Integral de la Familia (National System of Integral Development Services of the Family)

EZLN   Ejército Zapatista de Liberación Nacional (Zapatista Army of National Liberation

FNDALIDM Frente Nacional de la Liberación y Derechos de la Mujer (National Front for the Liberation and Rights of Women)

FTAA   Free Trade Area of the Americas

ILO   International Labor Organization

INI   Instituto Nacional Indigenista (National Indigenist Institute)

IUD   Intrauterine device

Maya-ICBG Maya International Cooperative Biodiversity Group

NAFTA   North American Free Trade Agreement

OCEZ   Organización Campesina Emiliano Zapata (Emiliano Zapata Peasant Organization)

OIMI   Organización Independiente de Mujeres Indígenas (Independent Organization of Indigenous Women)

OMIECH   Organización de Médicos Indígenas del Estado de Chiapas (Organization of Indigenous Healers of Chiapas)

PRD   Partido de la Revolución Democrática (Party of the Democratic Revolution)

PRI   Partido Revolucionario Institucional (Institutional Revolutionary Party)

PROGRESA Programa de Educación, Salud y Alimentación (Program for Education, Health, and Nutrition)

PRONASOL Programa Nacional de Solidaridad (National Solidarity Program)

PVEM   Partido Verde Ecologista de Mexico (Green Party of Mexico)

RAPS   Regiones Autónomas Pluriétnicas (Pluriethnic Autonomous Regions)

SER   Servicios del Pueblo Mixe (Services of the Mixe People)

UCIZONI   Unión de Comunidades Indígenas de la Zona Norte del Istmo (Union of Indigenous Communities of the Northern Zone of the Isthmus)

UP   Unión del Pueblo (The People's Union)

UU   Unión de Uniones y Grupos Campesinos Solidarios de Chiapas (Union of Ejidal Unions and United Peasants of Chiapas)

INDIGENOUS ORGANIZING AND THE EZLN IN THE CONTEXT OF NEOLIBERALISM IN MEXICO

LYNN M. STEPHEN, SHANNON SPEED, AND
R. AÍDA HERNÁNDEZ CASTILLO

The public appearance of the Zapatista National Liberation Army (EZLN) in 1994 served as a catalyst in the organization of indigenous women in Mexico. Zapatista women became important advocates of indigenous women's rights through the Women's Revolutionary Law.[1] This charter, written in consultation with Tojola'bal, Chol, Tzotzil, and Tzeltal women who were members of the EZLN, was made public on January 1, 1994, and has been of great symbolic importance for thousands of indigenous women in peasant, political, and cooperative organizations. Women from throughout Mexico have voiced their support for the demands of their *compañeros* (brothers and sisters in struggle) and the collective interests of their communities. Parallel to their participation in the struggle for land and democracy, these women have begun to demand the democratization of gender relations within the family, the community, and social and political organizations. Indigenous women have also developed and practiced strategies of everyday resistance. In some cases, they have been able to appropriate spaces in policy and decision making that previously had been the sole province of the state. Both through collective organizing and through individual actions in their daily lives, indigenous women have been confronting hegemonic ideologies that legitimate and perpetuate the subordination of women.

The women's organizing described in this book has taken place in two key contexts: the most highly developed and coordinated national indigenous movement for self-determination and rights in Mexico's history and the consolidation of the neoliberal economic model in Mexico. Here, we provide a brief description of the political, economic, and cultural context that led to the emergence of the EZLN in 1994 and its links to the neoliberal economic model implemented in the 1980s in Mexico.

ANTECEDENTS OF THE ZAPATISTA UPRISING

The 1960s, 1970s, and 1980s in Chiapas were marked by several distinct processes and events that were critical to the emergence of the Zapatista movement. Samuel Ruiz became bishop of the Catholic diocese of San Cristóbal de las Casas in 1960. In collaboration with Marist priests and nuns he opened up catechist schools, and by the early 1970s he had trained thousands of young, indigenous men and women in liberation theology. In 1974 the statewide Indian Congress organized by Bishop Ruiz with the help of Marist priests and nuns, schoolteachers, catechists, and advisers from the Maoist People's Union (UP), provided the first-ever forum in which 1,230 Tzeltal, Tzotzil, Tojola'bal, and Chol delegates from 327 communities came together to discuss issues of land, commerce, education, and health in their own languages (see Stephen 2002:115–119). Speeches at the congress called for indigenous peoples to unify across ethnic lines, to organize themselves, and to defend their own rights, rather than depend on others. Following the congress, a wide range of new organizations emerged, often under the banner of "peasant" rights and concerns. Outside grassroots organizers from various strands of the left came to encourage the formation of unions of *ejidos,* regional organizations composed of two or more agrarian reform communities that give its constituents more bargaining power as a group.[2] Several of these unions made up primarily of indigenous members formed in Chiapas in the mid-1970s in areas that later became important sites of EZLN organizing (see Harvey 1998:81–82). As these organizations grew, so did the population in the lowland jungle, making it necessary for many communities to petition for extensions of their *ejido* land grants as new generations came of age (see Stephen 2002:120–124).

In 1980 several *ejido* unions combined to produce a larger and more powerful independent organization called the Union of Ejidal Unions and United Peasants of Chiapas (UU; also known as the Union of Unions). The UU, comprising 12,000 families from more than 180 communities, represented a new level of organization for the indigenous peoples of Chiapas. In 1988 the UU joined with other organizations to form the ARIC-Union of Unions (ARIC-UU), which became the de facto subterranean government of a large region of the Lacandon jungle.

The anthropologist Xochitl Leyva Solano (2003) has argued that the emergence of the ARIC-UU resulted in political homogenization that was possible in part because of the absence of political parties in the region and the fact that its membership was almost entirely indigenous—unlike the composition of municipal governments in many other places in Chiapas. The UU-ARIC integrated four paths of change, "the Catholic faith, Guevarist and Maoist socialist ideologies, and an ethnic consciousness opposed to Ladinos [persons of nonindigenous descent]" (Leyva Solano 2003:164). Throughout the highlands and elsewhere in Chiapas, other types of indigenous organizations also prospered, among them writers' cooperatives, radio shows, theater groups, and history projects (see Benjamin 2000).

Mexico's adoption of neoliberalism began in the mid-1980s and was consolidated under the North American Free Trade Agreement (NAFTA). This economic system built on free trade policies benefited a few, but for the most part, it disadvantaged Mexico in relation to the United States; and most Mexicans, especially the rural poor, lost ground. In 1989, when the International Coffee Organization failed to agree on production quotas, prices fell by 50 percent. For the thousands of indigenous small coffee producers in Chiapas, the drop in prices was devastating. The inability of regional peasant organizations that had emerged in the 1970s and 1980s to resolve the problem convinced some to begin to listen to an alternative peasant organization, the Alianza Nacional Campesina Independiente "Emiliano Zapata" (Emiliano Zapata Independent Peasant Alliance), or ANCIEZ, that was serving as a cover for the growing ranks of the clandestine Zapatista National Liberation Army.

NEOLIBERALISM IN MEXICO AND THE EMERGENCE OF THE EZLN

The 1980s, a decade of crisis and change in Mexico, culminated in the conditions that would impel the Zapatista uprising. Mexico's ruling party, the Partido Revolucionario Institucional (Institutional Revolutionary Party), or PRI, had been able to maintain its hegemony for close to seven decades by developing a corporatist state that managed internal dissent through co-optation (and turned to coercion and repression when co-optation failed). Corporatism drew sectors of the population, in particular rebellious sectors, into the state project. For example, labor was drawn in through massive, state-sponsored unions; and indigenous people were engaged principally through the National Indigenous Institute (INI), whose goals were assimilation and modernization. However, the economic crisis of the 1980s left the Mexican state increasingly limited in its capacity to finance such social pacts (Collier 1994).

As in a number of other Latin American countries, neoliberal restructuring under way since the late 1970s was accelerated in the late 1980s. In Mexico, this program was carried out by President Carlos Salinas de Gortari. Mexico began to vie openly for a privileged place in the new global order. Through constitutional reform, policy changes were implemented to open markets (including privatization of sectors of the economy nationalized during the era of Lázaro Cardenas and the opening of Mexican markets to imported goods, such as grains, produced more cheaply in the United States) and to shrink the government's role in providing social services and subsidies. Together, these policy changes dealt a severe blow to many Mexicans, especially rural farmers, who depended on domestic markets to sell their grain and on state subsidies for production. Importantly, they signaled the end of the social pact of public welfare provided by the state that had been established after the revolution. Thus, the changes leading up to NAFTA brought Mexico into the emergent global order, ended decades of corporatist rule, and fundamentally altered relations between the state and civil society.

In late 1991 the Mexican government announced a forthcoming amendment to Article 27 of the Constitution calling for the end of land redistribution and the regularizing of all landholdings. As more than 25 percent of Mexico's unresolved land disputes were centered in Chiapas, the forthcoming reform was not welcome news there. For many, it meant the end of any hope of resolving social inequalities or injustices by petitioning the state for land reform. Soon after the announcement, a new peasant organization, the ANCIEZ, emerged in the Lacandon region, the highlands, and the northern region of Chiapas. It quickly began to pull people away from long-established regional peasant organizations and attracted interest from some catechists as well. Before going underground and reemerging as the EZLN in 1994, it held several large public demonstrations in 1992 to protest the revisions to Article 27, NAFTA, and the celebration of the 500th anniversary of Columbus's landing in the Americas. According to the EZLN, in the intervening two years, communities working with the social organization of the EZLN voted to go to war and prepared to do so. The Women's Revolutionary Law was also developed and debated during this time. It was distributed simultaneously with the first Lacandon declaration of the EZLN.

On January 1, 1994, Mexico awakened to news of the Zapatista rebellion—a rebellion that in many ways had already taken place in Chiapas and now encompassed the rest of the country. Armed and unarmed troops of Tzeltal, Tzotzil, Tojola'bal, Chol, and Mam Indians from the central highlands of Chiapas and the Lacandon jungle had taken over five county seats in Chiapas. The group's name, method, and message invoked the spirit of the Mexican Revolution as it put forward a platform of work, land, housing, food, health, education, independence, liberty, democracy, justice, and peace. Twelve days into an armed confrontation between the very poorly equipped EZLN and the Mexican Army, the government came to the negotiating table.

Soon after the EZLN's public emergence in January 1994, demands for indigenous rights and self-determination began to take center stage in the Zapatistas' negotiations with the government and later grew to include a wide range of indigenous communities, organizations, and movements that eventually consolidated into a national network. The Zapatista rebellion of 1994 initiated a nationwide reassessment of the relationship between the Mexican state and indigenous peoples. On the government side, there were two rounds of peace talks that ended optimistically in February 1996 with the signing of the San Andrés Accords on Indigenous Rights and Culture by the Mexican government and the EZLN. The accords recognize the rights of indigenous peoples to "develop their specific forms of social, cultural, political and economic organization," "to obtain recognition of their internal normative systems for regulation and sanction insofar as they are not contrary to constitutional guarantees and human rights, especially those of women," "to freely designate their representatives within the community as well as in their municipal government bodies as well as the leaders of their *pueblos indígenas* in accordance with the institutions and traditions of each pueblo," and "to promote and develop their languages, cultures, as well as their political, social, economic, religious, and cultural customs and traditions" (San Andrés Accords 1999:35). The accords further specify that the Mexican Constitution should "guarantee the organization of their own elections or leadership selection processes within communities or *pueblos indígenas,* recognize the procedures of cargo systems and other forms of organization, methods of representatives and decision making by assembly and through popular consultation," and "establish that municipal agents or other [local municipal] leaders be elected, or, when appropriate, named by the respective pueblos and communities" (35).

The euphoria following the signing of the accords was short-lived; it became evident that the administration of Ernesto Zedillo had no intention of implementing them. It was not until Vicente Fox took office in 2000—ending more than seven decades of PRI rule—that there was any movement in translating the accords into legislation. However, the outcome was a bitter disappointment to indigenous peoples throughout

Mexico (see Sierra 2002). After a national bus tour by the EZLN that retraced Emiliano Zapata's entry into Mexico City, an address to the Mexican Congress by Tzeltal Comandanta Esthér, and an outpouring of national support for legislation of the 1996 San Andrés Accords, the Mexican Congress passed a greatly watered down version of the original accords that left most of the specifics regarding how indigenous autonomy might be realized to individual state legislatures. Comandanta Esthér's address to the Mexican Congress was a historical first—an indigenous women at the seat of national government addressing primarily nonindigenous officials on the topic of rights and citizenship.

The so-called Law on Indigenous Rights and Culture, approved in April 2001 by the legislative branch and sanctioned by the executive branch, places a series of restrictions on the demands of indigenous peoples for autonomy, betraying the spirit of the San Andrés Accords.[3] Although Zapatista Autonomous Municipalities and Regions had been declared in December 1994, they did not become the heart of the Zapatista project until after the government failed to implement the peace accords it signed in 1996. Communities in Chiapas and elsewhere declared themselves Autonomous Regions and began to implement parallel governments and set up their own systems of education, health care, and agriculture. The declarations and experiments in autonomy at the local level in Chiapas connected to a larger national movement for indigenous self-determination and rights. This is an important part of the context of women's organizing in Chiapas in the 1990s.

After 2000, the Fox administration responded to the demands for autonomy and the broader international movement favoring multiculturalism by making a rhetorical commitment to the cultural rights of indigenous peoples. This "commitment" is manifested not only in legislative reform but also in a series of *indigenista* programs that combine old developmentalism with a liberal multiculturalist discourse having little to do with the real demands of indigenous peoples (see Hernández Castillo, Paz, and Sierra 2004). Borrowing a phrase from the Zapatistas, President Fox promised "Never again a Mexico without you" in the opening of his National Program for the Development of Indigenous Peoples 2001–2006.

In August 2003, the Zapatistas announced the creation of five *caracoles* (literally "spiral shells" but meaning points of communication) that are the seats for five Juntas de Buen Gobierno (Good Governance Councils).[4] Each of the five juntas is composed of one to three delegates from each of the already existing autonomous councils in each zone. Currently there are thirty Zapatista Autonomous Municipalities in Rebellion that are governed by the five juntas. Among other things, the functions of the juntas are to monitor projects and community works in Zapatista Autonomous Municipalities in Rebellion; monitor the implementation of laws that have been agreed to by the communities in their jurisdictions; resolve conflicts and disputes resolution in their jurisdictions; and govern Zapatista territory in rebellion under the logic of *mandar obedeciendo* (rule by obeying), a keystone of "good" governance that holds that authorities are to carry out decisions arrived at by consensus, not make them. At the celebration for the new Juntas de Buen Gobierno, Comandanta Esthér—who addressed the Mexican Congress in 2001 urging them to implement the San Andrés Accords— captured the sentiment of other indigenous women and men who had decided to establish their own systems of government and justice:

> Now we ourselves must exercise our rights. We do not need permission from anyone, especially not from politicians who only deceive the people and steal money. That is why, indigenous brothers and sisters of the people of Mexico, we are calling on all of you to enforce the law of the San Andrés Accords.
>
> We have the right to govern and to govern ourselves according to our own thoughts in every municipality and in every state in the Mexican Republic. No one can prevent us, let alone imprison us, for exercising rights which we deserve. Now is the time to put the autonomy of the indigenous peoples into practice and to act on it throughout the entire country of Mexico. No one needs to ask permission for their autonomous municipalities. (ZNET/Chiapas Watch 2003)

Esthér's words mark the assertion of a system of government and laws governing people's behavior that is redefining the meaning of citizenship as a concept embedded not only in relations between the individual citizen and the state but also in collective identities, rights, and responsibilities determined at the local level and shaped by local ethnic and cultural conventions. Although the five *caracoles* are gathered under the umbrella of one system of regional government, local cultural differences may influence the way communities are governed, the way authority is constituted, and the specifics of local legal systems. Thus while all communities governed by the Juntas de Buen Gobierno must follow Zapatista revolutionary law (the Women's Revolutionary Law, the Agrarian Revolutionary Law,[5] and others), the cultural forms through which these laws are interpreted can vary. For example, in the Tzotzil highland community of Oventik, the traditional authority of elders who assume civil and religious *cargos* (responsibilities) is honored. In lowland Tojola'bal communities, structures emerging from the *ejido* system have more weight in local governance (see chapter 5, this volume; Mattiace 2003b). For women who have often been excluded from traditional forms of government, newer hybrid political forms that involve men, women, and children in community assemblies as well as in formal committees and organizations offer avenues for increased participation. Although women may be empowered by these opportunities (see chapters 5 and 6, this volume), they may also find that discussions that arise on difficult issues, such as domestic violence, do not have the results they desire (see chapters 7 and 8, this volume).

The Zapatista rebellion and the emergence of national networks dedicated to the struggle for indigenous rights and autonomy have deeply marked the 1990s in Mexico in the larger context of economic neoliberalism. Within these two processes, indigenous women have emerged as creative political forces in Mexico, providing new models for governance, for conceptions of citizenship and rights, and for economic development and cultural autonomy. They are dissidents across many spheres of life. This book is dedicated to their spirit, leadership, and inspiring visions of how to build a better and more just world.

NOTES

1. This document, along with three other important statements by indigenous women on the issues discussed in this book, is included in the section "Key Women's Documents" following this preface.

2. *Ejidos* are lands redistributed by the government from large landholders to peasants. They were created after the Mexican Revolution to satisfy the demands of landless peasants who had seen their communal village lands eaten up by large agricultural estates and/or who had served as laborers on those estates. For many communities, *ejido* land refers to territory tied to the community. Since the Mexican Revolution, more than 70 million hectares have been transferred from large estates to slightly more than 3 million peasant beneficiaries. In 1992, however, the Mexican government implemented a revision in Article 27 of the Mexican Constitution that eliminated the government's obligation to redistribute land.

3. For example, the responsibility for determining the form in which the autonomy of indigenous peoples will be recognized is granted to state-level legislatures, the collective right to lands and territories is not recognized, and legal status is denied for their normative systems. As most of the state-level legislatures continue to be under the control of regional caciques (long-term political bosses), the autonomy acknowledged in paragraph A of the second article of

the new law will remain an empty concept if there is no legal backing for its implementation. Perhaps most problematic is that the law deems indigenous peoples subjects of "public interest" (*interés público*), a category also occupied by orphans, rather than "public right or law" (*derecho público*). In this manner, the reforms fail to recognize indigenous collectivities as subjects of legal rights (see Regino 2001).

4. In poetic prose, Subcomandante Marcos introduced the concept "caracol" in July 2003: "They say that the most ancient ones said that others, more ancient than they, appreciated the figure of the *caracol*. They say that they say that they said that the *caracol* represented entering the heart, that this was what the first to have knowledge said. And they say that they say that they said that the *caracol* also represented the heart going forth to walk through the world, that was what they said, the first to live. And not only that, they say that they say that they said that with the *caracol* they called to the collective so that the word would be one and agreement would be born. And they also say that they say that they said that the *caracol* helped the ear to hear even the most distant word. That is what they say that they said" ("Chiapas, la treceava estela: Un caracol," *La Jornada*, July 24, 2003).

5. The Agrarian Revolutionary Law, created by the EZLN, calls for land to be redistributed to all types of people regardless of their political affiliation, religious creed, sex, race, or color; and to be redistributed to landless peasants and farmworkers who apply for it as collective property for the formation of cooperatives, peasant societies, or farms and ranching collectives that must be worked collectively and must be used for production of foods necessary for the Mexican people. Further, individual monopolization of land and means of production are not permitted (EZLN 1999:253–254).

ACKNOWLEDGMENTS

First and foremost, I am grateful to the women of Nicolás Ruiz who generously shared their experiences with me and whose strength and commitment remain an inspiration. To protect their identities, I will not mention them by name. Also, thanks are due to Rubén Moreno Méndez and Herón Moreno Moreno, community human rights defenders, whose help was invaluable in Nicolás Ruiz. The Presidencia Municipal and Bienes Comunales of Nicolás Ruiz facilitated my research in the community, shared their perspectives, and opened their archives to me.

In Chiapas, I am fortunate to find an institutional home at CIESAS-Sureste, and I gratefully acknowledge the support and intellectual community they have provided to me over the years. I also have a home at the Red de Defensores Comunitarios por los Derechos Humanos; my experience with this organization of highly committed indigenous and nonindigenous human rights defenders is the foundation for much of my thinking about Chiapas, indigenous rights, and autonomy.

The research for my contribution to this book was conducted with support from two Mellon Faculty Summer Research Fellowships from the Teresa Lozano Long Institute of Latin American Studies at the University of Texas at Austin and a Social Science Research Council–MacArthur Foundation Fellowship on Peace and Security in a Changing World.

A number of friends and colleagues have contributed to the ideas expressed in this volume; among them are Kathleen Dill, Charlie Hale, Melissa Forbis, and Victoria Sanford. Two women who have had tremendous influence on my thinking on gender issues in Mexico are, I am pleased to say, my coeditors, Aída Hérnandez and Lynn Stephen. I am fortunate to enjoy their friendship and to have had the opportunity to work with them on this volume.

Finally, I wish to thank my husband, Miguel Angel de los Santos, whose love and support sustains me, and my daughter, Camila de los Santos Speed, who brings joy and meaning to my life.

SHANNON SPEED

~

I am grateful to the participants in the collective project under my co-ordination, "New and Old Spaces of Power: Indigenous Women, Collective Organization and Resistance": Patricia Artía, Ixkic Duarte, Margara Millán, Susana Mejía, Beatriz Canabal, Lina Rosa Berrio Palomo, Silvia Soriano, Morna MacLeod, Adriana Terven, Sandra Cañas, and Violeta Zylberberg. They have been a research team but also a support group in which we have shared our theoretical searches and our commitment to a feminist perspective that recognizes cultural and historical differences and believes in the possibility of political alliances. I am also grateful to the members of the CIESAS seminar "Gender and Ethnicity" for their insights, which were fundamental to my contributions to this book.

In Chiapas, my ten years of activism in the San Cristobal de las Casas Women's Group (COLEM) taught me more than any academic seminar on gender studies; I learned from both our achievements and our failures. I am especially grateful to Guadalupe Cárdenas Zitle, Graciela Freyermuth, and Anna María Garza for teaching me three different ways to understand feminist commitment.

In Mexico City, my dear friends and colleagues Teresa Sierra and Olivia Gall helped me to overcome my nostalgia for Chiapas and taught me much during our theoretical dialogues and long conversations about love, life, and motherhood.

Funding for my research and writing was provided by the Center of Advanced Studies in Social Anthropology (CIESAS) and by the Consejo Nacional de Ciencia y Tecnología (CONACYT) (Fellowship 38784-S), which also paid for the translations from Spanish to English included in this book. Maria Vinós skillfully translated three of the chapters, and Alicia Gómez patiently helped us with the secretarial work.

My mother, Doña Chava Castillo Viuda de Hernández, and my four sisters, Alma, Evelia, Angélica, and Alina, were my first women's support group. They taught me about empowerment and everyday forms of resistance. My father, Don Efrén Hernández Flores, and my two brothers, Mario and Efrén, did not understand or share my feminist ideas but always supported me in my nontraditional decisions.

It has been a great pleasure to work with Lynn Stephen and Shannon Speed. This edited volume is proof that three hyperactive and overworked women can accomplish a collective task and preserve solidarity and friendship.

Without the love and support of my two men, Rodrigo and Alejandro, none of my academic work would have been possible.

R. AÍDA HERNÁNDEZ CASTILLO

~

My twenty years of conducting research in Mexico are in many ways reflected in this project. Old friends who continue to be key to my life in Oaxaca include Margarita Dalton, Teresa Pardo, Paola Sesia, and Julia Barco. Juanita Ramírez is a dear friend who helps to make life possible in Oaxaca on a daily basis. Alejandro de Ávila, the father of my children, has provided key support through the years that contributed to this project in both Oaxaca and Chiapas.

In Teotitlán del Valle, my longtime friends and compadres Paco Gonzalez and Petra Vicente and my other compadres Andrés Gutiérrez and Margarita Alavez opened their homes and hearts to me and my family. Efrain Gutiérrez Alavez and Aurora Lazo González have become good friends, and I thank them for their contribution to my new research in Teotitlán. I would especially like to thank a group of women who are active in the cooperatives for their invitation to carry out a new project and for their enthusiasm and support: Aurora Bazan López, Aurora Contreras, Reina González Martínez, Isabel Hernández, Pastora Gutiérrez Reyes, Josefina Jímenez, Guadalupe Ruiz Soza, Fransisca Ruiz García, and Violeta Vásquez Gutiérrez. Moisés Lazo González offered very helpful perspectives on his and other cooperatives' histories and challenges. Arnulfo Mendoza and Mary Jane Gagnier were particularly generous with their time. Finally, I want to thank my old friends Francisco Soza and his family.

In Chiapas, Gabi Vargas-Cetina, Aida Hernández Castillo, Ron Nigh, and Stefan Igor Ayora Díaz provided intellectual support and friendship when I was conducting fieldwork in the 1990s. The men and women of Guadalupe Tepeyac and La Realidad were generous with their time and discussions on several field trips. To protect their identities there, I will not single out particular individuals.

Funding for research and writing was provided by the Center for U.S.-Mexican Studies through the Ejido Reform Research Project, the

Wenner Gren Foundation for Anthropological Research (Grant 6168, in 1997), a National Endowment for the Humanities Fellowship for University Teachers (FA-34700), a research grant from the Center for the Study of Women at the University of Oregon, and a Summer Research Award for Faculty from the University of Oregon.

As always, I treasure the support of my family. My sons, Gabriel and José Angel, were with me on many research trips and provided joy and insight in Mexico and at home. My partner, Ellen Herman, is the reason I am able to do much of what I do; I thank her for ongoing support, love, and commitment.

Finally, I want to express my pleasure at working with my two coeditors and my admiration for their research and intellectual contributions represented here and elsewhere. Our friendship has solidified through our collaboration on this book.   LYNN M. STEPHEN

DISSIDENT WOMEN

KEY WOMEN'S DOCUMENTS

WOMEN'S REVOLUTIONARY LAW

In the just fight for the liberation of our people, the EZLN incorporates women into the revolutionary struggle, regardless of their race, creed, color or political affiliation, requiring only that they share the demands of the exploited people and that they commit to the laws and regulations of the revolution. In addition, taking into account the situation of the woman worker in Mexico, the revolution supports their just demands for equality and justice in the following Women's Revolutionary Law.

First: Women, regardless of their race, creed, color or political affiliation, have the right to participate in the revolutionary struggle in a way determined by their desire and capacity.

Second: Women have the right to work and receive a just salary.

Third: Women have the right to decide the number of children they will have and care for.

Fourth: Women have the right to participate in the affairs of the community and hold positions of authority if they are freely and democratically elected.

Fifth: Women and their children have the right to primary attention in matters of health and nutrition.

Sixth: Women have the right to education.

Seventh: Women have the right to choose their romantic partner, and are not to be forced into marriage.

Eighth: Women shall not be beaten or physically mistreated by their family members or by strangers. Rape and attempted rape will be severely punished.

Ninth: Women will be able to occupy positions of leadership in the organization and hold military ranks in the revolutionary armed forces.

Tenth: Women will have all the rights and obligations elaborated in the Revolutionary Laws and regulations.

WOMEN'S RIGHTS IN OUR TRADITIONS AND CUSTOMS

TRANSLATED BY MARÍA VINÓS

[In May 1994, Tzotzil, Tzeltal, Tojola'bal, and Mam women met in San Cristóbal de las Casas, Chiapas, to make clear to the government and to peasant organizations that women have a great deal to say about constitutional amendments and to offer at the negotiating tables, popular polls, and forums in which these changes are planned and discussed. The document that we reproduce here—for the first time in English—is the product of this encounter. It is a historic document that, with the Women's Revolutionary Law, represents the first written text in which Maya women express their specific gender demands.][1]

We indigenous women have begun to reflect on our rights and the rights of our people. That was the purpose of the workshop "Women's Rights in Our Traditions and Customs." About fifty women from the Tzotzil, Tzeltal, Tojola'bal and Mam ethnic groups came together in the city of San Cristóbal on May 19 and 20. We came from communities in the municipalities of San Juan Chamula, San Cristóbal de las Casas, Motozintla, La Independencia, Oxchuc, Teopisca, Ocosingo, Chenalhó, Chanal, and Pantelhó. We talked about the poverty, discrimination, and injustice suffered by indigenous peoples, and we talked about violence and the mistreatment of women.

We talked of the things we are unable to do now, the things we are prevented from doing. We talked about the rights denied to indigenous peoples and to women by the authorities, by the Kaxlanes [nonindigenous people], by poverty. We talked of the rights denied to women by the community, by our husbands, by our parents, even by ourselves.

5

We have been taught since childhood to be obedient, to silence our complaints, to put up and shut up, to refrain from speaking or participating. But we do not want to be left behind, we do not want to be stepped over. Both as indigenous people and as women, we demand respect for ourselves and for all our rights. We want our customs to be respected, those customs that the community deems are good for women, men, and children alike. We want to take part in the making of laws that take women and indigenous people into account, and which respect our rights. We want to organize more gatherings to reflect together on Article 4 of the Constitution of Mexico, and on other laws, so that indigenous peoples, both men and women, are able to make the law according to our own understanding. With courage and determination we offer this document with our ideas and our proposals to end the mistreatment and injustice suffered by women. In this document we talk first about our lives and our rights, then talk about what we wish Article 4 expressed.

ABOUT OUR LIVES AND RIGHTS

Women must be taken into account. Unless we come to the meetings, we will never be able to change things. We must share our thoughts. Women must participate, not just men. Women can think and decide: we are the same in our bodies and our blood. When we participate and gather with other women, our hearts feel strong. If there is no organizing, no talking, our eyes feel closed. If I don't listen, I don't know how to defend myself: I sit there holding out. The struggle for freedom can take many forms. It can happen with ideas, with participation in our organizations, working for health care; it can happen in the community and in the home. It is important to be determined. Women must have leadership positions in the community and the organizations, and they must be respected by men. All the authorities are men now, but women must come to hold positions of authority. We need women leaders so that we can organize ourselves better, so that the voice of women can be heard loudly, and so that we can have more rights. When we take a leadership position in the community we shall be as committed to the job as are men. It is impossible to advance if we are not committed.

Women don't get the same wages as men. Even though our strength and work are the same, we get less pay. When we make up our minds to look for work we don't get a fair wage; sometimes we are paid as little as eighty new pesos for a full month of domestic service. Or we are offered one amount and paid a different one. In any case, what we are paid is not enough to support ourselves and our children. Rich people want to have employees, but they don't want to pay: we are making them richer with our work. In some communities, women are not allowed to work. Or women must hand their wages over to their husbands, who decide how to spend the money. That is not fair. Work allows us to go out of our communities, to travel, to see and buy things. We want a salary to support ourselves, to buy our clothes and our food. Women have a right to work and to receive a fair wage for our labor, as well as to sell our products at a fair price.

Women have a right to decide how many children to bear, and when to bear them. Women who have too many children suffer in order to raise and feed them. Having children also limits our ability to participate. We women don't want to have too many children: we get very tired, very sick. Our wombs become soft, and we have no strength left to bear the babies. We die in childbirth.

Men want many children because they don't think, they don't care. They don't feel the pain of pregnancy, of childbirth, of raising and feeding children. This is how we are killing ourselves, how we are forcing ourselves to die. Sometimes husbands are angry when we have baby girls, because girls don't go out to work with their papas. There must be agreement between a man and a woman on the number of children wanted. We need to know our bodies to be able to take good care of them. We need education; true and complete information. We need doctors to inform us but not to decide for us. Sometimes doctors ask women to sign papers to agree to have their tubes tied without telling them what they are signing.

It is important that women hold leadership posts, so we can demonstrate that we are valuable, that we are wise. Not just men can think. We women can think just as well—better, because most of us don't drink *posh* [an alcoholic beverage]. Sometimes, when we hold a position, men don't respect us. We want the women who have positions to participate more; we want them to be respected, to be defended, to speak well. We want a woman in a position of authority, because often men are disrespectful and don't listen, and a woman would listen, because she knows the needs, the customs. That woman would have to be someone who knows the law and knows the community. We want to attend school so that we can be chosen for positions of authority. We have gained some space, some of us are chairpersons, treasurers, or secretaries, or participate in other ways in community projects. We women must have determination, courage, and strength. We have the right to participate in the decisions of the community in the election of the municipal agent, the *comisario ejidal,* the municipal president, the governor, or the president of the nation, as in the elections of August 21 this year [1994]. And we can also be elected by the people for any of those posts, or to be teachers or health care workers, or to work in *ejido,* neighborhood, or area organizations.

There are no health clinics in our communities, no doctors. Where there are, they are disrespectful and keep us waiting for a long time. They don't want to let us in because they see we are Indians. Sometimes we are sent away with a prescription, and they don't care if we have the money to get the medicine. Medicines are very expensive in the communities. Those communities that have good health services have women participating on health committees and have midwives. In hospitals they laugh at us; they don't respect our customs, or even try to help us. The worst service is at the IMSS-Solidaridad [government] clinics. It's also expensive to seek attention outside of the community. We need more clinics, more attention, more medicines, better treatment. We want to be given the right drugs, not just any pill that takes the pain away but doesn't cure the ailment. Hospitals and clinics need translators, so that doctors can understand us and give us proper attention. Doctors are paid by the government, but they don't do a good job. The government should pay midwives, because they do very important work for the community, and the women they help are poor and cannot pay. Midwives help women more. Doctors are quick to cut a woman up if the baby is not coming, if the baby is late, or if there is a breach birth. They say that's what the knife is for. A midwife tries to move the baby, tries to help so there can be a good birth. She never cuts with a knife. We want the government to pay for midwives. We want the doctors to help more. Doctors and midwives together could give better care. We also need more food and care when we are pregnant. Women and children have a right to enough food to avoid malnutrition.

Our parents would not allow us to attend school. Education was not compulsory before; our parents were like us, they had no schooling. Parents think it is better to work in the field than to go to school. We don't think like that, because knowledge helps us to work better. We want to send our children to school. But getting to school is expensive, then there are the uniforms, the notebooks—we can't send our children to school if we are poor. We would like schools for adult education in our communities. We don't have any, and we would like to learn. In the few places where the INEA [National Institute for Adult Education] has branches, they only make up lists of names to justify their work and earn their wages, but they don't teach anything. People say when we go to school as adults we are going only to flirt with the teacher. It is important to send our daughters to school, and to go ourselves. Even if we are old women—like some of us here—we can still learn. Women who have attended school should teach the others the little they know. But men say no, women have enough work and have no time for learning. Women are afraid of their husbands. Girls need support to learn. We need to ask for higher education in our communities, because it is very difficult to commute. It is not enough to have schools; we need money to be able to study, and we need schools that teach well. Schools should teach both in Spanish and in our own languages.

Sometimes we are forced into marriage in our communities. Sometimes they trade women for cows. This is not fair. We are mistreated when we are forced into marriage. A daughter's decision should be respected, and marriage should be solely the choice of the couple. When a woman is against a marriage there is trouble, and domestic violence comes easily. The parents are to blame here, for marrying the daughter by force, because it is part of our custom. Sometimes parents want their daughters to serve for a while as their servants, and that is why they won't let them marry even if the man they want offers to pay for them. Women have the right to choose whom they marry and must not be made to marry someone they don't want, or be taken by force, or sold.

Our husbands, children, fathers, mothers, in-laws, brothers-in-law: they must not beat us or mistreat us, and neither must the police, the soldiers, or any person. A husband's beatings are not right; we don't marry to get battered. It is good that a batterer is punished, but jail is not enough. When he comes out of jail, he'll only beat his wife again. The authorities should put these men in jail and grant us a separation and take care that they don't come back, because they could even kill us. Those who attempt to rape a woman or who actually rape her should be severely punished. A rapist should stay in prison for a good long time, far away and outside the community, all the way to Cerro Hueco. We have the right to be protected from rape whether we are single or married. Not even our husbands can force us to lie with them if we don't wish it. Sometimes even our parents don't support us. There are fathers who rape their daughters, brothers who rape their sisters, sons-in-law who rape their mothers-in-law. It is important that women support women.

Women have rights and responsibilities, just as do men. Women should know the law so that it is not exclusively in the hands of men, so that they [men] do not behave proudly. We propose a law that will give property to women, because women also work, eat, and have needs. The youngest men may have land; it should be the same for boys and girls. We ought to have the right to inherit land, to have credit, to have good-quality homes of our own, to promote and direct our own production. Women should have the right to buy and hold land, homes, and everything else, and not be stripped of our possessions by our husbands. Widows should have support to live better, because life is hard.

ABOUT ARTICLE 4 OF THE CONSTITUTION

On January 28, 1992, *Diario Official de la Nación* published the text of an amendment to Article 4 of the Constitution whose first paragraph now reads as follows:

> The Mexican nation has a multicultural composition originally founded on its indigenous peoples. The law shall protect and promote the development of their languages, cultures, ways, customs, resources and specific forms of social organization, and shall guarantee its members effective access to state law. In the actions and procedures regarding land in which they take part, their judicial practices and traditions shall be taken into account in the terms established by law.

The people of Mexico have different traditions, different languages, different ways of dressing. They have different ways of working and celebrating, different organizations and religions, different foods. The homes and the climate in which the peoples of Mexico live are not all the same. There are different ways of thinking. In Chiapas there are Mam, Zoque, Tojola'bal, Tzotzil, Tzeltal, and other ethnic groups. Tzotzil, Tzeltal, Spanish, and Tojola'bal are spoken. The way we live in our communities is also different. Not all our customs are the same, each place has its own tradition. This is the heritage of our ancestors, and we should preserve it. We agree that the law should recognize different ways of living.

Until now the law has not made good on its promise to respect custom. We can't read, and the law has abandoned us. Among ourselves, no one knows the law or what it stands for. When we have problems with the Kaxlanes, the authorities don't listen to us. The courts don't listen when a battered woman wants to make a statement, even if she brings a translator. We are not respected when we travel. When we shop for something, the salespeople don't care what we want; they give us whatever they like. Even other women treat us badly.

The education of men and women should be guaranteed, so that we may learn and know the law. We should be justly protected by the law everywhere in the nation. We need to support our daughters so that they will go to school and learn, so that they will have a better life and won't be humiliated.

It is good that we preserve our language, to show we are indigenous and think differently than those who speak only Spanish. But we need to learn Spanish, so that we can go to other places, so that we are not ashamed and afraid to speak to other people.

People have children and teach them their language, and only that language is spoken. It is only in school that they learn some Spanish. People ask that the teachers teach Spanish. But it is also important that the government pay for teachers who speak our languages and that there are books in our languages. Indigenous women want to have access to primary, secondary, and higher education. We want to go to university. We want to write stories and novels and know the laws that refer to women. We want to learn politics. We want to paint, draw, design clothes, and engage in sports.

Our customs are different. The Kaxlan speaks Spanish. The Kaxlan buys medicine at the pharmacy. We go to healers, cure ourselves with plants and with prayers. We want official medicine to respect traditional medicine. But we also want to have access to doctors who understand our culture and translators to help us communicate with the doctors. We want resources: ambulances, pharmacies, radio communication, good roads to travel, and everything that facilitates our health care.

There are things in our customs that are good. We should work the land with care, to preserve it, and we should not burn the fields. We should not use Gramaxon [a pesticide]. If we don't respect the land, it will gradually die. The food grown with pesticides poisons rather than nurtures our bodies. We should learn to eat healthy food and not canned foods or meat from animals fed chemicals. Our ancestors used manure and organic fertilizers and respected the land. The work of the loom is also good work.

The laws should consider the needs of rural communities. We need support from good programs to sell our products. We want the Regional Funds to continue, in the hands of our people. We want to handle our resources and not have to rely on a middleman or cacique.

We want to continue to organize our social life around communal and *ejido* land, and we don't want to be under pressure to join a political party.

In spite of all the differences, we all deserve respect, and women deserve respect. We are flesh-and-blood people just like the Kaxlan. The Kaxlan is not made of gold or silver. And it is not true, as some mestizos think, that we traditionally eat only vegetables and *pozol*. We want the right to eat meat, to drink milk, to prevent our children from dying of malnutrition and women from dying in childbirth.

If we want to know the law, we must become organized. We need pamphlets, bulletins, radio programs, meetings, all in the language of the community. We need men and women lawyers and translators who can speak our language and understand our culture. If we don't have lawyers, nothing will change. The law must not be written by the lawyers in their offices. Their heart is not in the same place as ours.

It is good that there are laws that support us in our work, that our conversations, our thoughts, and our experiences are shared to make the law better. We want to have meetings and encounters so that we can consider the laws together. We want to speak to the indigenous peoples of Campeche, Yucatán, Sinaloa, and all the other places where there are indigenous peoples, so that it is we who set the law straight.

We also have to think about which of our customs need to be changed. The law should protect and promote only those customs that have been deemed by the communities and organizations, after examination, to be beneficial. Our customs should not hurt anyone. We don't like it when the authorities exclude us from decisions regarding how to distribute the land. The authorities do what they like, and we can't always defend ourselves. We need the law to be enforced, even if we have to rally the support and effort of other communities.

We propose that authorities are elected by the men and women of the community, so that they are people who know our poverty and suffering. We don't want to have caciques. We want to put a stop to so much exploitation.

In some places women are respected; they get land, and when the community has to pitch in to cover costs or help someone who is ill, everyone gives. But it is not so everywhere. In some places daughters don't get anything; only male children inherit land. The problem here is that if the authorities say that women can't own land, Article 4 will allow this. And if we are widowed or have many children, we won't have any land of our own. The custom regarding land needs to be changed, so that it is the same for men and women. We want women to be taken into account in all issues regarding land—credit, land distribution, inheritance. We want production and economic projects that include the construction of roads so that we can sell our products. We need money so that we can pay land taxes, utilities, and services.

Perhaps this amendment goes with the amendment to Article 27, which is not beneficial to women, families, men, or communities.

The authorities of the community do not help women to request credit or to do the paperwork necessary for finding work or housing. They do take us into account at first, when it's about getting approval to receive funds or services from a program, but later, even if we are part of the organization, they forget us. They don't like women to be organized, and they don't let us be signatories. This is why it is important that women become leaders in our organizations.

It is better that we women put down on paper that there are some customs that do not respect us and that we want them changed. Violence—battering and rape—is not right. We don't want to be traded for money. Those are the customs of the past, but we must change them. If we don't want to marry, we should tell our parents and tell the men. We must not be forced into marriage, because this is how women's lives are ruined. Later, if there are children, it's worse. A "custom" that won't allow us to be representatives or to own land is not a good custom. We don't like the custom of men drinking too much, because they fight or batter their wives and spend money that is needed for food. The government itself sets up businesses or gives permits for selling alcohol. We don't want any bad customs.

We feel more confident among other women. We would like to see *compañeras* from other organizations, invite them to talk to women about their rights, teach those women who believe they don't have rights, show them the law, because they are asleep. As they are now, people can take advantage of them and they won't even notice.

Women can take part in meetings and encounters. Women can organize with women from other states or speak to the municipal president, the governor, or the nation's president. The laws could be written correctly, and we can discuss them. We want women to be allowed to participate in any institution and create projects for women, so that we may be well organized to defend our group and our people.

This is the outcome of the first workshop, which lasted two days. There is still much to be said. We need to hear from other municipalities, other communities, other *ejidos,* other indigenous peoples, other women. The government and the organizations must listen to women. Consultations with indigenous people must be more comprehensive and include translators, and they need to be done with respect. And the laws should be made with our own proposals.

NOTE

1. This text was first published in Spanish by the Grupo de Mujeres de San Cristóbal de las Casas in mimeograph form, under the title *Record of the Encounter-Workshop, "Women's Rights in Our Ways and Traditions" San Cristóbal de las Casas, May 19 and 20, 1994, San Cristóbal Women's Group.* Portions were published as "El grito de la luna. Mujeres: Derecho y tradición," *Ojarasca* (August–September 1994). In 1995 the Grupo de Mujeres de San Cristóbal produced a video about the document under the title *Sentimos fuerte nuestro corazón: Los derechos de las mujeres en nuestras costumbres y tradiciones.* The translation of this document into English was sponsored by CONACYT as part of the research project, "New and Old Spaces of Power: Indigenous Women, Collective Organization and Resistance" (38784-S).

COMANDANTA ESTHER: SPEECH BEFORE THE MEXICAN CONGRESS

ORIGINAL TRANSLATION BY IRLANDESA

[On March 28, 2001, after a mobilization involving thousands, four members of the Zapatista Comandancia spoke to the Mexican Congress to ask them to pass a law (called the Cocopa Law) recognizing indigenous rights and culture in the constitution. Here is the first speech from that session.]

Honorable Congress of the Union:

Legislators, Men and Women, from the Political Coordinating Committee of the Chamber of Deputies:

Legislators, Men and Women, from the Joint Committees of Constitutional Issues and of Indigenous Affairs of the Chamber of Deputies:

Legislators, Men and Women, from the Committees of Constitutional Issues, of Indigenous Affairs and of Legislative Studies of the Senate:

Legislators, Men and Women, of the Commission of Concordance and Peace:

Deputies:

Senators:

Brothers and Sisters from the National Indigenous Congress:

Brothers and Sisters of all the Indian Peoples of Mexico:

Brothers and Sisters from other countries:

People of Mexico:

Through my voice speaks the voice of the Zapatista National Liberation Army.

The word that our voice is bringing is an outcry.

But our word is one of respect for this legislative body and for all of those who are listening. You will not receive insults or rudeness from us.

We shall not do the same thing that took place on December 1, 2000, in disrespect of these legislative halls.

The word we bring is true.

We did not come to humiliate anyone.

We did not come to defeat anyone.

We did not come to replace anyone.

We did not come to legislate.

We came so that you could listen to us and we could listen to you.

We came to engage in dialogue.

We realize that our presence in this room led to bitter discussions and confrontations.

There were those who believed we would use this opportunity to insult or to settle overdue accounts, that it was all part of a strategy to gain public popularity.

Those who thought like that are not present.

But there were those who counted on and trusted our word. It was they who opened this door of dialogue for us, and they are the ones who are present.

We are Zapatistas.

We shall not betray the trust and faith that many in this parliament and among the people of Mexico put in our word.

Those who chose to lend an attentive ear to our respectful word won.

Those who chose to close the doors to dialogue because they feared a confrontation lost.

Because the Zapatistas are bringing the word of truth and respect.

Some might have thought that this platform would be occupied by Sup Marcos and that it would be he who would be giving this main message of the Zapatistas.

You can now see that it is not so.

Subcomandante Insurgente Marcos is that, a Subcomandante.

We are the Comandantes, those who lead jointly, the ones who govern our peoples, by obeying.

We gave the Sup and those who share hopes and dreams with him the mission of bringing us to this Congress.

They, our guerreros and guerreras, accomplished that mission, thanks to the support of the popular mobilization in Mexico and in the world.

Now it is our hour.

The respect we are offering the Congress of the Union is one of content, but also of form.

The military chief of a rebel army is not present.

The ones who represent the civilian arm of the EZLN are here, the political and organizational leadership of a legitimate, honest, and consistent movement is here, which is, in addition, a movement that is legal, due to the Law for Dialogue, Conciliation, and a Dignified Peace in Chiapas.

We are thus demonstrating that we are not interested in provoking resentments or suspicions in anyone.

And so it is I, an indigenous woman.

No one will have any reason to feel attacked, humiliated, or degraded by my occupying this podium and speaking today.

Those who are not here now already knew that they would refuse to listen to what an indigenous woman was coming to say to them, and they would refuse to speak because it would be I who was listening to them.

My name is Esther, but that is not important now.

I am a Zapatista, but that is not important at this moment either.

This platform is a symbol.

That is why it caused so much controversy.

That is why we wanted to speak from it, and that is why some did not want us to be here.

And it is also a symbol that it is I, a poor, indigenous, Zapatista woman, who would be having the first word, and that the main message of our word as Zapatistas would be mine.

A few days ago, in these legislative halls, there was a very heated discussion, and, in a very close vote, the majority position won.

Those who thought differently, and worked accordingly, were not sent to jail, nor were they pursued, let alone killed.

Here, in this Congress, there are marked differences, some of them even contradictory, and there is respect for those differences.

But, even with these differences, the Congress does not come apart, is not balkanized, does not fragment into many little congresses, but— and precisely through those differences—its laws are constructed.

And, without losing what makes each individual different, unity is maintained, and, with it, the possibility of advancing by mutual agreement.

That is the country we Zapatistas want.

A country where difference is recognized and respected.

Where being different and thinking differently is no reason for going to jail, for being persecuted, or for dying.

Here, in this legislative hall, there are seven empty places corresponding to the seven indigenous people who could not be present.

And they were not able to be here with us because the difference that makes us indigenous is not recognized or respected.

Of the seven who are absent, one died at the beginning of January 1994, two others are in prison for having opposed the felling of trees, another two are in jail for defending fishing as a means of livelihood and opposing pirate fishermen, and the remaining two have arrest warrants against them for the same reason.

As indigenous people, the seven fought for their rights, and as indigenous people, they were met with death, prison, and persecution.

In this Congress, there are various political forces, and each one of them both joins together and works with complete autonomy.

Their methods of reaching agreements and the rules of their internal coexistence can be looked upon with approval or disapproval, but they are respected, and no one is persecuted for being from one or the other parliamentary wing, for being from the right, from the center, or from the left.

At the point at which it becomes necessary, everyone reaches agreement, and they unite in order to achieve something they believe to be good for the country.

If they are not all in agreement, then the majority reaches agreement, and the minority accepts and works according to the majority agreement.

The legislators are from a political party, from a certain ideological orientation, and they are, at the same time, legislators of all Mexican men and women, regardless of political party or ideology.

That is how we Zapatistas want Mexico to be.

One where indigenous people will be indigenous and Mexican, one where respect for difference is balanced with respect for what makes us equals.

One where difference is not a reason for death, jail, persecution, mockery, humiliation, racism.

One where, always, formed by differences, ours is a sovereign and independent nation.

And not a colony where looting, unfairness, and shame abound.

One where, in the defining moments of our history, all of us rise above the differences to what we have in common, that is, being Mexican.

This is one of those historic moments.

In this Congress the federal Executive does not govern, nor do the Zapatistas.

Nor does any political party govern it.

The Congress of the Union is made up of differences, but everyone has in common the fact of their being legislators and having concern for the national well-being.

That difference and that equality are now presented with the opportunity to see very far ahead and to discern, at the present moment, the hour to come.

Our hour, the hour of the indigenous Mexican, has come.

We are asking that our differences and our being Mexicans be recognized.

Fortunately for the Indian peoples and for the country, a group of legislators like you drew up a proposal for constitutional reforms that safeguards recognition of indigenous peoples, as well as maintaining and reinforcing, along with that recognition, national sovereignty.

That is the "Cocopa Initiative," so named because it was members of the Commission of Concordance and Peace of the Congress of the Union, Deputies and Senators, who drew it up.

We are not unaware of the fact that the Cocopa Initiative has received some criticism.

For the past four years there has been a debate that no other legislative proposal has received throughout the history of the federal legislature in Mexico.

And, in this debate, all the criticisms were scrupulously refuted, both in theory and in practice.

This proposal has been accused of balkanizing the country, ignoring that the country is already divided.

One Mexico that produces wealth, another that appropriates that wealth, and another that has to stretch out its hand for charity.

We, the indigenous peoples, live in this fragmented country, condemned to shame for being the color we are, for the language we speak, the clothes that cover us, the music and dance that speak our sadness and joy, our history.

This proposal is accused of creating Indian reservations, ignoring that we indigenous peoples are already in fact living apart, separated from the rest of Mexicans, and, in addition, in danger of extinction.

This proposal is accused of promoting a backward legal system, ignoring that the current one only promotes confrontation, punishes the poor, and gives impunity to the rich. It condemns our color and turns our language into crime.

This proposal is accused of creating exceptions in political life, ignoring that in the current one the one who governs does not govern, rather he turns his public position into a source of his own wealth, and he knows himself to be beyond punishment and untouchable as long as his term in office lasts.

My indigenous brothers and sisters who will be following me in the use of the word will be speaking of this in more detail.

I would like to speak a little about the criticism of the Cocopa Initiative for legalizing discrimination and marginalization of the indigenous woman.

Deputies, Ladies and Gentlemen.

Senators.

I would like to explain to you the situation of the indigenous woman who is living in our communities, considering that respect for women is supposedly guaranteed in the Constitution.

The situation is very hard.

For many years we have suffered pain, forgetting, contempt, marginalization, and oppression.

We suffer from forgetting because no one remembers us.

They send us to live in the corners of the mountains of the country, so that no one will come any more to visit us or to see how we are living.

Meanwhile, we do not have drinkable water, electricity, schools, dignified housing, roads, clinics—let alone hospitals—while many of our sisters, women, children, and old ones, die from curable illnesses, malnutrition, and childbirth, because there are no clinics or hospitals where they can be treated.

Only in the city, where the rich live, do they indeed have hospitals with good care, and they have all the services.

For us, even in the city, we do not receive any benefits, because we do not have any money. There is no way to come back. If there were, we would not have come to the city. We return to the road, dead already.

Primarily the women, it is they who feel the pain of childbirth. They see their children die in their arms from malnutrition, for lack of care. They also see their children without shoes, without clothing, because they do not have enough money to buy them; because it is they who care for the homes, they see that they do not have enough for food.

They also carry water for two or three hours, walking, with pitchers, carrying their children, and they do everything that is to be done in the kitchen.

From the time we are very young, we begin doing simple things.

When we are older, we go out to work in the fields, to plant, to weed and carry our children.

Meanwhile the men go out to work in the coffee plantations and cane fields, to earn a little money in order to scrape by with their families. Sometimes they do not come back, because they die from illnesses.

They have no time to return to their homes, or, if they do return, they return sick, without money, sometimes already dead.

And so the woman is left with more pain, because she is left alone caring for her children.

We also suffer from contempt and marginalization from the moment we are born, because they do not take good care of us.

Since, as girls, they do not think we are worth anything. We do not know how to think, or work, how to live our lives.

That is why many of us women are illiterate, because we did not have the opportunity to go to school.

And then, when we are a bit older, our fathers force us to marry. It does not matter if we do not want to. They do not ask for our consent.

They abuse our decisions. As women, they beat us; we are mistreated by our own husbands or relatives. We cannot say anything, because they tell us we do not have a right to defend ourselves.

The mestizos and the wealthy mock us indigenous women because of our way of dressing, of speaking, our language, our way of praying and of curing, and for our color, which is the color of the earth we work.

Always in the land, because we live there. Nor do they allow us to participate in any other work.

They say we are filthy, because, since we are indigenous, we do not bathe.

We, the indigenous women, do not have the same opportunities as the men, who have the right to decide everything.

Only they have the right to the land, and women do not have rights since we do not work the land, and since we are not human beings, we suffer inequality.

The bad governments taught us this entire situation.

We indigenous women do not have good food. We do not have dignified housing. We do not have health services or education.

We have no work programs, and so we scrape by in poverty. This poverty is because of abandonment by the government, which has never taken notice of us as indigenous, and they have not taken us into account. They have treated us just like any other thing. They say they send us help like Progresa, but they do so for the purpose of destroying us and dividing us.

And that is simply the way life, and death, is for us, the indigenous women.

And they tell us that the Cocopa Initiative is going to make them marginalize us.

It is the current law that allows them to marginalize us and to humiliate us.

That is why we decided to organize in order to fight as Zapatista women.

In order to change the situation, because we are already tired of so much suffering, without having our rights.

I am not telling you all of this so that you will pity us or come to save us from those abuses.

We have fought to change that, and we will continue to do so.

But we need for our fight to be recognized in the laws, because up until now it has not been recognized.

It is, but only as women, and even then, not fully.

We, in addition to being women, are indigenous, and, as such, we are not recognized.

We know which are good and which are bad uses and customs.

The bad ones are hitting and beating a woman, buying and selling, marrying by force against her will, not being allowed to participate in the assembly, not being able to leave the house.

That is why we want the indigenous rights and culture law to be approved. It is very important for us, the indigenous women of all of Mexico.

It is going to serve for us to be recognized and respected as the women and indigenous we are.

That means that we want our manner of dressing recognized, of speaking, of governing, of organizing, of praying, of curing, our method of working in collectives, of respecting the land and of understanding life, which is nature, of which we are a part.

Our rights as women are also included in this law, so that no longer will it be possible to prevent our participation, our dignity and safety in any kind of work, the same as men.

That is why we want to tell all the Deputies and Senators to carry out their duties, to be true representatives of the people.

You said you were going to serve the people, that you are going to make laws for the people.

Carry out your word, what you committed yourselves to with the people.

It is the moment for approving the Cocopa legislative proposal.

Those who voted for you, and those who did not, but who are also people, continue to thirst for peace, for justice.

Do not allow anyone to any longer put our dignity to shame.

We are asking you as women, as poor, as indigenous people, and as Zapatistas.

Legislators, Ladies and Gentlemen:

You have been sensitive to an outcry that is not only the Zapatistas', or just of the Indian peoples, but of all the people of Mexico.

Not only of those who are poor like us, but also of people of comfortable means.

Your sensitivity as legislators allowed a light to illuminate the dark night in which we indigenous are born, grow up, live, and die.

That light is dialogue.

We are certain that you do not confuse justice with charity.

And that you have known to recognize in our difference the equality that, as human beings and as Mexicans, we share with you and with all the people of Mexico.

We applaud your listening to us, and that is why we want to take advantage of your attentive ear to tell you something important:

The announcement of the military vacating Guadalupe Tepeyac, La Garrucha, and Río Euseba and the measures that are being taken in order to carry this out have not gone unnoticed by the EZLN.

Señor Vicente Fox is responding now to one of the questions that our people made to him through us:

He is the supreme commander of the federal army, and the army follows his orders, for better or worse.

In this case, his orders have been a sign of peace, and that is why we, the Comandantes and Comandantas of the EZLN, are also giving orders of peace to our forces:

First. — We are ordering Subcomandante Insurgente Marcos, as military chief of the regular and irregular forces of the EZLN, to carry out whatever measures are necessary in order to see that no military advance by our troops is made into the positions that have been vacated by the federal army, and for him to order our forces to maintain their current positions in the mountains.

We will not respond to a sign of peace with a sign of war.

Zapatista arms will not replace government arms.

The civilian population living in those places vacated by the federal army has our word that our military forces will not be employed to resolve conflicts or disputes.

We are inviting national and international civil society to set up peace camps and observation posts in those places and to certify in that way that there is no armed presence by the Zapatistas.

Second. — We are giving instructions to architect Fernando Yañez Muñoz to, in the shortest possible time, put himself in contact with the Commission of Concordance and Peace and with government peace commissioner Senator Luis H. Alvarez and to propose that, together, they travel to the southeast state of Chiapas and certify personally that the seven positions are free of all military presence, and, thus, one of the three signs demanded by the EZLN for the resumption of dialogue.

Third. — We are also instructing architect Fernando Yañez Muñoz to become accredited with the federal government headed by Vicente Fox in the capacity of official liaison for the EZLN with the government peace commissioner, and to work in coordination in order to achieve the fulfillment, as quickly as possible, of the two remaining signs so that dialogue may be formally resumed: the release of all Zapatista prisoners and the constitutional recognition of indigenous rights and culture according to the Cocopa legislative proposal.

The federal Executive now has, from this moment on, a secure, trustworthy, and discreet means for making progress on the conditions that will allow direct dialogue between the peace commissioner and the EZLN. We hope he makes good use of him.

Fourth. — We are respectfully requesting the Congress of the Union, given that it is here where the door to dialogue and peace has been opened, to facilitate a place within its walls so that there can be—if the government peace commissioner accepts it—this first meeting between the federal government and the EZLN liaison.

In the event of a refusal by the Congress of the Union, which we would understand, architect Yañez is instructed to see that the meeting is held wherever is considered appropriate, always and when it is a neutral place, and the public is informed as to what is agreed upon there.

Legislators, Ladies and Gentlemen:

In this way we are making clear our desire for dialogue, for the building of accords, and for achieving peace.

If the path to peace in Chiapas can be seen with optimism now, it is thanks to the mobilization of many people in Mexico and in the world.

We would most especially like to thank them.

It has also been made possible by a group of legislators, men and women, who are now in front of me, who have known to open the space, their ears and their hearts, to a word that is legitimate and just.

To a word that has on its side reason, history, truth, and justice, but which, nonetheless, does not yet have the law on its side.

When indigenous rights and culture are constitutionally recognized in accordance with the Cocopa Initiative, the law will begin joining its hour with the hour of the Indian peoples.

The legislators who today opened their door and hearts to us will then have the satisfaction of having fulfilled their duties. And that is not measured in money but in dignity. Then, on that day, millions of Mexican men and women, and those from other countries, will know that all the suffering they have endured during these days, and in those to come, has not been in vain.

And if we are indigenous today, afterward we will be all those others who are dead, persecuted, and imprisoned because of their difference.

Legislators, Ladies and Gentlemen:

I am an indigenous and Zapatista woman.

Through my voice spoke not just the hundreds of thousands of Zapatistas of the Mexican southeast.

Millions of indigenous peoples from throughout the country and the majority of the Mexican people also spoke.

My voice did not lack respect for anyone, but nor did it come to ask for charity.

My voice came to ask for justice, liberty, and democracy for the Indian peoples.

My voice demanded, and demands, the constitutional recognition of our rights and our culture.

And I am going to end my word with a cry that all of you, those who are here and those who are not, are going to be in agreement with:

With the Indian Peoples!

Viva Mexico!

Viva Mexico!

Viva Mexico!

Democracy!

Liberty!

Justice!

From the San Lázaro Legislative Palace, Congress of the Union. Clandestine Revolutionary Indigenous Committee—General Command of the Zapatista National Liberation Army, Mexico, March 2001.

Thank you very much.

INTERNATIONAL DAY
OF THE REBEL WOMAN

Today, March 8, 2001, the international day of rebel women, Zapatista women, through three of their Comandantas who are members of the Clandestine Revolutionary Indigenous Committee—and who are all part of the Zapatista National Liberation Army delegation that is reaching the gates of Mexico City today—say their word.

COMANDANTA ESTHER

To women throughout the country, we are saying let us fight together. We have to fight more because as indigenous we are triply looked down upon: as indigenous women, as women, and as poor women. But women who are not indigenous also suffer. That is why we are inviting all of them to fight, so that we will not continue to suffer. It's not true that women don't know, that they're not good for anything except being in the home. That doesn't happen only in the indigenous communities but also in the cities.

When I was a little girl I was hungry and sick. Even though we didn't eat well, here we are. We go on.

I didn't know how to speak in Spanish. I went to school, but I didn't learn anything there. But when I entered the organization (EZLN) I learned to write and to speak Spanish, the little bit that I know. I'm engaged in the struggle.

Once I grew up I began to see that we didn't have adequate food, that others did and we didn't. Why didn't we? I saw that I had four or five little brothers and sisters who had died, that's when I realized, why were my little brothers and sisters dying? I saw that it was necessary to fight, because if I didn't do anything other brothers would keep on dying, and I decided. And not only me, there are women who decided to be soldiers, and those women now have the insurgent rank of captain, of major, of lieutenant. That's how we saw that women can indeed be strong.

In the beginning, I had to pay a price for the truth. The men didn't understand, even though I always explained to them that it was necessary to fight so that we wouldn't always be dying of hunger. The men didn't like the idea. According to them, women were only good for having children, and they should take care of them.

And there are also some women who have that idea in their heads. Then I didn't like them. Some men said it wasn't good, that women didn't have the right to participate, that women are stupid. Some *compañeras* said, 'I'm stupid.' I always confronted that. I explained to them that it wasn't true, that we are women, but we can do other work. Little by little the men began to understand, and the women also. That's why women are fighting now. That's why you know that in our fight it's not just the men who are fighting here, we're fighting together.

Since the war began, the bad government has been putting the armies in, but the ones who have had to confront that problem are the women. The militarization has been very hard, but the women haven't been afraid. They've gone out to run the soldiers off. And so we've seen that women do have strength, not with weapons, but with strength and with shouts. We see that as women we can be strong.

The truth is that we have resisted, even though it has been years since the war began. Despite the suffering, we are still here. If we hadn't resisted, we wouldn't still be here. Though a lot has happened to us, in spite of that, we haven't surrendered. We've been strong.

As Zapatista women we've made a little progress. We saw that we didn't have anything, and we asked ourselves, Who is going to give us anything if we don't do anything? We ourselves have to work, to help each other in order to have the little we need. The women began working in collectives, then, in bakeries, vegetable gardens, and other things.

Before, women didn't participate in meetings, in the assembly, because their husbands wouldn't let them. The men understand now; women can go to meetings, and men can stay at home taking care of the animals. Now if men see that there's a lot of work in the kitchen, they help their wives or their *compañeras*. They didn't do it before. Now they do. There's a change.

We ourselves explain to the boys and girls that there should be respect, that we are equal. The girls and boys go to school. And not just them, but the older women as well, because they learn well there. The men go also. Because we ourselves are organizing now, and we're not in the government schools anymore but in our own autonomous educational system. We all go there.

I believe we're going to achieve the change we want, if it's going to be achieved, because I see many women organizing themselves. We invite them also, and that way we'll have more strength. We're going to achieve it, with all of us.

We want the San Andrés Accords to be recognized. For us, as indigenous people, they are very important, because as long as we are not recognized we'll continue to be ignored. They don't recognize us, they don't take us into account. We want our method of speaking to be recognized, of dressing, of organizing ourselves. But we aren't going to continue the bad things.

We don't say that [President Vicente] Fox is here now and Mexico has changed now. No. Change itself isn't made by the government. Just because the PRI was brought down doesn't mean that there's going to be change, no matter who wins. We've already seen that. It's the people of Mexico who have to build the change they want.

We see that the Fox government doesn't want to carry out the three signals that we've asked for in order to engage in dialogue: that the troops be withdrawn from 7 of the 259 positions they occupy; that the Zapatista prisoners be released; and that the San Andrés Accords be recognized. They say he's already carried them out, but we see he hasn't.

COMANDANTA YOLANDA

We want the COCOPA Initiative to be approved because it protects women. It says that 'the Indian towns can choose their authorities and exercise their forms of internal government with autonomy, or in accordance with their customs and culture, but always safeguarding the participation of women, who are equal with men.' That means that the participation of indigenous women will be in the Constitution.

The COCOPA Initiative says quite clearly that 'the dignity and safety of women in the resolution of any problems' must be respected. It's true that there are customs that aren't good, drunkenness, for example. That's not good culture, nor is forced marriage. What we are doing is fighting to change it little by little, so that it improves. But in our methods of working, of making crafts and many other things, we have a culture that cannot be lost. We don't want to be a country apart. We want to be included in Mexican law.

Ever since I was little I've had a very hard life in my community and in my family. We didn't have maize or anything to eat. But I hadn't understood the situation. Even I believed that it was like that because the old ones had told a story that suffering exists because God wants it like that, that we must resign ourselves. When I was a bit older, I found the organization's words. Then I realized that it wasn't useful to be resigned, to die like that, in poverty. And that's when I also decided to join the struggle. I began talking with the towns and to encourage other women, until we had a broader understanding that we, as women, have a double suffering. It woke us up quite a bit.

The men are struggling to fully understand what we are asking for as women. We are asking to have rights and for men to give us liberty, and for them to understand that we have to fight for that along with them. We want them to not take our participation here badly, because, before, we never went to meetings and Encuentros. Now just a few of us go, but the path is opening up in all ways. There's more freedom. The men now take our words into consideration, and they understand that we, as women, have a place where we can present everything we feel and everything we are suffering.

We have been resisting for more than seven years, since the declaration of war. This has been quite difficult for us as women, with all the armies. In addition, the armies have caused the appearance of paramilitaries, who hide along the roads. We can't walk along the little roads now. They're there, masked, hiding.

COMANDANTA SUSANA

I've been working with women in the communities of the highlands for many years. I am Tzotzil. Since I'm illiterate and don't even know how to write, it's even more difficult to make the effort to talk. But we're making progress in the towns. I'm not saying it's a lot, but there's progress. As women, we suffer repression within the family, and an even greater one, in that we don't have any right to complain about everything we are suffering, everything we are feeling. There's still much work to be done. I can't say that it's here and everything's fine. More *compañeras* need to participate.

We have suffered from the presence of the armies all these years. And the ones who suffer the most are the women. We can't go out because we're afraid of the soldiers. We can't go out to bring in our firewood, our water, because they're always on the roads. In addition, they abuse the women sometimes. If we go along the road with our little things, they always stop us and search us. They take up our time. They threaten us. They really do make life hard for the women. We don't like their being here. We don't need them, because we know how to take care of ourselves.

We are all fighting together, all of Mexico, not just in Chiapas, not just in these communities. We want national and international civil society to help us. We are calling on everyone, because that's the most important thing.

We have hope that there's going to be a solution, that it's not going to be like this all the time. That the armies will have to get out, return to their barracks.

We've seen that Fox only makes promises, he just says his pretty words, but he doesn't carry them out. He says he's going to get rid of all the armies from the most important places, but he doesn't do it. The truth is that we don't trust Fox. He doesn't want to have dialogue, he just announces it.

We want indigenous rights to be respected, because our language is the most important thing. Because our language is very beautiful, our regional clothing. Because there are a lot of people who aren't wearing the clothing now; they say that they don't want to put it on, that they're ashamed to use it now. There are also people who are ashamed to speak in our own language. I don't think that's right, because we are indigenous, and we aren't going to be ashamed of being what we are, because everything we have is our culture and it's real.

It's not true that we want to be separate from Mexico. What we want is for them to recognize us as the indigenous people we are, but also as Mexicans, since we were born here, we live here.

INTRODUCTION

R. AÍDA HERNÁNDEZ CASTILLO,
LYNN M. STEPHEN, AND SHANNON SPEED

The emergence of indigenous women as new social actors is the expression of a long process of organizing and reflection involving Zapatista and non-Zapatista women that is analyzed by the contributors to this volume, who are activists and anthropologists with long-term field experience in Mayan communities. Through archival research and ethnographic data, they shed light on the emergence of gender-specific demands and the appropriation by indigenous women of discourses of human rights and women's rights. The result is a unique blend of gendered social movement activity that we have put forward as dissident women who defy categorization as traditionally "feminist" or "leftist." These dynamics reflect other transformations that are taking place in indigenous communities: economic change linked to free trade, widespread migration, and experience acquired through organizing that has been gestating since the 1970s. Mayan women have become important political actors in a regional and national indigenous movement, no longer simply accompanying their fathers, spouses, and sons but adding to community demands their own claims as indigenous women and struggling to change the elements of their "traditions" that exclude and oppress them.

DISSIDENTS OF MONOCULTURAL NATIONALISM: GENDER, ETHNICITY, AND NEW FORMS OF CITIZENSHIP

Like other women who have challenged conventional notions of politics narrowly focused on voting and formal political systems, Zapatista women and others inspired by them in Mexico are expanding the arena that constitutes politics and are also exploring new forms of citizenship, rights, and responsibilities. Among the key arenas through which citizenship is being redefined in Mexico are movements for indigenous autonomy and self-determination. The national indigenous autonomy movement has been centered in two national networks, the National Assembly for Autonomy (ANIPA) and the National Indigenous Congress (CNI) (see Gutiérrez and Palomo 1999; Hernández Castillo 1997). The ANIPA and the CNI, unfortunately, have emerged as competing national spaces for indigenous rights. The ANIPA grew out of non-EZLN autonomous municipalities in Chiapas—pluriethnic autonomous regions (RAPs)—based on a model developed by Tojola'bal and other ethnic groups related to that of the Atlantic coast of Nicaragua (Burguete Cal y Mayor 2003; Gómez Nuñez 2000; Díaz Polanco 1991; Mattiace 1998). The CNI came out of the Zapatista experience of autonomy and has been strongly influenced by Oaxacan monoethnic communities that often compete with one another (Stephen 1997b; Lomelí González 2000; Burguete Cal y Mayor 2003). Both of these networks have worked at the local, regional, and national levels to press for the implementation of the San Andrés Accords and have also been the sites of sustained efforts by indigenous women to reexamine what is meant by "indigenous customs and traditions" and to create avenues for increasing women's political participation in community assemblies.

At the national level, the autonomy movements and networks have pushed for the broadening of Mexican political institutions and representative bodies to include indigenous peoples as members and to address their concerns. It is from this dynamic perspective of culture that organized indigenous women are adding their voices to demands for recognition of the cultural, political, and social rights of indigenous peoples. They have joined the Zapatistas in saying "Never again a Mexico without us." This call has been taken up by indigenous women leaders and others who are demanding that the struggle for autonomy grapple seriously and centrally with the wide range of ways in which women have been excluded. They are making it clear that the nation's homogeneous, centralist model is invalid. The promises of equality in the liberal definition of citizenship have lost their appeal to a broad sector of the Mexican population whose freedom to develop "individual capacities" has been restricted by economic marginalization, racism, and the lack of cultural capital to actively exercise the civil, political, and social rights described by T. H. Marshall (1950) and unknown to the majority of indigenous Mexicans.

In both the larger movement for self-determination and women's struggle to attain representation, leadership, and authority, the notions of "social citizenship" and "social rights" have been central. Independent Mexico has distinguished itself from the United States by having granted formal citizenship to indigenous peoples since independence in 1821 (a right the U.S. government did not grant to Native Americans until 1924). However, in Mexico state building entails creating a homogeneous "Mexican" populace through the discourse of *mestizaje*. This notion of a racial mix of Spaniard and Indian into one mestizo race supported assimilationism by rendering Indians as part of the distant past in the national imaginary. The discursive erasure of indigenous peoples was linked to political and legal exclusion from the nation. In the Mexican Constitution, Indians were not recognized and all Mexicans—a homogeneous national identity category—were equal as individuals before law.

As has occurred in many other parts of the world, women and indigenous people have revealed the fallacies in the republican discourse on equality. For the first time in Mexico's political debate, there is recognition of the racism and ethnocentrism concealed in the nationalist discourse on *mestizaje* and citizen equality (Gall 2002). In the name of equality and the need to build a modern, homogeneous, mestizo nation, indigenous peoples were denied the right to speak their own languages, and Spanish was imposed as the national language. Laws they did not understand and that failed to consider the cultural context of the accused were introduced. The authority of their political-religious institutions was not recognized and mestizo municipal authorities, in whom the political and economic power in entire regions was concentrated, were imposed on them. All these impositions were made in the name of the "right to equality." All Mexicans had to be treated equally, without regard to their cultural, economic, and social differences, which were subordinated to this citizenship imposed by law.

In response to the exclusionary discourse of liberal citizenship, the Mexican indigenous movement together with the EZLN have proposed the need to link their demands for autonomy to the recognition of their cultural and political rights as peoples, or *pueblos indígenas*.[1] The struggle for autonomy is not only a struggle against the state but also for the construction of new collective imaginaries that will profoundly change the ethnic, gender, and national identities of participants in the movement as well as in Mexican society overall (Rus, Hernández Castillo, and Mattiace 2003). Moving beyond the formal designation of the individual rights of citizens as part of the nation and as part of the contract between the Mexican state and individual citizens, the movements for indigenous autonomy and of indigenous women are about the recognition of social and cultural rights—both individual and collective—that have not been formally legislated in the Constitution.

In contrast to undocumented Mexican migrants in the United States who are clearly not citizens but who are struggling to be recognized as legitimate political subjects claiming rights for themselves and their children based on their economic and cultural contributions regardless of their official legal status, Mexico's indigenous peoples are legal citizens but are struggling to establish larger social and cultural rights that are not formally defined as part of Mexican citizenship. Susan Eckstein and Timothy Wickham-Crowley (2003:1) point out that struggles for social rights (which might include rights to subsistence protection and social consumption, rights to work-linked benefits, rights based on gender, and rights based on race and ethnicity) are sociologically contingent and "the productions of social construction, negotiation, contestation and possible reconstruction." In addition, they remind us that "both conceptions and the actual enjoyment of rights also hinge on historical circumstances, along with people's positions in social hierarchies and group identities" (1). In the case of Mexico's indigenous peoples, the kind of social rights associated with the current autonomy movements are clearly linked to Mexico's specific colonial heritage, the current peak in the inequitable redistribution of income and wealth in Mexico, electoral processes that recently resulted in the removal of the PRI after seventy years of hegemony, and prior social movements involving peasants, indigenous peoples, women, labor, and other sectors. The specific set of social rights pushed forward by indigenous women is thus bound to specific circumstances within Mexico and the kinds of political openings and opportunities uniquely created from 1994 to the present, including those circumstances stemming from the Zapatista rebellion.

The concept of cultural citizenship associated in anthropology with the work of Renato Rosaldo (1997), William V. Flores and Rina Benmayor (1997), among others (in Mexico, Guillermo de la Peña [1999] has elaborated a similar concept of ethnic citizenship), is useful for understanding the strategy of the movements for indigenous autonomy based in Chiapas and women's place within it. It also suggests a way to reformulate our understanding of "the political" to extend to many cultural and social arenas of life. Cultural citizenship can be understood as everyday activities through which marginalized social groups can claim recognition, public space, and, eventually, specific rights (see Flores and Benmayor 1997). In the case of indigenous Mexicans, the notion of cultural citizenship emphasizes their struggle to achieve not only the enjoyment of rights already assigned to them as Mexican citizens but also to embody the concept of citizenship in culturally grounded terms that recognize ethnic differences and provide legal flexibility in terms of how the rights and responsibilities of citizenship are actualized in local systems of governance, justice, and political economy. Although the concept has not been vindicated by these movements, in practice we can see that their demands point to the construction of a new type of cultural citizenship, in which being different in ethnic or linguistic terms with respect to the community's dominant forms does not jeopardize the right to belong, in the sense of participating in the democratic processes of the nation-state (see Rosaldo 1997).

This is distinguished from the concept of multicultural citizenship as posited by Will Kymlicka (1997) and other liberal theorists of multiculturalism (Taylor 1994). Kymlicka argues that collective rights should be recognized by states, because the individual members of those collectivities have the need and right to have the significance of their cultural contexts taken into account. In other words, individuals can only exercise their right to liberty if they can freely exercise their culture. But in this formulation, the emphasis remains on the individual, and Kymlicka (1997:192) is clear that such group rights should not extend to self-government, which is "a threat to social unity." There has also been a consistent argument within multicultural theory that states should have the right to oversee and intervene in the practices of "minority" cultures when cultural norms violate liberal notions of individual human rights (what Kymlicka terms "external protections" [7]). The question at the heart of this matter is whether a group's rights, in the words of Susan Moller Okin (1999:11), "trump the individual rights of its members." Okin concludes in her influential essay, "Unless women . . . are fully represented in negotiations about group rights, their interests may be harmed rather than promoted by the granting of such rights" (24).

The specifically gendered debate within the cultural citizenship demands of the larger indigenous autonomy movement reflects the problematic of the liberal model that Okin highlighted but also suggests ways of moving beyond it, precisely because women are participating in the debate. During the 1990s, many women and some men were deeply involved in questioning the gender inequalities reflected in federal, state, and local law in relation to indigenous peoples. Women were involved in the process of formulating the San Andrés Accords from 1994 to 1996 (see Gutiérrez and Palomo 1999; Rojas 1996; Lovera and Palomo 1997), in attempting to operationalize autonomous townships in Chiapas, and in the revitalization and interpretation of local *usos y costumbres—*

loosely translated as "customs and traditions." Their questioning of federal and state laws regarding "Indigenous Rights and Culture" as well as local debates about "usos y costumbres" has covered a wide range of issues including domestic violence, forced marriage, equal participation in a wide range of political arenas, rights to housing, education, jobs, and medical care, and land rights (see Gutiérrez and Palomo 1999; Hernández Castillo 1997, 2002a). By insisting that discussions on autonomy address the multiple arenas of home, community, and nation, indigenous women have complicated the project of "Indian autonomy" by maintaining that ethnic rights and women's rights can be protected all at once. While many people have counterposed "ethnic" or "indigenous" rights as collective and women's rights as individual, indigenous women activists do not see this dichotomy and emphasize that both ethnic and gender rights potentially embrace collective and individual rights. Balancing the tensions between individual and collective rights and ethnic and women's rights is at the heart of many of the chapters in this book. Exploring this tension in home, community, and nation, as the contributors do here, provides a horizontal slice of the complexity involved in the everyday struggle of indigenous women to assert their cultural citizenship in a variety of arenas such as in the rights to political participation (see Stephen, Zylberberg Panebiano, Speed, this volume), rights to cultural recognition as healers and keepers of local knowledge (see Forbis, this volume), and rights to decision-making power within social movements at the national government level and internationally (see Blackwell, Hernández Castillo, Millán Moncayo, this volume).

Women in the de facto autonomous communities of Nicolás Ruiz, La Realidad, and Guadalupe Tepeyac (see Speed and Stephen, this volume); the county of 17 de Noviembre, the official township of Altamirano (see Forbis, this volume); and in the regional forums, the National Coordinating Group of Indigenous Women (Coordinadora Nacional de Mujeres Indígenas) and the Continental Network of Indigenous Women (Red Continental de Mujeres Indígenas) (see Millán Moncayo, Hernández Castillo, and Blackwell, this volume), are teaching us how to rethink—from a gender perspective—the politics of cultural recognition of human collectives. Their perspectives break with the dichotomies tradition/modernity, individual rights/collective rights, and domestic/public, and they give us some clues for finding a way out of the old anthropological debates over cultural relativism and conceptual universalism. At one extreme of this debate we find sectors that—based on a conception of culture as a homogeneous entity of shared values and customs that is located on the sidelines in terms of power relations—

propose the need to suspend any value judgment with regard to another culture; and in the political sphere, they often idealize the practices and institutions of cultures considered non-Western (reminiscent of Rousseau's ideal of the Noble Savage that the West continues to look for in its former colonies). At the other extreme we find sectors that, from their liberal perspective, deny the right to having one's own culture and, in the case of Latin America, the rights of indigenous peoples to autonomy; and they justify acculturation and integration on the basis of a vindication of republican values and an equalitarian discourse of citizenship, assumed as universal values. In their political practice and in their everyday struggle, organized indigenous women are trying to move away from this dilemma and are proposing more creative ways to rethink ethnic and gender identities and ways to build an identity politics that considers diversity within diversity.

The studies brought together in this volume illustrate that indigenous women are pointing the way toward a rethinking of multiculturalism and autonomy from a dynamic perspective on culture. Although they demand the right to self-determination, they make this demand from a conception of identity as a historical construction that is taking shape and reformulating itself day by day. Indigenous women are not only constructing cultural citizenship, but differentiated citizenship in which ethnic and gender specificities are taken into account in the construction of a public, heterogeneous space in which interest groups can work together while maintaining their identities (see Young 1990; see also Benhabib 2002).

GENDER AND ZAPATISMO: A DISSIDENT SOCIAL MOVEMENT?

In the 1990s intellectuals writing about social movements frequently debated the meaning of what many termed "new social movements." Ernesto Laclau and Chantall Mouffe (1985), for example, argued that such movements were no longer characterized by their focus on class-based, material demands but were really about creating new forms of democracy that came out of people's experience of multiple subjectivities in which one particular aspect of identity was not the driving force for movements. Others, such as Sonia E. Álvarez, Evelina Dagnino, and Arturo Escobar (1998), wrote about the importance of culture and identity politics as the driving force behind a wide range of movements in Latin America: indigenous rights, gay rights, environmental rights, women's rights. Lisa Lowe and David Lloyd (1997) also explored the rise of cultural politics, emphasizing the relationship between cultural difference and capitalism. They argued that the contradictory and uneven nature of the latest phase of capitalism (postmodernity) opens spaces in which "culture . . . constitutes a site in which the reproduction of contemporary capitalist social relations may be continually contested" (26).[2]

The Zapatista movement has often been termed the first "postmodern" social movement because of its use of the Internet as an organizing tool, its ability to put together national and international networks of support, and its mix of demands for indigenous rights and culture, for humanity, and against neoliberalism. Zapatista women have further complicated the labeling of the movement because of their insistence on examining women's rights in conjunction with ethnic rights for indigenous peoples. It is important to point out that some of the gendered issues raised by Zapatista women are quite consistent with other issues raised by nonindigenous women's movements in Mexico.

The second wave of Mexican feminism of the 1970s was first characterized by consciousness-raising groups of primarily middle-class women who also began to make cross-class connections in 1975, following the United Nations World Conference for International Women's Year. The issues on which feminists initially focused included legalization of abortion, stricter penalties for violence against women, support for rape victims, and connecting the personal and the political. The mid-1970s saw the first feminist publication, the creation of centers for rape victims, and a large number of public demonstrations and assemblies.

The 1970s also saw women's involvement in a range of other kinds of social movements, including relatives of the disappeared led by Rosaria Ibarra, women in leftist political groups, women as a part of liberation theology–inspired Christian base communities, in labor unions, and in grassroots urban organizations. These spaces for women's political participation were not explicitly feminist, and women in them did not come into contact with self-defined feminist organizers in a sustained way until the mid-1980s. The devastating earthquake of 1985 in Mexico City stands as a watershed for social movement organizing in Mexico. The enormous response of Mexico's citizens to the earthquake and the strong presence of women within these responses marks a new era of broader-based feminist organizing as well as the emergence of nongovernmental organizations (NGOs) specifically focused on women. These efforts built on earlier organizing efforts in the 1980s that resulted in several new loosely allied networks that included the Network Against Violence Toward Women, the Feminist Peasant Network, and the Network of Popular Educators (Lamas et al. 1995:336). These networks developed a discourse that by the late 1980s had come to be characterized as *feminismo popular,* or grassroots feminism, an important strain of second wave Mexican feminism that had lasting influence on rural women's organizing. Grassroots feminism "integrates a commitment to basic survival for women and their children with a challenge to the subordination of women to men" and "challenges the assumption that issues of sexual assault, violence against women, and reproductive control are divorced from women's concerns about housing, food, land, and healthcare" (Stephen 1997:2). It was not until the mid-1990s that ethnicity was included as an additional basis for women's inequality in the agenda of Mexico's women's movements, brought to the table by indigenous women from Chiapas and their nonindigenous, often openly feminist allies. The "feminismo popular" of the 1980s and early 1990s is clearly different from the "indigenous feminism" discussed below in terms of its content and origin but similar in the attempt to join women's rights with social rights from another arena.

Prior women's organizing around democracy in Mexico is also part of the context for the position on rights taken by Zapatista women in the 1990s. In 1987 women began to mobilize and participate in a widespread public debate about the importance and meaning of democracy in Mexico. Within organized women's sectors, "democracy at home" as well as "democracy in the government" were topics of heated discussion. Their focus was on building democratic processes at home, at work, and in the political system, working against all forms of violence, and generating conditions (economic and otherwise) that support life beyond survival (Maier 1994:41–45; Stephen 1989). While much of the successful coalition building between women's organizations was centered in the urban areas, the emergence of women's NGOs began to affect the kind of discourse and strategies promoted by some rural organizations that women were part of. Some of these connections also eventually filtered down to Chiapas, where women were a significant part of NGOs formed in the 1980s and 1990s.

The demands and framing of rights by Zapatista women as described here brings with it historical continuity both in terms of specific rural organizing in Chiapas (see Garza Caligaris and Toledo, this volume) and in terms of previous organizing done largely by urban women. The particular political juncture in Mexico that framed the emergence and maintenance of the Zapatista movement in Mexico in the 1990s and after 2000 and its insertion into an ongoing globalization process marked by significant speed-ups and interconnectivity in communications technology have also been significant in giving it a distinct content and strategy, in both its gendered and nongendered manifestations. The specifics of how Zapatista women have framed and organized for their rights is unique in Mexican history—especially with regard to the integration of ethnic and gendered rights as articulated at the grassroots level in indigenous communities in Chiapas. What remains important to keep in mind, however, is that this unique articulation of rights did not grow out of a vacuum but is connected to the larger context of rural and indigenous and feminist organizing in Mexico during the past thirty years.

ANTHROPOLOGIES OF INDIGENOUS WOMEN IN MEXICO

Anthropology of women in the 1970s and later feminist anthropology made it possible for us to hear voices and see experiences that had been silenced and concealed by earlier androcentrism (see Moore 1999). These perspectives illustrated to us the importance of women's work for the reproduction of domestic economies and for the production and reproduction of the labor force in the capitalist system (see Boserup 1970; Goody 1976; Young 1990). They helped us to look at rituals through a different lens, to see the importance of women in various religious traditions, and to see the complementary roles that allow for *cargo* systems (see Collier 1968; Nash 1970). In terms of Mesoamerican ethnography, it was beginning in the 1980s that a new assessment was made of the contexts in which indigenous women exercise power within their own cultures, and we were able to see the way in which this power was affected by changes in the domestic economies from the unequal insertion of these economies in capitalist relations (see Bossen 1983; Ehler 1990; Flood 1994; Nash 1993; Olivera 1989). Most of these works have focused on analyzing everyday life in which resistance and subordination are expressed and, in some cases, contextualizing these dynamics within national and global processes (see Eber 1995; Rosenbaum 1993; Stephen 1991). However, anthropological studies in Chiapas have paid little attention to the collective organizing that indigenous women have been carrying out for several decades now, and which, since the Zapatista uprising in 1994, has become highly visible.[3] This organizing made it possible for indigenous women to participate politically in a new way, and any attempt at silencing them in ethnographic terms became impossible.

Because of women's dramatic emergence into the public consciousness as members of the Zapatista National Liberation Army, some analyses have focused their attention on Zapatista women's role as guerril-las. In *Mujeres de maiz* (1994), Guiomar Rovira was able to give us an extraordinary early picture of the experience of women in the EZLN. Karen Kampwirth (2002) situated Zapatista women's experience in the context of women's participation in guerrilla movements more gener-ally, looking comparatively at Nicaragua, El Salvador, and Cuba, as well as Chiapas. Kampwirth suggests that the participation of women in the Zapatista army was similar in many ways to that of women in the earlier guerrilla movements, for example, in the percentage of women in the dif-ferent guerrilla armies: about 30 percent in each case. But what marked the Mexican case as distinct was the significant fact that the majority of the women participating in the Zapatista army were indigenous. Eber and Kovic (2000) provided a much-needed collection that highlighted the diversity of women's experience in Chiapas since the uprising.

DISSIDENTS OF COMMUNITY NORMS: REINVENTING TRADITION

In this volume we look specifically at women who have taken a dissi-dent position, not just as participants in the Zapatista movement or other organizations, but also in relation to community gender norms. Some of the women represented in this volume have abandoned the roles assigned to them by their culture—not to renounce their identity but rather to reinvent new traditions and reject "bad customs." We could say that these women are also dissidents in relation to a form of nationalism that is exclusive and monocultural and that has concealed its racism for decades behind its discourse on *mestizaje* and acculturation. They are also dissidents in relation to the Mexican state; some of them have opted to confront the state by taking up arms, others through political organiz-ing, thus revealing the limitations of a neoliberal economic model that fails to offer their peoples even the most minimal possibility for survival with dignity.

Each of these dissidences has involved decentering hegemonic dis-courses and confronting the relations of domination present at various scales of power (see Blackwell, this volume). Some of these women have been obliged to pay a high cost for "dissenting," for example, politi-cal violence from the army and paramilitary groups and even domestic violence from their own life partners (see Hernández Castillo 2001). Many others have had to confront subtler forms of symbolic violence: rejection in their communities that is manifested through isolation and

43

rumors circulated by those who consider them a "bad example" for other women in the community to follow (see Artía Rodríguez 2001; Sánchez Nestor 2001; Hernández Castillo and Zylberberg 2004; Speed, this volume).

Various chapters in this volume refer to the Women's Revolutionary Law made public by the EZLN on January 1, 1994, and reproduced here in Section 1. This law recognizes the rights of indigenous women to hold public positions, to inherit land, and to make decisions regarding their own bodies—rights that in many cases imply breaking with community tradition. As Margara Millán Moncayo points out here, this is a law that destabilizes the very core of patriarchal domination, implying a loss of control for the male head of the family in relation to daughters' marriages and material resources, especially land, and giving women the opportunity to exercise local power. This law has symbolic importance, not only for Zapatista women, but also for many indigenous women who view it as a legitimation of the demands around which they have been organizing for several decades (see Garza Caligaris and Toledo and Hernández Castillo, this volume).

Paradoxically, at the same time that these women have been organizing to change community traditions and structures that exclude them, they are demanding the right to their own culture. The contributors to this volume analyze the various organizational contexts in which indigenous women, both Zapatista and non-Zapatista, have taken up the demand for the self-determination of indigenous peoples, while in their communities and organizations they are critically proposing changes in their own normative systems. In response to both autonomous and government discourse, organized indigenous women have pointed to the way in which gender inequalities are equally apparent in national law and in what is referred to as indigenous law (see speech by Comandanta Esthér, Section 1). Confronting the essentialist approaches by some sectors in the Indian movement that mythologize cultural traditions, these women have responded: "This is why we, together with other organized indigenous sisters who persistently advocate for changing customs, say that we want to open up a new path for thinking about customs from another perspective in which our rights are not violated, in which we are allowed our dignity, and we are respected as indigenous women. We want to change the customs that damage our dignity."[4]

By questioning the dichotomy between tradition and modernity, these voices decentered the official discourse on indigenous cultures of indigenism and of many conservative sectors in their own communities, according to which there are only two options—to remain the same through tradition or to change through modernity (see Millán Moncayo and Hernández Castillo, this volume). Through testimonies, political documents, and life histories, we show how indigenous women are vindicating their right to cultural differences while demanding the right to change the traditions that oppress or exclude them.

In response to racist discourse that uses a caricatured, ahistorical vision of what are referred to as "indigenous traditions and customs" to discredit the Zapatista demand for autonomy (see Speed, this volume), indigenous women have pointed to the dynamism of their normative systems, reminding us that these social constructions emerged in contexts of power relations and, like national law, have suffered constant modifications, reflecting the complex social processes experienced by indigenous peoples.[5]

In the Zapatista Autonomous Regions established in large areas of Chiapas under EZLN control, state powers are no longer recognized, and new local power structures and new community normativities have been established, most of which include an opening to participation by women.[6] Lynn Stephen shows us how in the cases of La Realidad and Guadalupe Tepeyac the Tojola'bal women already had skills obtained through their participation in the colonization of the jungle and in the formation of new *ejidos,* as well as in other local power contexts, and this is what made it possible for them to assume the new opportunities for participation opened up by Zapatismo. The new "traditions and customs," such as consensus building in mixed community assemblies (with participation by both men and women), were enriched by the experiences and skills acquired by women in what were considered traditionally female contexts. Violeta Zylberberg suggests the unevenness of the processes of women trying to assume new roles and authority as they make some gains in individual communities while simultaneously facing consistent backlash and resistance both from men and from other women, often female relatives.

These processes of reinventing tradition have been extensively analyzed by historians and anthropologists, especially in regard to their political uses in colonialism (see Hobsbawm and Ranger 1983; Mani 1998). These works have demonstrated to us that we cannot continue to look for the factors determining the validity of traditions by focusing on the point in time in which they originated. In this sense, tradition should be considered not so much a descriptive term of an "essence" but an interpretive term for referring to a process (Handler and Linnekin 1984). Given that cultures are engaged in constant change, when we conceptualize something as being traditional, this does not so much refer to a particular sense of time but rather grants it a specific symbolic value. When a specific practice is conceived of as "tradition," the very contents of the practice are altered. "Cultural categories such as that of tradition have a reflexive nature; we invent them to the degree that we experience them and think about them; the consciousness that people have of them as categories affects their contents" (Linnekin 1982:250). Once we have recognized that traditions and what are referred to as legal customs are socially constructed, the challenge is to identify these constructions in the framework of power relations, and this will make it possible for us to understand why certain inventions are legitimized and others are not (see Ulin 1995). In this book we address the struggle that organized indigenous women are waging in their own communities as well as with the state, with the aim of legitimizing their new traditions.

DISSIDENTS IN RELATION TO THE NEOLIBERAL STATE: DEMANDING AUTONOMY

Indigenous demands for "inclusion" in the Mexican nation go beyond giving indigenous people representation in local, state, and federal governments and a new pact between indigenous citizens and the Mexican state. It includes the recognition of collective rights for indigenous peoples, which suggests a profound transformation in the very conception of the nation—something the neoliberal Mexican state has not been willing to accept. This is in marked contrast to other states in Latin America such as Colombia, Ecuador, Bolivia, and Guatemala that engaged in constitutional reform to recognize collective rights for indigenous peoples precisely in the process of neoliberalizing.

That the Zapatista movement made itself known publicly on January 1, 1994—on precisely the day the free trade agreement between Mexico, the United States, and Canada went into effect—made explicit its intention to link the struggle for indigenous rights with an anti-neoliberal struggle. The Zapatistas have focused their demands on achieving recognition of the political and cultural rights of indigenous peoples and to simultaneously promote the distribution of wealth by rejecting the economic model promoted by financial agencies such as the International Monetary Fund and the World Bank. In the ten-year political struggle following the ten days of armed confrontation with Mexico's national army, the EZLN has become a symbol around the world of the fight against neoliberalism. The Forum Against Neoliberalism and for Humanity, held in 1997 in the heart of the Lacandon jungle and attended by representatives from social movements in five continents, has been followed by many other initiatives, including the formation of regional coalitions against macrodevelopment projects such as the Plan Puebla Panama and trade agreements such as the Free Trade Area of the Americas (FTAA). In all these contexts, indigenous women have actively participated, taking their specific experiences of the way that economic policies are affecting their daily lives to roundtable sessions and workshop discussions (see Blackwell, this volume).

The Zapatistas' political agenda has revealed the false dichotomy between recognition of cultural rights and redistribution of wealth. On one side are those who prioritize redistribution and focus on the struggle for economic equality and against labor exploitation while often disregarding the importance of cultural demands. On the other side are those social movements that give exclusive (or nearly exclusive) priority to the struggle against cultural domination and to the vindication of differences founded on nationality, ethnicity, gender, and sexuality (see Fraser 1996; Hobsbawm 1996) while leaving behind any reference to economic inequality.

The Zapatista movement's demand for autonomy, which has been taken up by a major sector of the national indigenous movement, synthesizes the search for cultural recognition with redistribution of wealth. From the Zapatistas' perspective, advocating autonomy entails the need to promote sustainable development that takes into account indigenous traditional agricultural practices and also other proposals for organic agriculture, thus confronting agrochemical transnational corporations. This is not easy to do, and many indigenous communities have come to believe that petrochemical inputs and mechanized agriculture are better than all traditional methods. The EZLN also proposes an economic autonomy that will allow them to appropriate the means for marketing their basic products such as coffee, eliminating the need for intermediaries. The vindication of their normative systems and forms of government places doubt on whether electoral democracy is the only road to broad-based political participation. By demanding recognition for their indigenous languages and cultural practices, they are not only asking for new legislation in this regard but also proposing the need to restructure the educational and health systems at the national level, to include recognition of diversity.[7]

Further, alongside their demands to the state, the Zapatistas have continued to pursue their autonomy project unilaterally, in practice. Given the government's reticence about recognizing indigenous rights and autonomy (as reflected in the Indigenous Law of 2001 that effectively set indigenous rights back in Mexico), the Zapatistas are now defining their autonomy without the component of state recognition. This is a significant departure from the constitutionalist models that have accompanied the establishment of indigenous rights in other neoliberalizing Latin American countries, such as Nicaragua, Colombia, Ecuador, and Bolivia (see Van Cott 2000a, 2001), and may reflect new directions in the definition and pursuit of indigenous autonomy.

ENGAGED FEMINIST ANTHROPOLOGY

The contributors to this volume share a commitment to the struggle for indigenous rights and for gender equality. Feminist theory, unlike some other forms of theorizing, is always explicitly tied to political struggle—the struggle for gender justice. In a recent volume titled *Gender's Place: Feminist Anthropologies of Latin America,* Rosario Montoya, Leslie Jo Frazier, and Janise Hurtig argue that "gendered ethnographic accounts produce critical analysis toward social change" because of the ethnographers' long-term commitment to and ongoing relationships with the communities involved, combined with "a methodological and political principle" of directly engaging our "ethnographic subjects" (2002:4, 5).

But our feminist engagement is based in a political perspective that considers the plurality of experiences that mark gender identities. Several postcolonial feminists have coincided in pointing out that academic feminist discourses reproduce the same problems as modernist metadiscourses when, through an ethnocentric and heterosexist perspective, they assume that the experience of Western, white, middle-class women is the experience of women in general (see Alarcón 1990; Alexander and Mohanty 1997; Mohanty 1991; Trinh 1988).

We recognize that these "sisterhood"-promoting metanarratives can debilitate feminist struggle by excluding the experiences of other women and, by focusing exclusive analytic attention on a homogeneous understanding of gender as the main axis of domination, fail to create the necessary conditions to establish broader political alliances. An engaged feminist ethnography must recognize cultural and historical differences with the goal of being able to build larger political alliances.

Kay Warren and Jean Jackson (2002:3) suggest that the challenge for us as anthropologists is to "document more fully than other observers can" indigenous activism. Here, we would like to contribute a fine-grained anthropological documentation of the struggle of indigenous women for their rights, and to do so in a way that is "engaged," taking into consideration the politics of doing anthropological field research, representing others in our writing, and of the knowledge we produce. While pursuing different modes of engagement, the contributors to this volume share a commitment to the individuals, communities, and organizations that are the focus of our research. We seek to bring a critical analysis to processes of change to which we are, sometimes directly, often indirectly, committed. At times combining scholarly pursuits with other forms of activism, we also recognize that the knowledge we produce has political effects (whether intended or not) and thus can contribute to social change. In the latter sense, our research is what Hale (2001) calls "activist research," in which "activist" is an adjective modifying research; it is thus not scholarship by researchers who are activists on the side but rather by researchers committed to creating knowledge that is of use to their "subjects" in struggles that they (the researchers) support.

An engaged approach also compels us to continually recognize the power differentials that inhere in the relationships we form with our collaborators in the field. While we may share some political goals and commitments, in many cases the researcher enjoys greater access to resources, greater mobility, and greater valorization of their forms of knowledge and communication. We cannot eliminate these inequities, but it is nonetheless important to keep them visible and open to discussion when possible throughout the research process. We share a conviction that a committed, engaged feminist research can contribute to greater social justice in both the forms of research it undertakes and the knowledge it produces.

THE STRUCTURE OF THE BOOK

This volume is organized in three sections. The first section highlights four key documents, The Women's Revolutionary Law, Comandanta Esther's 2001 speech to the Mexican National Congress, Women's Rights in Our Traditions and Customs, and statements by three members of the Clandestine Revolutionary Indigenous Committee on the occasion of the International Day of the Rebel Woman, March 8, 2001.

The second section presents broad, historical discussions, preparing the terrain for the more focused ethnographic case studies of the third section. Below are brief descriptions of Sections 2 and 3.

Section Two: Indigenous Women's Organizing in Chiapas and Mexico: Historical Trajectories, Border Crossings

This section opens with an analysis by R. Aída Hernández Castillo of the impact of the Zapatista uprising on the emergence of a national indigenous women's movement. This movement incorporates women from different indigenous regions of Mexico who are working together through the Coordinadora Nacional de Mujeres Indígenas (National Council of Indigenous Women, CNMI) and have taken up the challenge of reconciling two of the main demands of the Zapatista movement: the recognition of indigenous self-determination and a critical rethinking of prevailing normative gender systems. Hernández Castillo describes how the women in this movement are claiming the right to their own culture, but from an expanded definition of culture, and through their struggle are redefining the concept of multiculturalism from a gendered perspective, thus challenging cultural reductionism and contributing to the national debate about cultural citizenship and collective versus individual rights.

Through a case study in a Tojola'bal community in Chiapas, Margara Millán Moncayo analyzes the ways in which "Zapatismo" has made an impact on how "Indianness," or indigenous ethnicity, is now understood in Mexico and the ways in which gender has only been partially incorporated into that discussion. Like Hernández Castillo, she notes the two distinct types of rights implied in Zapatista discourse—women's and indigenous—and suggests that the political strategies attached to these two types of rights have not been well integrated. This chapter points to the difficulties that the mobilization of women and the Zapatista discourse of gender equity have created, noting that in many communities they have produced multiple tensions and contradictions. The author argues through a case study in one community that while creating new spaces of participation for young women, the Zapatista movement has also redefined the terms of their subordination to older men and women and to their partners.

Anna María Garza Caligaris and Sonia Toledo Tello's genealogy of women's organizing in Chiapas provides the context out of which the post-Zapatista (after 1994) organizing emerged. They follow the processes in which, during the 1970s and 1980s, Chiapas (as other states in Mexico) was shaken by intense social mobilizations. This chapter demonstrates that women actively participated in peasant and indigenous organizations, even if they were not at that time making claims of their own, and that these experiences were the early part of the political training of many of those who today make up the women's movements in the state. By exploring three key political events of the 1980s, the analysis highlights the tension between the stereotypes of women projected in these key events and the concrete political experiences women feel they gained by participating in them. Emphasizing the continuities between these past organizations and new ones formed in the past decade, the authors illustrate the roots of some of the specific demands and strategies present in contemporary indigenous women's organizing in Chiapas.

We close this section with Maylei Blackwell's chapter, which widens the lens of gender and cultural politics in Chiapas to the transnational arena by tracing the powerful reverberations of women's presence in the EZLN and the formation of the national indigenous women's movement in Mexico. The analysis focuses on how indigenous women, as the most marginalized sector of Mexican society, weave in and between local, national, and transnational scales of power to create new spaces of participation as well as new forms of consciousness, identities, and discourse. Blackwell suggests how indigenous women organizers are effectively using interstitial spaces to create new modes of participation and organizational spaces at the intersections of local, regional, and national politics.

Section Three: Rights and Gender in Ethnographic Context

In this section, we move to the local level in fine-grained case studies of the differential gendered impact of Zapatismo in specific communities. Lynn Stephen's chapter compares indigenous women's political activism in a Zapotec community in Oaxaca with that of the women in a Tojola'bal Zapatista community in Chiapas in order to answer the question of what makes the organizing successful in each case. Looking at community-specific gender roles for women in what have often been called "traditional" forms of local governance and at how women's roles in such institutions interact with other forms of organizing at the local level, Stephen suggests that the capacity for indigenous women to be successful in opening up local political systems to their participation and leadership is predicated on the recognition of specific skills and experience they develop in local, ethnic-linked forms of governance—even if such systems formally exclude women. She argues that such capacity is rooted in their ability to connect local gendered contests over political power and ethnic and cultural rights with regional and national forms of association that offer a different set of gendered political roles and often emphasize a specific ethnic identity or a pan-indigenous form of identity as a basis for organization.

Melissa M. Forbis analyzes how women health promoters (*promotoras*) working in the Zapatista Autonomous Municipalities in Chiapas have begun the process of recuperating traditional medical knowledge as part of a movement toward community self-sufficiency. These *promotoras* characterize themselves as healers who are working collectively and using local natural resources in service to their communities. The valorization of this work by the Autonomous Municipalities has strengthened local indigenous identities through a linkage to "ancestral knowledge" and to local intellectual property rights. In describing the personal consequences of their mobilizations and how this work has opened up other spaces for women's organizing, Forbis argues that this work has enabled women to confront and renegotiate gender and ethnic relations within their families, their communities, and beyond.

Shannon Speed considers the recent organizing of women in one community, where a conflict between women's groups reflects larger dynamics of reemergent ethnic identifications, newly voiced gender demands, and ultimately the contentious issue of collective versus individual rights. Speed argues that indigenous women—in their insistence on struggling simultaneously for their communities' collective right to define themselves and determine their own futures and for change within the community to meet their gender demands as individual women—are rendering an individual rights/collective rights dichotomy irrelevant. She further suggests that by refusing to separate out the various aspects of their experience as human beings and members of a community into the conceptual categories of liberal legal thought (individual vs. collective rights), these women are also challenging the precepts that underpin the logic of the neoliberal state in Mexico.

Section Three closes with Violeta Zylberberg Panebiano's exploration, through a case study of a Tzeltal community in the Lacandon rain forest, of some of the challenges that Zapatista communities have faced in their attempts to eliminate gender inequality. Since the introduction of the Women's Revolutionary Law in the community in 1994, some community norms have changed. Zylberberg Panebiano describes, for example, how domestic violence has decreased but has not vanished as some women are still afraid of male retaliation. One of the most significant changes in the community has been to raise the age of marriage from fourteen to sixteen years of age to twenty or older. Younger women are now choosing their own spouses and even have access to birth control pills. Such changes are significant, but they exist in an overall context in which women often have to continue to fight for their rights both in their community and in the larger region they live in.

Taken together, these chapters bring historical and ethnographic depth to the processes of social construction and social change that characterize the situation of indigenous women in Chiapas today. Mapping both the ways in which indigenous women's dissident discourses and actions can disrupt, challenge, and potentially transform oppressive power relations and the manner in which power relations become reconfigured and reinscribed in new forms, the volume highlights indigenous women's agency in creating their own futures in complex and contradictory terrain. Because we agree with Chandra Talpade Mohanty (2003:33) that "it is only by understanding the contradictions inherent in women's location within various structures that effective political action and challenges can be devised," we offer this mapping of women's multiple locations to provide critical understandings toward more effective political action and greater social justice.

NOTES

1. The word *pueblos* in Spanish has multiple meanings: indigenous nations, indigenous peoples, or specific indigenous communities. In this discourse, it refers to indigenous peoples.

2. Charles R. Hale (2004:3) has deemed this view "dangerously sanguine" because it seriously underestimates the extent to which these collective actions have already been *acted upon,* yielding political spaces that are at once empowering and constrained.

3. Since the Zapatista uprising, a number of books have been published that address political organizing by indigenous women. See Eber and Kovic 2003; Hernández Castillo 1998b; Lovera and Palomo 1997; Nash 2001; Rovira 1994; Stephen 2002.

4. *Propuestas de las mujeres indígenas al Congreso Nacional Indígena (Proposals from Indigenous Women to the National Indigenous Congress).* From the seminar "Reformas al Artículo 4to. Constitucional" (Reforms to Article 4 of the Constitution), October 8–12, 1996, Mexico City.

5. For a historical perspective of indigenous normative systems, see, for San Pedro Chenalhó, Garza Caligaris and Toledo 2002; for San Juan Chamula, Rus 1990; for New Guinea, Fitzpatrick 1980; and for Africa, Comaroff and Comaroff 1992; and Cooper and Stoler 1989.

6. The extent to which women have been included in Zapatista communities has depended on the type of preexisting local power structure, the level of organization and political consciousness that women had before Zapatismo, and the political history of the communities. For other experiences, see Eber 2001; Hernández Castillo and Zylberberg 2001; Olivera 2004.

7. The various proposals and concrete experiences in indigenous autonomy are addressed in Díaz Polanco 1997; Rus, Hernández Castillo, and Mattiace 2003.

INDIGENOUS WOMEN'S ORGANIZING IN CHIAPAS AND MEXICO

Historical Trajectories, Border Crossings

ONE

BETWEEN FEMINIST ETHNOCENTRICITY AND ETHNIC ESSENTIALISM

The Zapatistas' Demands and the National Indigenous Women's Movement

R. AÍDA HERNÁNDEZ CASTILLO

I've had enough
I'm sick of seeing and touching
Both sides of things
Sick of being the damn bridge for everybody

Nobody
Can talk to anybody
Without me

Right?

I explain my mother to my father my father to my little sister
My little sister to my brother my brother to the white feminists
The white feminists to the Black church folks the Black church folks
To the ex-hippies the ex-hippies to the Black separatists the
Black separatists to the artists the artists to my friends' parents . . .

Then I've got to explain myself
To everybody
I do more translating
Than the Gawdamn U.N.

KATE RUSHIN, FROM *THE BRIDGE POEM*

Kate Rushin's poem refers to the frustrations and difficulties of many black feminists during the 1970s in the United States. It tells of being a "bridge" between several struggles, of having to "explain" to the black movement the importance of feminist demands and to the feminist movement the relevance of the fight against racism. Speaking at a

university forum, Candida Jiménez, Mixe leader of the National Council of Indigenous Women (Coordinadora Nacional de Mujeres Indígenas, CNMI), and Alma López, Quiché member of the municipal government of Quetzaltenango, described experiences similar to Rushin's.
They have fought to bridge the gap between an indigenous movement
that refuses to acknowledge its sexism and a feminist movement that
cannot see its own ethnocentricity.[1] The testimonies of these women are
a wake-up call to urban feminists about the need to construct a feminism of diversity (*feminismo de la diversidad*) that recognizes the different ways in which Mexican women imagine their gender identities and
conceive their strategies in the struggle. This chapter analyzes how the
incipient national movement of indigenous women is affecting feminist,
indigenous, and nationalist discourses.

One group of women, still a minority, began to be heard after the
Zapatista uprising on January 1, 1994. From many different parts of
the country and with diverse organizational histories, these women presented a political agenda that combined specific gender demands with
demands for the autonomy of their peoples. It has been a fight on many
fronts. On one side, organized indigenous women have joined with the
national indigenous movement in their protest against the economic oppression and racism that disadvantages indigenous peoples. In parallel,
these women are developing their own political discourse and practice
from a culturally situated gender perspective that questions equally the
sexism and essentialism of indigenous organizations and the ethnocentricity of hegemonic feminism.

An analysis of their demands and strategies points to the emergence
of a new kind of indigenous feminism. Although it may coincide in some
respects with the demands of some sectors of the national feminist
movement, there are substantial differences. The economic and cultural
context in which indigenous women have constructed their gender identities marks the specific forms taken by their struggles, their concepts of
women's dignity, and their ways of forming political alliances. Ethnic,
gender, and class identities have determined the strategies of these
women; they have opted for incorporating themselves into the broadest
struggles of their peoples while creating specific spaces for reflection on
their experiences of exclusion on the grounds of sex and ethnicity.

BACKGROUND

Although the Zapatista movement was a catalyst for indigenous women and made their demands more visible, their newfound activism must be seen from the perspective of the indigenous and peasant struggles of the past two decades.

Beginning mainly in the 1970s, there emerged an important indigenous movement that questioned the official ideology that Mexico is a homogeneous mestizo nation. Hand in hand with demands for land came cultural and political demands, which would evolve into the struggle for autonomy of the indigenous peoples. During this time, there were important changes in the domestic economy, and new spaces emerged for collective reflection, of which indigenous women were a part.

In the case of Chiapas, the so-called Indigenous Congress (Congreso Indígena) of 1974, in which Tzotzil, Tzeltal, Chol, and Tojola'bal people took part, is considered a watershed in the history of indigenous peoples. Dating from this congress peasant demands for fairer distribution of land were accompanied by cultural demands. Though academic studies of the period make no mention of the participation of women, we know from firsthand accounts that women took charge of the logistics of many of the marches, sit-downs, and meetings that these studies document.[2] This role of "accompaniment" continued to exclude indigenous women from decision making and active participation in their organizations, but it did permit them to gather and share their experiences with other indigenous women from different regions of the state.

Alongside women's active participation in peasant movements, changes in the Mexican domestic economy were bringing larger numbers of women into the informal economy through the sale of agricultural and handcrafted products at local markets. At the same time, the "oil boom" combined with the scarcity of cultivable lands caused many men from the states of Chiapas, Oaxaca, Tabasco, and Veracruz to migrate to the oil fields, leaving their wives in charge of the family economy.[3] This monetarization of the indigenous economy has been seen as a factor that takes power away from women within the family, as their domestic work becomes less indispensable for the reproduction of the workforce. According to this perspective, as wage work became more readily available, cash-based transactions between people began to replace exchanges of services and obligations, and purchased foods and commodities began to replace those grown and made at home, such as corn tortillas, by indigenous women (Collier 1994; Flood 1994). However, for many women, the process has been exactly the opposite: their position within the family has been restructured, but their involvement with informal commerce has led to increased contact with other indigenous and mestizo women and to the organization of cooperatives that later became spaces for collective reflection (Nash 1993).

The Catholic Church, through priests and nuns linked to liberation theology, also played an important part in the promotion of these spaces of reflection, above all in the areas of influence of the San Cristóbal (Chiapas), Oaxaca and Tehuantepec (Oaxaca), and Tlapa (Guerrero) dioceses. Although liberation theology does not promote reflection on gender issues, its courses and workshops, which analyze the social inequality and racism of mestizo society, have led indigenous women to also question the inequalities of gender in their own communities. The workshops also provided many women with their first experiences with public speaking and in some cases taught indigenous women how to read and write in Spanish.

In Chiapas at the end of the 1980s a group of nuns together with lay religious activists began to support this line of questioning, pointing to the need to establish a women's area in the diocese of San Cristóbal. Elsewhere I have analyzed in detail this encounter between religious and indigenous women, which resulted in the creation of the Diocesan Council of Women (Coordinadora Diocesana de Mujeres, CODIMUJ), a principal organization of Chiapanecan indigenous women (see Hernández Castillo 1998b, 2004; Gil 1991). These women have had an important role in the wider women's movement. At the same time, feminist nongovernmental organizations (NGOs) began working in rural areas, combining their support for indigenous women's economic participation with the promotion of gender consciousness.

I am a member of this generation that developed its feminism through dialogue with indigenous and peasant women in various regions of the country. Many of us had participated in leftist movements, in solidarity with national liberation struggles in Central America or in political organizations working with popular and peasant sectors in Mexico. Based on the lessons we learned with rural women, we felt the feminist agenda should be closely linked to a process of reflecting on the economic and social inequalities that defined their lives. The history of Mexican feminism has been characterized by the tension between those who have placed the legalization of abortion at the center of their feminist struggle and those who have insisted that a feminist agenda should focus on transforming gender and class inequalities. This has been one of the many challenges we have confronted in constructing a national feminist movement.

With the creation of the Feminist Women's Coalition (Coalición de Mujeres Feministas) in 1976 and then the National Front for the Liberation and Rights of Women (Frente Nacional por la Liberación y los Derechos de las Mujeres, FNALIDM) in 1979, the legalization of abortion and the fight against domestic violence were the two demands that united hegemonic feminism in Mexico. This feminism—fundamentally urban, theorized from an academic perspective, and constructed in central Mexico—has maintained its hegemony vis-à-vis other popular and rural feminisms, whose ideas have not been heard at major international feminist events. The political practices of these other feminisms have been developed outside the influence of international funding agencies, and their history has yet to be written.[4]

To date histories of Mexican feminism written by academics (Lamas 1992, 1994; González 2001; Lau 2002; Bartra 2002) continue to use the term "popular feminisms" to refer to NGOs that, beginning in the 1980s, supported organizing among poor urban and rural women but not to refer to women from the popular sectors who developed their own critical posture with regard to gender inequalities. The latter are represented as passive women who are in need of "consciousness-raising" by feminists, and their actions are described as corresponding exclusively to practical demands.[5] Gisela Espinosa Damián (2005:85), who has witnessed and participated in the construction of this feminism from the bottom up states the following in this regard: "The appellation 'popular feminism' should not be applied to civil organizations, since women from poor urban neighborhoods were those who coined this term and assumed this identity." She proposes differentiating between civil feminism, composed of civil organizations with members who are generally middle-class professionals who work with popular sectors, and popular feminism, which she would use to refer to "processes led by women from popular sectors who are the key players, and who create their own organizations, but also participate in mixed organizations and combine the struggle to transform gender inequalities and to work toward a more favorable position for women with other types of demands" (Espinosa Damián 2005:87).

Indigenous and peasant women have joined with women from the popular sectors in a number of historic events, such as the First National Women's Conference (Primer Encuentro Nacional de Mujeres), held in 1980 and attended by, for example, indigenous women from Chiapas belonging to the Emiliano Zapata Peasant Organization (Organización Campesina "Emiliano Zapata," OCEZ).[6] However, indigenous women's movements in Chiapas have followed their own courses, independent of urban popular feminisms in central Mexico.

In Chiapas, it was in the context of the peasant movement during the 1980s that indigenous women from various regions came together in conferences, workshops, and congresses. Independently from the official agendas of those events, which were focused on agrarian problems, these women began to share experiences and reflect on their lives. Inequalities within the family, community, and political organizations became the topic of conversation in the hallways during these meetings. As advisers to organizations, pastoral agents linked to liberation theology, and academics with a social commitment, we not only witnessed and participated in this dialogue, we also constructed our own feminist agenda, expanding on the criticisms pointing to the inequality of the "capitalist system" and reflecting on gender exclusion and racism.

An important event that defined this meeting point between civil feminism in a process of construction and an indigenous women's movement was the First Conference of Indigenous and Peasant Women of Chiapas (Primer Encuentro de Mujeres Indígenas y Campesinas de Chiapas), held in San Cristóbal de las Casas in 1986 and organized by academics and activists at the Autonomous University of Chiapas (Universidad Autónoma de Chiapas, UNACH) and the Organization of Indigenous Healers of the State of Chiapas (Organización de Médicos Indígenas del Estado de Chiapas, OMIECH). Sonia Toledo and Anna María Garza Caligaris, who promoted this event, explain the way in which methodologies from popular education were used to explore together with indigenous women their own conceptions of women's bodies, sexuality, and suffering (Garza Caligaris and Toledo 2005). They state:

> The idea was to build relations different from those characterizing organizations traditionally dominated by men. Even though we have inherited and re-created the distinction between those giving and those receiving advice, and even though certain tensions and conflicts were also generated, this type of encounter makes it possible to create new dynamics for reflection and coexistence. Value was placed on political work and participation by women; emphasis was placed on the expression of emotions and on personal self-esteem. (213)

Despite the structural inequalities separating professional women from indigenous women, these dialogues defined the organizational processes and political agendas of both sectors.

Emerging from these dialogues were various feminist associations that chose to devote themselves to organizing and assisting indigenous and peasant women. I developed my position as a feminist within the framework of one of these organizations, the Women's Group of San Cristóbal de las Casas (Grupo de Mujeres de San Cristóbal de las Casas), founded in 1989 (and renamed COLEM in 1994) after a series of rapes in 1988 and 1989 of NGO women. We initially organized as a broad-based front against sexual and domestic violence. Over time our work expanded into the educational, legal, and health realms, including workshops for promoting gender awareness.[7] Similar experiences took place in other indigenous regions in the country, as in the case of Comaletzin, founded in 1987, whose members promoted development based on a gender perspective with indigenous groups and peasants in the states of Morelos, Puebla, Sonora and Chiapas;[8] the Center for Research and Action for Women (Centro de Investigación y Acción para la Mujer, CIAM), founded in 1989 to support organizing among indigenous women in the Altos region of Chiapas and Guatemalan refugee women;[9] Women for Dialogue (Mujeres por el Diálogo), which worked in the states of Veracruz and Oaxaca; and advisers from the Women's Solidarity Action Team (Equipo de Mujeres en Acción Solidaria) who worked with Purepecha women in Michoacán.[10]

Discourses centering on women's dignity promoted by the Catholic Church began to be supplanted by a discourse centering on women's rights and by new views on gender. Indigenous women appropriated and reinterpreted these ideas from their dialogues with feminists.[11]

Migration, organizing, religious groups, feminist NGOs, and even official development programs have all influenced how indigenous men and women have restructured their relations within the family and reworked their strategies. But it was the Zapatista National Liberation Army (Ejército Zapatista de Liberación Nacional, EZLN) that first provided a public forum for indigenous women.[12]

Under the influence of the Zapatistas, a movement of national dimensions has emerged for the first time in Mexico—still embryonic and full of contradictions—in which the various local forces are arguing for the incorporation of gender demands into the political agenda of the indigenous movement. In 1997, at the National Encounter of Indigenous Women "Building Our History" (Construyendo Nuestra Historia), the National Council of Indigenous Women was founded (see chapter 4, this volume). This organization has been vital to the promotion of a gendered perspective within the national indigenous movement. The voices of many of its members have been raised in the National Indigenous Congress (Congreso Nacional Indígena, CNI) and in the national debate on the Law of Indigenous Rights and Culture (Ley de Derecho y Cultura Indígena), questioning static representations of tradition and recovering the right to "cambiar permaneciendo y permanecer cambiando" (to change while remaining and to remain changing).

UP AGAINST FEMINIST ETHNOCENTRICITY AND ETHNIC ESSENTIALISM

Indigenous women have linked their gender struggles to the struggle for the autonomy of their peoples—hence their desire to continue as part of the National Indigenous Congress, the main organization of indigenous peoples of Mexico that was established to support the Zapatistas' demands. Nevertheless, this policy has faced considerable resistance, as much from the feminist movement as from the indigenous movement. In our view, both movements have benefited from this double activism: different kinds of feminists have been stimulated to incorporate cultural and ethnic diversity into their analysis of gender inequality, and the indigenous movement has had to incorporate gender into their perspectives on the ethnic and class discrimination against their peoples.

Mexican academic feminism, mainly through the work of anthropologists in the 1980s, had already modified its definition of gender to include the diverse contexts in which it is constructed. It was recognized that "asymmetry between men and women signifies different things in different places. Hence the position, activities, limitations and possibilities of women vary from culture to culture" (Lamas 1986:184). However, this recognition did not lead to an inclusive feminist agenda that would meet the specific needs of indigenous women. The hegemonic feminist agenda has focused on demands for voluntary maternity, recognition of reproductive rights, and the struggle against sexual and domestic violence (Lamas 1992; González 2001; Lau 2002; Bartra 2002; Tuñón 1997; Marcos 1999). While it is true that indigenous women voice many of these demands, in their case they are always accompanied by economic and cultural demands, products of the racism and exploitation that have configured their gender identities. In this sense we can apply to Mexican hegemonic feminism's ethnocentricity the same criticism that Judith Butler (2001:9) leveled at North American academic feminism's homophobia: "Any feminist theory that restricts the meaning of gender to the presuppositions of its own practice establishes exclusive gender norms in the bosom of feminism, usually with homophobic consequences." In our case, the consequences are ethnocentric.

Even those of us who have been working with indigenous women in rural areas since the 1980s have been doing so from the basis of our own feminist agendas and out of definitions of gender and self-esteem that arise from our own experiences. Projects for popular education and co-participative investigation popularized in South America by Paulo Freire influenced our methodologies in working with rural women.[13] Although this model of investigation and education proposed to "democratize" the hierarchical relationship of the investigator and the investigated, the educator and the educated, the theoretical-political premise inherited from Marxism that the intellectual can awaken the consciousness of the "oppressed" assumed a paternalistic view of the popular sectors. When we met in workshops with indigenous women during the 1980s, this was a legacy that we found ourselves reproducing and gradually confronting. Inherent in the idea that our feminist mandate consisted of "raising the awareness" of indigenous women was the perspective that a "false consciousness" existed that had to be confronted. Processes of self-evaluation and reformulation of methodologies began to be developed during the 1990s, and constructive dialogue with organized indigenous women has been essential throughout.[14]

Feminist anthropology in Mexico has also been developing a line of analysis that tries to reach problems specific to indigenous women. Beginning mainly in the 1970s, feminism joined forces with anthropology in the study of the indigenous peoples of Mesoamerica. The oppression of indigenous women was studied from two perspectives: one that emphasized the importance of the patriarchy as a system of inequality that furthered the "universal oppression of the woman" (Chiñas 1975; Dalton and Musalem 1992) and one that, under the influence of Marxism, focused on the impact of capitalist development and modernization on gender relations among indigenous peoples. It is this second, political economy line of analysis that has had more influence on feminist ethnographies of Mesoamerica. Among these are studies on Mazahua and Otomí women by Lourdes Arizpe (1980), on Mam women by Laurel Bossen (1983) and Tracy Ehler (1990), and on Tzotzil women by Mercedes Olivera Bustamante (1979), June Nash (1993), and Merielle Flood (1994). The main argument was that the introduction of capitalist relations among indigenous peoples had transformed gender relations, substituting the complementary roles characteristic of self-sufficient economies for less equal relationships. According to these perspectives, in the new economic context women lose autonomy through increased dependence on their husbands' wages or through being placed in a more marginal position in the capitalist economy. Although some of these perspectives recognize possibilities for resistance against the powerful forces of capital (Eber 1995; Nash 1993; Rosenbaum 1993; Stephen 1991), the social agency of indigenous women almost disappears in the face of the emphasis on the structures of domination that mark their lives.

In spite of the efforts of feminist anthropology to create a space where indigenous women could speak out, for decades its representations portrayed them as passive subjects, victims of patriarchy or the forces of capitalism. Not until 1994 have representations of indigenous women as political actors and constructors of their own history begun to appear in Mexican social science.[15] In this theoretical reformulation of the concept of gender as a multidimensional category and in the recognition of the importance of ethnic and class issues in understanding identity processes in multicultural Mexico, input from indigenous women has been fundamental. Their voices can be heard in documents emanating from their encounters, workshops, and congresses and in statements and interviews that have been published in feminist periodicals and in the national press.[16]

In parallel with this dialogue with feminism, indigenous women have maintained an exchange with the national indigenous movement of which they are an active part through their participation in the CNI. There they have had to confront the idyllic visions of indigenous culture that permeate the political discourse of many CNI members, many indigenous leaders, and many of their advisers.

Although we can understand that during certain phases in the development of social movements a discourse that essentializes "lo propio" (what is ours) and excludes the "other," as in some sectors of the radical Afro-American movement in the United States or in the initial radical segregationism of the feminist movement, may emerge, experience has taught us that such strategies only bring isolation and cancel the possibilities for forging political alliances. On many occasions indigenous women have opted to vindicate the historic and malleable character of their cultures and to condemn those "uses and customs" that offend their dignity. It is a battle on two fronts: claiming from the state the right to cultural differences and fighting within their communities to change the traditions that they see as infringements of their rights. Their struggle is not one for the recognition of an essentialized culture but for the right to reconstruct, confront, and reproduce that culture, not on terms established by the state but on terms established by the indigenous peoples themselves in the context of their own internal plurality.

FROM "FEMINISM" TO FEMINISMS

Although the construction of more egalitarian relationships between women and men has become a central point in the struggle of organized indigenous women, the concept of feminism has not been appropriated in their political discourse. This concept continues to be identified with urban liberal feminism, which for many of them carries separatist connotations that do not fit with their ideas of the need to join with their male indigenous comrades.

Those of us who arrived at feminism through the experience of militant leftist groups know the ideological force of discourses that represent feminism as a bourgeois ideology, divisionist and individualist, that separates women from the struggles of their peoples. The experiences of Anglo-Saxon liberal feminism, which in fact arose from an individualistic view of "citizens' rights," have been used to create a homogeneous representation of feminism.[17] Appropriating this concept and giving it new meanings has been the struggle of the various Mexican feminisms that have been growing up in recent decades. An "indigenous feminism" will be possible only insofar as indigenous women give their own content to the concept of feminism and find it useful in creating alliances with other organized women.

At present, many of their demands—both those directed at the state and those directed at their organizations and communities—continue to center on recovering the dignity of women and on the construction of a more just life for all men and women. The Zapatista Women's Revolutionary Law (Ley Revolucionaria de Mujeres) is one of the many documents that express these new gender demands. (See chapter 2, this volume.) Although all indigenous women do not know this law in detail, it has become a symbol of the possibility of a better life.

These new gender demands have been expressed in different forms in workshops, forums, and congresses organized since 1994, and question equally the essentialist perspectives of the indigenous movement and feminism's generalizing discourses—which emphasize the right to equality without considering the way in which class and ethnicity mark the identities of indigenous women.

At the forefront of the indigenous movement, these new voices have struggled for the recognition and elimination of the inequalities that characterize gender relations within their communities and organizations. At the same time, they have revealed the dichotomy between tradition and modernity that is reproduced by the official indigenous movement—and to a certain degree the autonomy movement as well—according to which there are only two options: stand by tradition or embrace modernity. Indigenous women claim their right to cultural difference while demanding the right to change those traditions that oppress or exclude them. "We must also think about what needs to be made new in our customs. The law should protect and promote only the modes and customs that women, communities, and organizations agree are good to have. The customs we have should not hurt anyone."[18]

Indigenous women are also questioning the universal concept "Woman" promoted in some urban feminist discourses. Here their voices echo the criticisms of women of color against North American radical and liberal feminism in presenting a homogenizing vision of women without recognizing that gender is constructed in different ways in different historical contexts.[19]

The assertion of a culturally situated analysis of gender has been central for the CNMI (see chapter 4, this volume), among whose objectives are the following: "Strengthen the leadership of indigenous women from a gender perspective based in our cultural identity. Establish a network of communication at a national level among indigenous women. Train indigenous women at a national level. Raise the consciousnesses of indigenous peoples and national society regarding respect for the human rights of indigenous women, including a vision of gender. With regard to training, methodologies appropriate to identity and gender will be used according to our worldview."[20] This is evidently a feminist platform that questions the hegemonic definitions of the term "feminism."

THE CULTURE GAP BETWEEN INDIGENOUS AND NONINDIGENOUS WOMEN

The lack of cultural sensitivity in the face of specific problems and worldviews has often hindered dialogue between urban feminists and indigenous women. The temptation to assume that we are united through the common experience of patriarchy is always present. It is this lack of recognition, in part, that has impeded the construction of an inclusive national feminist movement.

One example of the failed attempts to form a broad movement is the September 1994 State Convention of Chiapanecan Women (Convención

Estatal de Mujeres Chiapanecas). Prior to the National Democratic Convention (Convención Nacional Democrática) convened by the EZLN, women from NGOs, cooperatives, and peasant organizations gathered to write a document to be presented at the convention enumerating the specific demands of the women of Chiapas. This was the seed of the State Convention of Chiapanecan Women, a politically and ideologically heterogeneous cultural space. Urban women from NGOs and feminists and nonfeminists from ecclesiastical base communities (comunidades eclesiales de base, CEBs) met with monolingual women from the highlands, principally Tzeltal and Tzotzil; with Tojola'bal, Chol, and Tzeltal women from the jungle region; and with Mam indigenous women from the Sierra. The convention was short-lived; only three ordinary meetings and one special meeting took place before its dissolution. A historical reconstruction of this broad movement that would analyze the strategies of urban feminism to create bridges of communication with indigenous women remains to be done. However, it is noteworthy that mestizo women, though a minority, assumed positions of leadership in an internal hierarchy that was not openly recognized.

Many members of the convention were later invited by the EZLN to advise or participate in a panel on indigenous culture and rights formed in 1995 in San Cristóbal de las Casas, within which a special panel was set up titled "Situation, Rights and Culture of the Indigenous Woman." In this panel, the nonindigenous women organizers in charge of reporting the findings omitted detailed descriptions by indigenous women of their day-to-day problems, instead including only their general demands for demilitarization and their criticisms of neoliberalism. It is through these daily experiences, erased from the records of encounters, that indigenous women have constructed their gender identities in a manner different from urban feminists, and it is only through these experiences that we can understand the specificity of their demands and their struggles.

It is not surprising, then, that when in October 1997 the First National Congress of Indigenous Women (Primer Congreso Nacional de Mujeres Indígenas) was held, the members decided that nonindigenous women present could participate only as observers. This decision was called separatist and even racist by some feminists who found themselves silenced for the first time by indigenous women. Their arguments are similar to those used against women when we demand our own space within political organizations.

Despite our best intentions, it is usually the case that nonindigenous women, who have a superior command of Spanish and the written word, dominate discussions when sharing space with indigenous women. For this reason, it is essential to respect the creation of separate spaces and to wait for the best time to form alliances. Purépecha, Totonaca, Tzotzil, Tzeltal, Tojolabal, Mazateca, Cucateca, Otomí, Triqui, Nahua, Zapoteca, Zoque, Chol, Tlapaneca, Mam, Chatina, Popoluca, Amuzga, and Mazahua women who gathered in Oaxaca at that first national meeting of indigenous women are undergoing their own processes of change that do not always obey the times and agendas of urban feminists.

An example of the cultural breach between urban mestizos and the indigenous is found in the harsh criticism by some feminists of the Second Women's Revolutionary Law (Segunda Ley Revolucionaria de Mujeres) proposed by the Zapatistas because it included an article prohibiting adultery (see Rojas 1996). This modification of the First Women's Revolutionary Law (Primera Ley Revolucionaria de Mujeres) was considered a conservative measure resulting from the influence of the church over indigenous communities. Critics should instead see the indigenous women's demand as a protest against the cultural justification of male infidelity and bigamy, which is closely linked to domestic violence. A prohibition that may seem moralistic and retrograde to urban women is perhaps for many indigenous women a way of rejecting a "tradition" that makes them vulnerable within both family and community.

Another example is legislation on domestic violence. For several years, urban feminists in Chiapas fought for harsher penalties against wife-batterers, with eventual success in the modification in 1998 of Article 122 of the penal code. For indigenous women who are financially independent, the harsher penalties mean considerable hardship. The case of alimony and child support is similar: as long as their husbands are without lands and steady work, indigenous women will not be helped by legislated penalties.

The words of Chandra Mohanty (1991:67) are valuable with regard to domestic violence in multicultural contexts: "Masculine violence must be interpreted within specific societies so as to understand it better and organize ourselves more effectively to fight it." If recognition of the similarities among women allows us to form political alliances, recognition of our differences is vital in the construction of a respectful dialogue and in the search for strategies more in keeping with differing cultural realities.

This attempt to reformulate feminism in the context of indigenous culture has advanced more from the other side. The Quiché councilor Alma López described these new concepts:

> As an indigenous feminist, I try to recover the philosophical principles of my culture and ground them in the realities of the twenty-first century.

That means I criticize what I don't like about my culture while proudly accepting that I belong to it. Indigenous feminism for me grows from a principle: women are working toward the objective of constructing ourselves as independent people formed in community, people who can give to others without forgetting about themselves. The philosophical principles that I would recover from my culture are equality, the complementarity between men and women, between women and women, and between men and men. At present, this famous complementarity of the Mayan culture does not exist; to claim the opposite is an aggression. It exists only in history. Currently, we have total inequality. But complementarity and equality can be built.

I would also recover the idea of the double vision, the *cabawil*; he who at the same time sees forward and backward, who sees one side and the other, sees black and sees white. Recovering this ideal in terms of women means recognizing all that is sad and terrible forming my reality as a woman, and rebuilding myself with all the good that I have. It means recognizing that there are women different from me, indigenous and *ladina*, black, urban and peasant women.[21]

Perhaps the building of this respectful and constructive intercultural dialogue will contribute to the formation of a new indigenous feminism based on respect for difference and rejection of inequality.

NOTES

An earlier version of this article was published in Spanish in the feminist journal *Debate Feminista* 12, no. 24 (October 2001):206–230. I am grateful to the members of the CIESAS seminar "Gender and Diversity," Patricia Artía, Ixkic Duarte, Margara Millán, Jules Soro, Teresa Sierra, Beatriz Canabal, Lina Rose Berrio Palomo, Silvia Soriano, Morna MacLeod, and Violeta Zylberberg, for the reflections shared in this space, which were fundamental to the development of this chapter. This chapter is a product of the collective research "New and Old Spaces of Power: Indigenous Women, Collective Organization, and Resistance" sponsored by CONACYT (38784-S).

1. Both leaders participated in the Foro Interdisciplinario de Estudios de Género (Interdisciplinary Forum on Gender Studies), which took place at the Escuela Nacional de Antropología e Historia (National School of Anthropology and History) in April 2001.

2. Although some feminists have tried to note the participation of women in these movements in nonacademic publications, academic works published to date silence the voices of indigenous women. For example, on the peasant and indige-

nous movement at the national level, see Mejia and Sarmiento 1987; and on the indigenous movement in Chiapas in the 1970s, see Morales Bermúdez 1992.

3. For an analysis of the impact of these changes on the peasant economy, see Collier 1994; Rus 1990.

4. There is some pioneering work on the history of popular urban feminism and its links to civil feminism (e.g., Alejandra Massolo 1991; Espinoza and Paz Paredes 1992; Espinoza Damián 1993). However, the history of rural and indigenous feminism is still in the process of systematization through a number of doctoral dissertations (see Espinosa Damián 2005; Mejia 2005) and research projects in progress (see, e.g., advances from the project "Viejos y nuevos espacios de poder: Mujeres indígenas, resistencia cotidiana y organización colectiva" under the section "Proyectos Especiales" at www.ciesas.edu.mx).

5. These representations of women from the popular sectors in the histories of Mexican feminism appear to reproduce a rather hegemonic tendency in the literature on social movements. They establish typologies that implicitly hierarchize these movements, from lesser to greater potential for emancipation, and they tend to reify the dichotomy between material demands and cultural demands as mutually exclusive. The organizing experiences we present in this book reveal the limitations of perspectives in which the utopian values and horizons of the analyst are used as universal parameters for measuring social actors' capacities for transformation. The closer the political agenda of these perspectives is to that of the analyst, the greater the potential for transgression, leading to ethnocentric representations of social movements in Latin America. Alan Touraine (1987), for example, stated that there were no social movements in Latin America, since collective actions around economic needs lacked a sense of *historicity* that would make for a more comprehensive political project.

Feminist analyses have not been exempt from this "political evolutionism" in their typification of women's movements in Latin America, and the clearest example is the so-called paradigm of interests popularized through the works of Maxine Molyneux (1985, 2003). This paradigm once again proposes a division between poor women who mobilize around practical interests and feminist women who mobilize around strategic interests. *Practical interests* are defined as those based on the satisfaction of needs emerging from women's position within the gender-based division of labor; *strategic interests,* as those involving demands for transforming unequal gender relations. Here, strategic interests are the only interests considered intrinsically political in nature and potentially transforming. Similarly, Sheila Rowbotham (1992) differentiates between "women in movement," referring to those women who work together to achieve common objectives, and limited the use of the concept "women's movement" to refer to those making gender demands of a feminist nature.

These dichotomous typifications have been seriously questioned by other feminist perspectives (Álvarez 1990; Kabeer 1992; Stephen 1997; Wieringa 1994; Hernández Castillo forthcoming), which have pointed out that these visions underestimate the critical contributions that organized poor women, in this case indigenous women, can make to the destabilization of the social order by failing to discuss how, within the framework of their strategies for survival, these women negotiate power and reconstruct their collective identities.

6. This event is considered to have been a turning point in the history of popular feminism and was organized by groups linked to liberation theology and feminist civil associations such as Comunicación, Intercambio y Desarrollo Humano en América Latina (CIDHAL). Approximately five hundred women from both the urban and rural sectors attended, and one of their objectives was to discuss the role and problems of women in popular movements.

7. For a history of this organization, see Freyermuth and Fernández 1995; and for a self-critical reflection on my own experiences in this organization and the work with indigenous women, see Hernández Castillo forthcoming.

8. Comaletzin was officially constituted in 1987. Its principal lines of action are "training, organization, education, and investigation, with gender as a focus of analysis" (Comaletzin manifesto, 1999). This organization played an important role in the formation of the National Network of Rural Advocates and Advisors (Red Nacional de Asesoras y Promotoras Rurales) in 1987 by organizations concerned with gender and development issues in various rural areas of Mexico.

9. CIAM was founded in 1989 by Gloria Sierra, Begoña de Agustín, Pilar Jaime, and Mercedes Olivera, with members in Nicaragua, Mexico, and Guatemala. The initial objective was to work with women displaced by armed conflict (refugees, the displaced, and the returned) in Central America and Mexico and, through socially committed research, help them to develop gender identity and consciousness, stand up for their rights as refugee women, and defend those rights in UNHCR, in their own refugee organizations, and in their countries of refuge. They worked principally with organized women in popular movements; exiles in Mexico, Nicaragua, Costa Rica, Honduras, Belize, and Panama; and displaced women in El Salvador, Nicaragua, and Guatemala. (Thanks to Mercedes Olivera for this information.) These experiences were preceded by various efforts to promote reflection on women's rights within peasant organizations such as the Independent Confederation of Agricultural Workers and Peasants (Central Independiente de Obreros Agrícolas y Campesinos, CIOAC) and the Emiliano Zapata Peasant Organization (OCEZ-CNPA). For an account of these initial efforts in the early 1980s, see Garza Caligaris and Toledo 2004.

10. The Women's Solidarity Action Team (Equipo de Mujeres en Acción Solidaria) was founded in February 1985. It defined its areas of work as health and popular education with popular sectors in Mexico City and with indigenous women in various parts of the country.

11. This is by no means an exhaustive list of the work of feminist organizations in rural areas. Many others have followed these pioneer organizations and have established constructive dialogues with indigenous women. An important example is the work of K'inal Antzetik with the women of the CNMI and that of many other feminist organizations belonging to the National Network of Rural Advisors and Advocates.

12. This public participation has been answered with repression both from the state and from their own communities and partners. For an analysis of the

violence confronting organized women, see Hernández Castillo (1998b). For an analysis of other problems facing indigenous women in their attempts to organize, see Magallón 1988.

13. Co-participative investigation and the projects of popular education developed in the late 1970s and the 1980s in rural Mexico stem from a reworking of Freire's investigative model. Considered by many to be Latin America's contribution to world social science, co-participative investigation, also known as action-investigation, became popular as a methodology that sought to further science that was committed to the popular sectors. In 1977 investigators from five continents formed the Participative Investigation Network (Red de Investigación Participativa), headed by the Latin Americans Fals Borda, Francisco Vio Grossi, and Carlos Rodríguez Brandao.

14. A critical reflection on the relation between mestizo counselors and indigenous peasants during the 1980s may be found in Garza Caligaris and Toledo 2004. I have taken part in self-evaluation of feminist methodologies with colleagues in Comaletzin and COLEM. These lines of reflection have also been developed in Latin American feminist encounters; see the contents of the Taller sobre Feminismo y Diversidad Cultural (Workshop on Feminism and Cultural Diversity), organized by Sylvia Marcos in the VIII Congreso Latinoamericano y del Caribe, in Marcos 1999a.

15. For the point of view of journalists, see Lovera and Palomo 1999; Rojas 1994; Rovira 1997; Marcos 1997; and various issues of the periodical *Cuadernos Feministas,* 1997 to the present. For the academic view, see Alberti Manzanares 1997; Bonfil 1997; Garza Caligaris 2002; Hernández Castillo 1994a, 1994b, 1996, 1998a, 1998b; Millán 1996a, 1996b, 1997.

16. A collection of these documents may be found in Lovera and Palomo 1999; see also Sánchez Nestor 2001.

17. Liberal feminism argues that equality for women can be achieved through legal means and social reform and that men as a group need not be challenged. It leans toward an equality of sameness with men and conceives politics in individualistic terms, looking to reform present "liberal" practices in society rather than advocating a radical change. The pro-choice agenda is central in the struggle of liberal feminism using the argument that every individual should have control over his or her own body and that this also affords them the right to make medical decisions. An important theoretician of liberal feminism is Betty Friedman.

18. See "Women's Rights in Our Traditions and Customs" in Section 1 of this volume.

19. For a critique of Western feminism, see Trinh 1988; Alarcón 1990; Mohanty 1991.

20. Document of presentation of the CNMI.

21. Duarte Bastian 2002:27.

TWO

INDIGENOUS WOMEN AND ZAPATISMO

New Horizons of Visibility

MÁRGARA MILLÁN MONCAYO,
TRANSLATED BY MARÍA VINÓS

Women have become visible in contemporary Zapatismo in various ways, a fact that this movement has had to grapple with. Subcomandante Marcos is not making light of the issue when he states that women belong in Zapatismo not because it is a feminist movement but because they have earned their place in it. Women have articulated this space with specific demands that have made them visible in a new light and—most important—in their own eyes. This chapter discusses the forms of visibility that indigenous women have adopted and explores how they have gradually altered traditional gender relations by redefining female indigenous subjectivity and by transforming the way they are perceived by Mexican society.

SOCIOECONOMIC AND ORGANIZATIONAL ENVIRONMENT

The presence and participation of women in Chiapas's social conflicts predates their public appearance as part of the organized Zapatista movement. The armed uprising took place in the context of a long tradition of organization and mobilization among a sector of the peasant movement, a tradition recognized in the demands of the Zapatistas, whose strategies have been implemented since 1994 through Zapatista civil resistance. The strategies comprise a series of organized actions such as the occupation of land and government halls, hunger strikes, organized ballot abstention (or, where appropriate, suffrage), and the protection of open dialogue, which entails the constant presence of a human chain formed by indigenous people wherever negotiations are taking place. In all these actions—and especially after 1992, in the marches to occupy San Cristóbal de las Casas—indigenous women of all ages, many of them carrying small children, have had an overwhelming presence. It is estimated that women comprise about 30 percent of the membership of the Zapatista National Liberation Army (EZLN), but it is also acknowledged that the percentage is much higher among the support base.

Present-day Chiapas is diverse. Along with the state of Oaxaca, it has the largest indigenous population in Mexico and is also one of the most marginalized from the benefits of development. It has seen soaring rates of congenital malnutrition, infant and adult mortality from preventable disease—so-called poverty deaths—and illiteracy and continuing social and economic marginalization and cultural segregation. Life expectancy in indigenous communities is forty-four years, whereas the national average is seventy years.[1] In Chiapas, 150 babies die for every 1,000 live births, whereas the average in the rest of the nation has been reduced to 45. Chiapas is simultaneously one of the states with the greatest wealth in natural resources and the one with the highest poverty index. This situation is evidence of the dominance of racist and discriminatory policies in Mexican society and of the contradictions of global capitalism.

Women are the most seriously affected by poverty and marginalization. Their greater vulnerability is conditioned by class, race, and gender, and it is translated in the ways women live and die in Chiapas. In the region of the Cañadas, the overall annual fertility rate for women of childbearing age is 7.32; that is, women may have more than seven children, of whom on average two survive. The main causes of women's death are related to reproductive health. According to the Mexican Foundation for Indigenous Children's Health, half of the total indigenous population is malnourished, and among these, girls are usually more severely affected.[2] Poor nutrition and congenital malnutrition have affected the growth of indigenous peoples, especially of women over the age of fifteen, who a decade ago averaged 142 centimeters and today average only 132 centimeters. Chiapas, Guerrero, and Mexico State have the highest rate of maternal mortality (Espinoza Damián 2004:172–173).

The sociopolitical conditions in Chiapas are complex. The forced migration of people from diverse ethnic groups into the jungle region has given rise to a lifestyle that combines community affirmation with the exercise of pluralist forms of political, cultural, and productive organization (Leyva Solano 1994b). Grassroots groups with varied ideologies have been added to this mix. These regions are in effect a social laboratory: interethnic exchange combines with progressive and leftist religious ideologies, including some officialist ideologies, all, however, related to the defense and reconstruction of community. This has promoted a high degree of social and dynamic cohesion by matching traditional authority and community structures with basic demands—democracy, justice, and dignity. This process has seen the important construction of new identity spaces where indigenous men and women are modernizing the ways in which their community and culture work.

The demands of Zapatismo contain both an affirmation and a redefinition of what is *indigenous*. Recently, the indigenous movement has become politicized by rearticulating its traditional forms around the most important contemporary debates. Indigenous peoples have thus shown their ability to keep pace with the modern nation and destabilize the dominant notion of indigenousness as premodern, archaic, or even authentic. At the same time, the larger society must do its part: it must recognize the reality of contemporary indigenous peoples and modernize its views so that indigenous peoples are seen as citizens whose rights are equal to those of other citizens but who also have specific ethnic and cultural rights.

THE FIRST HORIZON OF VISIBILITY

Indigenous women have gradually articulated a discourse that strikes precisely on the relevance of their link to change and tradition and focuses on the idea of updating the meaning of indigenousness through the affirmation and transformation of tradition. On this issue, as in others, the EZLN acts as a magnet for the rest of the indigenous movement, as a symbolic reference point that unites diverse and contradictory experiences.

There are several ways in which women have joined with the tradition of organization and struggle with which the peasants of Chiapas have confronted the "policies of modernization and development" imposed by the national government. During the 1970s, Chiapas saw the rise of peasant groups that became part of three national organizations: the Organización Campesina "Emiliano Zapata" (Emiliano Zapata Peasant Organization, OCEZ), the Coordinadora Nacional Plan de Ayala (Plan de Ayala National Council, CNPA), and the Central Independiente de Obreros Agrícolas y Campesinos (Independent Confederation of Agricultural Workers and Peasants, CIOAC). Women then began to form their own organizations, such as those comprising artisans or Christian women. In the past decade, women from nongovernmental organizations (NGOs) and academia have added a gender perspective to issues such as reproductive health, civil rights, and human rights. By the 1990s a number of mixed organizations had formed that have been defining women's claims, such as the comunidades eclesiales de base (ecclesiastical base communities, CEBs) and the Organización de Médicos Indígenas del Estado de Chiapas (Organization of Indigenous Healers of the State of Chiapas, OMIECH), as well as Mujeres de Motozintla, Mujeres de Margaritas, Mujeres de Ocosingo, and Mujeres de Jiquipilas. In addition, we have established cooperative and productive associations, such as the Organización de Mujeres Artesanas de Chiapas J'pas Joloviletik and J'pas Lumetik in the Chiapas highlands, the Organización Independiente de Mujeres Indígenas (OIMI), Nan Choch, and Indígenas de la Sierra Madre de Motozintla (ISMAM). The Coordinadora Diocesana de Mujeres (Diocesan Council of Women, CODIMUJ) has formed a broad human rights defense network in the jungle and the highlands. Another important experience that has helped women's organizational efforts in Chiapas has been contact with women refugees from Guatemala who have also called for gender and ethnic identity.

In recent years other organizations have formed, such as Grupo de Mujeres de San Cristóbal (San Cristóbal Women's Group), Centro de Investigación y Acción para la Mujer (Center of Investigation and Action for Women, CIAM), Centro de Capacitación para la Ecología y Salud de San Cristóbal (San Cristóbal Center for Ecology and Health, CCESC), Chiltak, and K'inal Antzetik. All these organizations provide support for communities and women's organizations with a gender perspective (Olivera Bustamante 1994; Hernández Castillo and Zylberberg 2004).

Women have also gained increased access to posts of social responsibility in their communities. As members of cooperatives, as health promoters, by creating savings cooperatives, and in many cases through direct negotiation with the authorities, they have transformed their position inside the community and have created spaces for their specific demands as women within the general set of demands. This process has to a greater or lesser degree developed everywhere. In the highlands, a more traditional region than the jungle, organization has come as a result of artisans' cooperatives, in which the participation of Tzotzil women, most of them monolingual, has increased. Women's spaces, like the Casas de la Mujer in the Tojola'bal *ejido* community in Santa Martha and El Porvenir settlement, both in the La Trinitaria municipality, and Poza Rica, in Las Margaritas municipality, have been created. These projects received the support of the CCESC for the purpose of creating community pharmacies (Hernández Castillo 1994b).

The point I want to make is that the context of women's Zapatismo is one in which women's incorporation in social and political work was already under way. It is in this context that, alongside the ethnic and community demands of Zapatismo, indigenous women in Chiapas began to develop gender demands: the construction of democratic relations within the family, the community, and local organizations; the participation of women in decision making related to both communal and organizational structure; the right to inherit land; the right to choose when and whom they marry; the right to receive an education and to work; the right to be respected by men when in positions of leadership; the need to change traditions and customs that disadvantage women.

A document in which it is possible to observe clearly the enunciation of the horizon of gender awareness among indigenous women of various ethnic groups is that produced in the workshop "Women's Rights in Our Traditions and Customs," held in San Cristóbal de las Casas on May 19 and 20, 1994, and promoted by several NGOs. The workshop was attended by more than fifty Tzotzil, Tzeltal, Tojola'bal, and Mam women from very different communities.[3] The document questions patriarchal "common sense"—on the state's part as much as on the part of the community—and articulates the discourse of women's new experience and new expectations. Below I focus on some of the demands; the full text can be found in Section 1 of this book.

a) Recognition of different structures that discriminate, segregate, or mistreat women: poverty, making the state responsible for; discrimination and racism, as rights denied indigenous women by authorities and cashlanes (mestizos); communities, meaning costumbre or indigenous law, also rights denied to women; and also, "our husbands, our children, our parents, and even by ourselves."

b) Education, tradition: "We have been taught from childhood to do as we are told, to be silent, to cope, to keep quiet, to bypass participation. But we no longer want to remain behind: we do not want to be walked on. We demand respect as indigenous peoples and as women. We demand that our rights be respected. We want respect for our traditions, those that are beneficial to all women, men, and children. We want to take part in the making of legislation that takes into consideration the rights of indigenous people and indigenous women. We want to enforce our rights." ("Women's Rights in Our Traditions and Customs")

Here we can see not only the subordination of indigenous life to national life but also the subordination of women in the traditional gender system—subordination that women will no longer accept. This document is the inner reflection, the counterpoint, of the Zapatista Women's Revolutionary Law.

In both of these documents, which indeed are in dialogue, we can see women wanting to be social agents, to transform their lives. We can also see women demanding recognition for their own cultural forms. This combination of community transformation and affirmation is what is particular to women's struggle. A detailed reading of "Women's Rights in Our Traditions and Customs" reveals this combination/appropriation of knowledge and practices, as, for example, in the proposal that physicians and midwives work together.

Generational change is also evident:

Our parents believe working in the fields as they do is more useful than going to school. We believe knowledge will allow us to work better. . . .

In our communities we are sometimes forced to marry. We are sometimes traded for a cow. This treatment is unfair, we are violated by forced marriage. A daughter's decision should be respected, and marriage should be only the couple's decision. When a woman is forced into marriage there are problems from the beginning and she is more exposed to the man's violence. The parents are to blame for marrying a daughter by force. This is part of our tradition. Sometimes what parents want is to have a servant for a while rather than a bride for their son. (29–30)

And what I will call the self-determination principle:

Women have the right to choose their husbands, and should not be made to marry someone they don't want, should not be taken by force or sold. The husband, children, father, mother, the parents or brothers-in-law: they have no right to mistreat or batter us, and neither do the police or the army or any other person. (30)

Clearly differentiated are the various planes in which women are subject to violence: family, community, Ladino society, the state. The need for support among women is also clearly stated.

Family structure works as a contradictory core: it is simultaneously a unit of solidarity and resistance, which implements cooperative strategies for survival and reproduction, and a power structure, which establishes the internal relations and women's place within them, where inequality is marked by gender and generation. Thus the authority that the older men exert over women and over the younger generations is established both in the domestic and in the political, religious, and community spheres. This authority operates through the control of sexuality, material resources, work, and participation in decision-making processes and government institutions.

Men's control of resources begins with their control over land and extends into the family. Soledad Gonzáles Montes writes:

> The position of women in relation to the authority hierarchy varies according to the stage of the domestic cycle women are in, to their age and to whether they are or not married. . . . Women's progression is not the same as men's. Most women will never be heads of the family or control a significant share of the more valued resources. As long as there is a man above them (father, father-in-law, husband), women are "not their own boss." (González Montes 1991:236)

The family structure may continue as a unit of solidarity, but the accompanying hierarchical structure will have to be gradually modified, because the demands of indigenous women today go to the very core of domination: elimination of control by the head of the family over children's marriages, transformation of the marriage standard, access to control of resources—most important, of land—and participation in community government.

It is women who are more sharply highlighting the relationship between change and tradition, and they are doing it from a perspective that reveals the complicity between a national culture of "respect for tradition" and the persistence of marginalization:

> It is not true, as some mestizos think, that our only tradition is to eat vegetables and *pozol*. We want the right to eat meat, to drink milk, to have our children not die of malnutrition, to have women not die in childbirth. ("El grito de la luna," 31)

And women are pointing the way toward an ethical norm for the modification of a specific tradition:

> We must also think about what needs to be remade in our tradition. The law [meaning national law] should protect only those traditions and ways

that are deemed beneficial by the community. Our traditions should not hurt anyone. (12)

THE SECOND HORIZON OF VISIBILITY: THE *INSURGENTAS*

The EZLN opens a space where indigenous women and men can have diverse experiences. There is a "frontier" between indigenous women who remain in their communities and those who have joined the rebels (*insurgentas*).[4] The experience of command, the undifferentiated work of men and women, and the control of their own individual sexuality are three practical dimensions of the redefinition of gender. It is, paradoxically, an exceptional situation, in which women, in the words of Marcos, "have had to stop being women to become soldiers," but also in which through this negation of "womanhood" they may access another kind of regulation and experience of the feminine.[5]

Zapatismo as a Way of Life

Captain Elisa, one of the twelve women who, along with one hundred armed revolutionary militia, attended a press conference on January 19, 1994, said: "When I was living with my family, I knew nothing. I could not read, I did not attend school. But when I joined the EZLN I learned to read and write, to speak Spanish, and I trained for war" (*La Jornada*, January 20, 1994). Laura, a twenty-one-year-old Tzeltal who has held the rank of captain of assault troops for three years, said:

> I attended school as far as fourth grade. I was very young when I heard about the EZLN. I was working the land with other women who got together to grow some food. That's where we started talking and began to understand why we live in poverty and cannot find a better way of living. . . . I joined out of conscience, to fight for the poor; it is not right that children go on dying. (*La Jornada*, January 20, 1994)

The great majority of women who join the armed movement are young, just girls. From the choices available to them, many preferred joining the Zapatistas to working in San Cristóbal as servants or remaining in their communities. Subcomandante Marcos reported:

When revolutionary women left for the mountain, the older women in the towns accused them, said they were going whoring, that there would be no one to look after them up there. Women would ask the women revolutionaries how they were treated. . . . "If you don't want to be taken, do they punish you?" "No, no one can take you if you don't wish to be taken." "If you don't want a man, can you not marry him?" "If you don't want to marry you don't marry. . . ." And so we started to get loads of women joining in. (Quoted in Durán de Huerta 1994:33–34)

Something similar happened to the men. They could hire out to work and bring in a bit of money, but joining the Zapatistas began to seem a more interesting option. A boy who came back to his town to get his papers and join the Mexican army was convinced by his parents to join the Zapatistas instead.

The Zapatista armed movement is a community movement. Its links are blood links: parents have two, three, or more children in the mountains. The community sets aside food for them and provides whatever is needed so that the organization can survive. Families have given their sons and daughters to the Zapatista army.

The young *insurgentas* begin to look different to their counterparts who have remained in the communities. They are women of eighteen or twenty who have not had multiple births, have eaten well, and speak Spanish. They speak with confidence. The difference is illustrated by Hermann Bellinghausen in his article on a Zapatista camp in the jungle:

María Elena can speak Tzeltal, although she is a Chol, and she is old. The women of the EZLN are educated and healthy. They have led for years a Spartan life, but have had regular meals and health care. Like Amalia, María Elena thinks she is better off than if she had stayed in her town. Had she stayed, she would be like those sad mothers, barefoot, thin, surrounded by sickly children; any mother older than twenty has lost one or more children already and speaks with a fixed sadness that María Elena doesn't have. In her conversation there is no fatalism or ideological stiffness. She speaks without pretension, but when asked specifically she answers that she fights so that people can live better. Dying in battle does not worry her, and she already had a close encounter on January 2. Today marks three months of borrowed life. (*La Jornada,* April 4, 1994)

Infantry Major Ana María, age twenty-five, arrived in San Cristóbal with Comandanta Ramona for the first negotiations with the federal government there. She told how she joined the EZLN when she was twelve or thirteen:

> The EZLN responds to my personal interests. We joined the fight more than ten years ago. At first we had peaceful struggles where I participated alongside my brothers and sisters. . . . When I joined, there were only two women. All together we were only eight or nine *compañeros* up in the hills. They taught us to walk in the mountain, to load a weapon, to hunt. They taught us military combat exercises, and when we had learned that, they taught us politics. Then we went to the communities to speak with our people, to tell of our struggle and how we could reach a solution, and many began to come to us: men, women, and children. Most of us are young. . . . [W]e need support, especially women, because women suffer the most. It is painful to see children die, die of malnutrition, of hunger, of preventable disease. Women suffer. And that is why we fight. (*La Jornada*, March 7, 1994)

Women's Place in the EZLN

Captain Laura, about twenty-one years old, sits on a rock and holds a weapon across her knees as she speaks with journalists. They ask her about Marcos, of whom she says, "He is a man who belongs to our struggle, although he is a mestizo, as you have seen." "How did you manage to defeat all those soldiers?" "Well, we earn our rank according to our experience in the mountains, our capacity to work, and how we handle responsibility. When you start working as a member you are just one more subordinate. Your superior observes your progress, starts to give you people for you to lead and command. That is how I rose, I got some people, they saw I did well, and gave me rank." She coordinates one hundred fifty militia members. (*Proceso* magazine, April 18, 1994, 29)

Women earn their place in the military structure. Major Ana María was commander of the operation to take the San Cristóbal City Hall. But what really demonstrated the Zapatista women's military importance was the fighting at Ocosingo.

> Before the war there was a lot of suspicion from men when a woman held a command post. It was havoc; I spent all my time straightening people out. They'd say, "No bitch is going to tell me what to do." Well, that is how they were educated. . . . The problem came to an end in Ocosingo,

because the women officers fought best there. They were the ones who brought the wounded back from the field, where we were surrounded . . . brought them back alive. That put an end to whether women are able to command troops or not. (Subcomandante Marcos, quoted in Durán de Huerta 1994:32–33)

In a set of laws first made public on January 1, 1994, the Zapatistas included a women's law. There are various testimonies indicating that the law was sketched out during extended consultations among Zapatista communities. The law (see Section 1, this volume) was published in the EZLN bulletin *El Despertador Mexicano,* along with the First Lacandon Jungle Declaration, "Today We Say Enough!"

Subcomandante Marcos referred to this law as the "first Zapatista uprising" in his comments on the passage of the law in March 1993 and pointed out how the law upset the traditional norms governing indigenous relationships.

In March 1993 we were discussing what would later become the revolutionary laws. . . . Susana [head of the women's commission of the Clandestine Revolutionary Indigenous Committee, CCRI) had the job of visiting dozens of communities to talk to women's groups and gather the content for the women's law. When the CCRI met to vote on the the laws, the commissions passed to the front one by one—the justice commission, the agrarian law commission, the war taxes commission, the rights and responsibilities commission, and the women's commission. Susana had to read the proposals she had written from the thoughts of thousands of indigenous women. . . . [S]he began to read, and as she read, the CCRI assembly grew restless. Voices whispered in Chol, Tzeltal, Tzotzil, Tojola'bal, Mam, Zoque, and Castilla. Comments flew from one end to the other. Susana did not falter, she went on, tearing down everything and everybody: "We don't want to be made to marry someone we don't want. We want to have the number of children we decide we can raise. We want the right to hold posts in the community. We want the right to speak and have our words respected. We want the right to go to school and even to be chauffeurs, if we choose." She continued until she was finished. There was a heavy silence. The Women's Revolutionary Law that Susana had just read meant a real revolution for indigenous communities. The men looked to one another, nervous, restless. Suddenly, all at the same time, the translators finished, and in a gradually increasing movement, women began to clap and speak among themselves. It goes without saying that the law was unanimously approved. A Tzeltal representative commented, "Thankfully my wife does not understand Spanish, otherwise . . ." And a revolutionary official, a female infantry major, exploded: "You're fucked, because we are going to translate it into every dialect." The representative lowered his gaze. The women were singing; men were scratching their heads. I prudently called for a recess. . . . That is the truth: the first Zapatista uprising was in March 1993 and was led by Zapatista women. There were no losses, and they won. Such things happen in this land. (*La Jornada,* January 30, 1994)

Subcomandante Marcos's description illustrates the tensions around women's demands inside the Zapatista movement. In this context, the Women's Revolutionary Law articulates women's relationship to Zapatismo. Unlike other revolutionary laws, it is not only a declaration to the government and the nation but also a demand to indigenous communities, to indigenous men, whether they are Zapatista or not. It is also a demand to the internal organization. Women are integrated as a sector, and their specific situation of discrimination is recognized, and therefore the corresponding responsibility for gender subordination is placed on men. By opening the space for its enunciation, the Women's Revolutionary Law puts into action within the Zapatista movement one of its own principles—listening to those who have no voice. The voice of women is the intimate voice of the personal and daily life of indigenous communities. It is the voice that questions the internal hierarchy and the places where gender difference and subordination are practiced. In this sense, the law is only a formal representation of a larger process in which women are speaking out to change their political condition at the same time that they are transforming their daily lives. Not with evident success, as is pointed out in the self-critical communiqué titled *Leer un video* (Reading a Video). In the second part of the communiqué, "Two Failures" (August 2004), Marcos points out that there has been little change in day-to-day gender relations in communities.

In a way, current conditions have stopped the processes of change in indigenous communities. These communities are preoccupied with resisting counterrevolutionary attacks and laying out strategies to achieve results on the national level. In this plane, the demands made by the Zapatistas to the Mexican government on behalf of women are very clear. They are basically contained in point 29, "Petition by Indigenous Women," of the thirty-four demands presented on March 1, 1994, by the Clandestine Revolutionary Committee, General Command of the EZLN, on the negotiation table of the Peace and Reconciliation Talks in

Chiapas. These demands form the basis of later debates on the issue of women. They are transcribed below.

> We indigenous peasant women request the immediate solution to our urgent needs, which the government has so far failed to meet.
> a) Childbirth clinics where qualified gynecologists give indigenous women necessary medical attention.
> b) Child care centers in our communities.
> c) We request from the government enough food for all children in rural communities: milk, cornmeal, rice, soy beans, cooking oil, beans, cheese, eggs, sugar, soup, oats, etc.
> d) Well-equipped community kitchens and dinners for our children.
> e) Nixtamal (corn-paste) mills and tortilla factories in each community, depending on the size of the population.
> f) Farm projects (chickens, rabbits, sheep, pigs, etc.) with technical and veterinarian assistance.
> g) Bakery projects with ovens and basic materials.
> h) Artisan workshops with equipment and basic materials.
> i) Fair market prices for our crafted products.
> j) Technical schools for women.
> k) Early education (nursery and preschool) rural centers where our children can enjoy a healthy moral and physical start to education.
> l) As women, adequate transportation to travel and take the products from our various projects.

The difference between this petition and the Women's Revolutionary Law is clear. Subcomandante Marcos explains:

> Why is the Women's Law—which the women *imposed* on us—on March 8, 1993, not among the demands to the government? Zapatista women replied: "Some things must be asked for, and others must be imposed. We ask for minimal material conditions. . . . But our freedom and dignity are things which we shall impose, whether or not they are recognized by the government or by our partners." And they are advancing, in spite of the newspapers, churches, laws and our own resistance—we need to recognize this—as men to be thrown out of the dominant position we have inherited. Women have a long way to go still, but I don't see the least sign that they might be getting tired. (*La Jornada*, May 11, 1994)

THE THIRD HORIZON OF VISIBILITY: GENDER NEGOTIATION AT THE COMMUNITY LEVEL IN THE ZAPATISTA CONTEXT

Periodically from 1997 to 2004 I visited a community in the Tojola'bal highlands of Chiapas. During this time, I met and interviewed the women of the community many times. The main tensions I found with regard to what was gradually defined as "women's rights" were related to marriage, to the role of the man as the woman's "educator," and to women's political participation. I also uncovered what I will refer to as the figures of the new possible order.

Renegotiating Marriage

Taking part in the Zapatista movement requires that communities assign new activities, or "charges," to women, which in turn requires that they remain single for a longer period. In the community I studied there is a group of women between the ages of eighteen and twenty-five who have remained single and who defend this status as a right. This has been possible because of the new "possibilities" the movement has created and because the women's families have accepted the new rules.

Daría is the eldest of Zoila's twelve children. Zoila is proud that all her children "are still alive" and considers her family richer for that fact.

I have known Daría since she was eighteen. I have seen her grow stronger in her defense of her "right" to postpone marriage and decide who she will marry. These rights are clearly stated in the Women's Revolutionary Law. She represents a generation of young women who have charges in the organization. Daría participated in the women's commission and traveled to Aguascalientes and to Caracoles.[6] At present she is in charge of the Autonomous Municipality women's store, which is near her community. Below is a portion of the interview I conducted with her.

> MM: Don't your parents tell you that you have to get married?
> Daría: No, because they have no right to do so. Whoever wants to get married it is up to them, but they can't make me get married because they have no right, so I am not getting married.
> MM: Are you happy?
> Daría: Yes, I am happy. I'm going to play when I want to play [basketball]; not every afternoon, tomorrow we are going with the women. I'm not going to marry because then I won't be free to attend meetings, to visit other communities, whereas like I am, I can go to my meeting, I

can stay and chat, but if I had a husband he wouldn't let me, so I don't marry.

MM: Never?

Daría: I don't know, maybe . . .

MM: And do men think the same way? That they won't marry just yet?

Daría: Yes, there are men who are twenty-four, twenty-five years old, and still single. They think, when they have a family of their own, sometimes their family gets sick, then we can't go out . . .

MM: Did your sister choose a husband?

Daría: Yes.

MM: And is she still participating?

Daría: No, he won't let her.

MM: And your brother, does he allow Carmelina to participate?

Daría: No. She wants to, but he doesn't. That's how it is. People change a lot when they marry.

This interview took place on July 15, 1999.

Daría works in her household, but because of her responsibilities in the community, it is primarily her sisters who make the tortillas, work in the field, and bring in firewood and water.

Their husbands' "permission" is not the only obstacle to married women's participation. There are a series of responsibilities in a married woman's life that stand in the way: preparing food for her family, caring for her children, and working in the home of her parents-in-law, as is traditional. All of this makes married women think twice before accepting a position in the organization, even if they support the movement. Practical life is difficult; there is no time for organizing.

Still, some married women do participate. In these cases, the husband's agreement, his help with domestic tasks that are traditionally reserved for women, and his encouragement are important. Two couples in the community stand out.

One of these couples is the *koltanum*[7] and his wife, who also "talks the word of God." This couple is representative of another process that has upheld indigenous Zapatismo: religious practice committed to the poor. For this couple, there is no clash between their religious practice and the Zapatista struggle; they see them as having the common goal of dignifying indigenous life.

For years I have seen them participating in the movement, raising their five children in the Zapatista struggle. It is common to see the *koltanum* minding all five of them. Previously, when there weren't so many children, his wife went to meetings and he stayed home with their daughters. He also helps with traditionally female tasks, such as carrying water from the river, or firewood. The *koltanum* is a gentle person. His way of speaking and expressing himself shows a masculinity that is not based on exaltation. He cultivates the Tojola'bal quality of temperance.

The other couple is much younger and recently married. The woman, whose name is Teresa, is a friend of Daría's, but she is more reserved with me than her friend. Still, during one of my first visits, in April 1997, Teresa told me what her day is like: "I work in the house and in the field, I work all day. I am seventeen years old, and I have younger brothers. I get up at four o'clock, drink my coffee, make my tortilla, sweep up, serve my father . . ." By October 2004, Teresa had married a "true Zapatista," a twenty-four-year-old man, and they had a six-month-old baby daughter. This has made her more firm in her decision to participate in the movement. She is less reserved and speaks better Spanish than before. Since the birth of her daughter, she has not gone on "long outings," but she represents the women in her community and tries to encourage others to participate.

This is how, little by little, the idea of organization as something that relates to every man and woman in the community is absorbed. The movement demands that it be so: autonomy is not a simple project. The division of political labor requires every member's participation and, very important, women's participation.

Domestic Violence

Women's participation has another limitation that some of them pointed out: the jealousy of their husbands. On different occasions, women told me that their absence had been immediately interpreted as deceit and infidelity by their husbands, that they were considered to have done wrong and that the situation often became violent. Alcohol is often part of this picture.

Women are increasingly seeking the help of collective institutions to arbitrate cases of domestic violence. Zapatista rules prohibit alcohol consumption, and this is one rule with which many women are very much in agreement, because they feel it benefits them directly in daily life. We could go so far as to say that it is one of the benefits they see in Zapatismo, that men are pressured from other fronts not to get drunk. This fact has been described in many written testimonies, and the interviews in this community provide ample evidence for it.

Furthermore, in general, alcohol is known to have a clear relationship to violence.

In the interviews with men in the community, they immediately associated "women's rights" with the right not to be battered. This idea has spread quickly in indigenous communities, which is not to say that violence is not part of everyday life, but rather that the pressure to avoid situations in which women are subject to violence is greater today than before. When such a situation occurs, it is taken before the community institution, like any other conflict, and a punishment is meted out.

Women's Rights

To illustrate the two previous points, I would like to recount some of the discussions from three women's meetings between 1997 and 1999 where the subject was the Women's Revolutionary Law. Women's conflicting positions were defined gradually and generally along generational lines. Two positions emerged after the general acceptance of the law. The comments below are representative of the views of older women and younger women, respectively.

> The Law is good, because women's work has value too. But we should not exaggerate. Women have duties. Now they don't want to comply any more. That's why men hit.

> Men don't have the right to hit women, regardless of whether they are fathers, brothers, or husbands, and whether or not they are in the right; that's what talk is for.

The women also talked about other sensitive issues in the law: the lack of economic opportunities and resources; the way the central government (the bad government) treats both men and women and their communities; and the need for men to stop drinking, because alcohol results in violence.

The younger women felt strongly about being able to choose their husbands. The subject of deciding how many children they wish to have is also appropriated but not in practical terms (what contraception methods to use, sex education, etc.) Something similar happens with regard to the issue of women's inheritance of land. So the issues that remained central were violence and decision-making power. As the discussion proceeded, the tone of the older women became more cautious, even threatening: it's good that women are claiming their rights, but they should not ask for everything or oppose men.

The meetings also became, at times, a space for accusations: Have men changed? Only a little, they were still drinking, and when they drank, they hit. Morale was are not very high. They seemed to agree that very gradually men were changing. They mentioned that women were still ashamed, that they could not "speak" very well.

Martín, a man in his mid-twenties, arrived at the end of one of the meetings. He is a one of the political representatives of the organization, is married, and has three children. Martín spoke about how it is important to change, to respect women, and to respect women's rights. He said that women need to participate more. He spoke of the Women's Revolutionary Law and of how Zapatismo also seeks to make relations between men and women equitable. The women listened to him.

During the last meeting, thanks to the assistance of a Tojola'bal interpreter, communication flowed more easily. In contrast to the earlier polarized views—young women demanding their rights versus older women seeking to circumscribe those rights—the older women took a more moderate stance: Women should not stop "being women"; "men need to command"; sometimes hitting is needed for a woman's education. What should be done if the woman is not carrying out her duties? There has to be some punishment. This is the dominant commonsense voice, the voice of the gender *doxa,* as used by Bourdieu (1980), the social law always "naturalized" and the voice of cultural precept.

Younger women take a different position. Those who clearly promote the movement, like Daría, also assert and define their discourse: no man, especially a husband, has the right to hit a woman. Zapatista law says that everything should be even. The women asked Daría, mockingly, whether she was never getting married. And she responded, "I will marry, but I will choose my husband very carefully." "Well," the women said, "You will choose well, but once you are married, he's going to hit you anyway!" They say this and laugh. Daría laughs with them.

Laughter here shows their sense of irony and their full awareness that the dominant order cannot be changed just by insisting that it do so. The Women's Revolutionary Law has limitations, and they recognize the delicate balance of forces between the sexes.

Daría represents the re/vision of the law, or more precisely, the enunciation of a new law that would modify cultural precepts, not in their essence—women have responsibilities and duties that make them women—but in its procedures—men don't have the right to hit women; women have the right not to be hit.

Each of those statements affects different spaces of the community *doxa*. The authority that community structures confer on the male as father, brother, or husband is accepted. However, having authority does not make physical punishment valid. Even if a woman is at fault, that is, when she has not fulfilled the duties that the community assigns to her as a woman (whether as daughter, sister, mother, wife, or grandmother), she still has the right to her physical integrity, under any circumstance. This is a right that belongs to her as a person, because she exists. It is not a circumstantial or negotiable right.

Tradition is ambiguous in regard to the right of people to their physical integrity, because there are responsibilities and hierarchies that are understood as educational. How can a woman be shown how to be "a complete woman"? There are some circumstances in which the *doxa* justifies physical punishment of a woman by her father, brother, or husband.

However, the person who can teach and relate to others, both in public and in private, without screaming, shouting, or hitting is held in high cultural regard. Temperance is a valuable quality among the Tojola'bal, just as good behavior—within a rather strict framework of gender representations—is appreciated. Thus in cases of physical violence the community considers the reasons and circumstances and often punishes both members of the couple in a sort of exhortation to do better by each other.

As we have seen so far, the Zapatista process unleashes a tension inside the community we studied: people recognize, albeit rhetorically, that women's rights are part of the demands of the movement in its search for a more just and democratic society. At the same time, this is to a certain extent in contradiction with the *doxa* or the instituted common sense.

During the discussion we generated, the contradiction was represented mainly in the discourse of some of the older women, who think that younger women should be under some sort of authority that ensures that they fulfill their duties. Younger women and the movement's political participants created a discourse according to which there was no authority that would justify physical battering of women.

A recurrent metaphor of Zapatismo is that of "awakening." Even their newspaper is called the *Zapatista Awakener*. It would seem, then, that Zapatista awakening is also the awakening of an indigenous feminist consciousness[8] that introduces a tension between tradition and change, affirmed both in cultural and in community forms. Indigenous women are demanding cultural and community change so as to fit better inside them as the feminine subject that at present they want to be.

The appropriation of "rights" that revolve around the physical security of women is, no doubt, a fundamental principle intended to broaden
the sphere of individuality, an individuality that would seem to be completely overwhelmed by cultural precepts. In this way there is the potential for a "feminine individuality" that complies with community norms
but modifies tradition. Understanding physical integrity as a right and
having the power to decide when and whom to marry are spaces in
which individuality is growing within the framework of community recognition; that is, it is an individuality that is seeking legitimation under the new order unleashed by Zapatismo. Social movements are also
spaces of cultural creation, of reinvention of subjectivities, of contestation of the social order that has been naturalized (Álvarez, Dagnino,
and Escobar 1998). If the nation can grant justice to indigenous people,
then there should also be justice between indigenous men and women.
If nondiscrimination is at the core of the Zapatista agenda, this should
be translated also as gender justice in communities.

The more conservative women's discourse sets a limit on women's
possible visions. The inertia and the power of symbolic order, on the
one hand, and of everyday practice, on the other, can be recognized in
the ironic laughter of the young women. There is no revolutionary law
that can guarantee that the respectful man you choose through the exercise of your rights will not turn into a batterer after marriage.

Still, the law is the beginning of the enunciation of possible horizons, of envisioned forms, of acquired powers and expressed desires. In
everyday micropolitics, this allows more space for the processes of self-
representation of indigenous women. These are spaces founded in the
positive valuing of feminine subjectivity, its capacities and powers, its
specific weight in the processes of community reproduction.

One of the most interesting things about Zapatismo in relation to
women is the two levels on which the movement is articulated: the statement of indigenous demands is expressed from the marginalized collectivity to the nation; the same structure of organization has an effect
on its members that alters and underlines the relevance of gender order,
between the ranks and between community members.

Two things are happening at this point: it is recognized that wom-
en's rights are part of the movement's demands in its search for a more
just and democratic society, and the main subject of those rights is the
women themselves, who must—and do, in fact—act on their own
rights and against the dominant tradition, culture, and education.

It would seem that the Zapatista awakening is also an awakening of
feminine indigenous awareness. It is an awakening that, based as it is on

existing cultural and community ways, demands their transformation in order for women to better fit in them as their newly defined subjects. The axis around which the women's movement is explained inside the Zapatista organization is democracy. It might be that the issue for organizations with close links to the Zapatista movement is to consider the type of structures, spaces, and dynamics that better realize indigenous women's progress in the formulation of their own rights, needs, and desires.

What is happening in Chiapas sets forth many challenges to the Mexican nation in the twenty-first century. Foremost among them is the possibility that indigenous groups, today marginalized from resources, may be integrated into the nation in a way that *they agree and decide* is better for them. This depends also on the ability of the movement itself to make room for the demands and expectations of women, who are "marginalized among the poor," "subordinated among the oppressed." This means having the ability to articulate the specific differences between the movement's components and to reverse the patriarchal and paternalistic constitution of dominant culture. This depends also on the ability of indigenous women and of the nonindigenous women with whom they have built networks to go deeper into the process of political and subjective self-representation that is now under way. This process of self-representation is based on a positive valuation of feminine subjectivity, of its abilities and powers, of its specific bearing in the processes of community reproduction.

Against the old belief in the absolute subordination of indigenous women and their inability to transcend it, the Zapatista women's movement shows a combative resistance that, not without difficulty and contradiction, seeks to develop a new kind of politics, that is, a politics without gender subordination.

Today these social liberation processes face the threat of low-intensity warfare and the international polarization of the fight against terrorism. However much the Mexican political transition gave Chiapas the chance to catch its breath, conditions in the world at large are not very promising. Nevertheless, against the general flow, indigenous women's own affirmation seems to grow every day.

NOTES

An earlier version of this chapter was published in Cuadernos Agrarios 13 (1966). The research for this chapter and its translation were sponsored by

CONACYT as part of the collective research "New and Old Spaces of Power: Indigenous Women, Collective Organization, and Resistance" (38784-S).

1. *La Jornada,* April 8, 1995.

2. "Health in Indigenous Children," *La Jornada,* October 5, 1994, 24.

3. Record of the Encounter-Workshop "Women's Rights in Our Ways and Traditions," which took place in San Cristóbal de las Casas on May 19 and 20, 1994.

4. *Insurgentas* are female members of the EZLN who go to the mountains, leaving their families and communities. This section is based on press interviews with these women.

5. As formulated in Subcomandante Marcos's speech during his intervention on March 1994 in San Cristóbal de las Casas: "Why is it necessary to die and kill so Ramona may come here and you may listen to what she has to say? Why is it necessary that Laura, Ana María, Irma, Elisa, and so many other indigenous women take up arms and become soldiers instead of becoming doctors, lawyers, engineers, or teachers?"

6 Aguascalientes first and now Caracoles are regional political centers of Zapatismo.

7. The koltanum is the preacher, the representative of the diocese to the community, according to the indigenous theology of the San Cristóbal Diocese.

8. Aída Hernández Castillo uses the term "indigenous feminism." See chapter 1, this volume.

THREE

GENDER AND STEREOTYPES IN THE SOCIAL MOVEMENTS OF CHIAPAS

SONIA TOLEDO TELLO AND
ANNA MARÍA GARZA CALIGARIS

Recent social movement history in Chiapas begins with the 1970s and 1980s. The peasant movement dominated the Chiapanecan political landscape of that time, and agrarian struggles became the centerpiece of social programs. Women participated actively in a wide range of peasant organizations; although they did not make gender demands or form part of the leadership, their experiences are the basis for the political formation of many of those who today comprise the women's movement in Chiapas (Garza Caligaris 2000). The long road that indigenous and peasant women had to walk before they were recognized as political actors has been little explored. The analysis of this process presented in this chapter provides important insights into current scholarship on indigenous and peasant women's activism in Chiapas. We begin our analysis by reflecting on some of the stereotypical representations of indigenous women that dominated the early years of the peasant movement and on how these representations were used by the agrarian social movement in their confrontation with government officials and political elites. We center our analysis on two events: an indigenous peasant march to Mexico City in 1983 and the organization of peasant towns to reclaim land they felt was rightfully theirs and to resist repression in the 1980s.

The representations of indigenous women that we focus on here were constructed from different perspectives, but they stand for widely used categories and social relations that reach much further than our personal experiences. While they do not embrace the experiences of all women in peasant movements in Chiapas in the 1970s and 1980s, they do reflect the kind of experience and treatment many received as a result of their political activism during this time. What is striking is that very similar images have operated in the conflicts that have developed since

1994. We therefore point out the parallels that we find between the rural social movements of the 1980s and the 1990s in Chiapas and women's places in them during these two historical moments. We do not intend to make an exhaustive comparison; instead we want to point out that these representations are linked to deeply rooted social relations that tend to be reaffirmed when used. There are, however, spaces within which challenges may take place; this is why it is so important to discuss the tensions that exist between these stereotypes and women's concrete political experiences.

CHIAPAS AT THE END OF THE TWENTIETH CENTURY

The last thirty years of the twentieth century brought a series of crises and deep changes to Chiapas. The peasant movement there coincided with teachers' protests, religious conflicts, and the banishment of many indigenous families from the Chiapas Highlands due to religious conflicts that were also political. In addition, migration changed the demographic makeup of the state as well as land use, the economic structure, and social relations. In the early 1980s, thousands of Guatemalans fled into the jungle on the Mexican border to escape repression. The confrontations, encounters, and negotiations that resulted from all these processes contributed to a political transformation. Women participated in all these processes, and in a general way conditions emerged that allowed women to express their own demands and build political spaces that included them.

The rise of the peasant movement was expressed differently in different regions of Mexico according to different immediate causes, specific demands, and enemies (Bartra 1985:104–105). In Chiapas, land and peasants were the two main symbols around which an array of demands, discourses, identities, and actions were structured. These were the referents, with varied meanings, from which people started on diverging paths.[1] The first "invasions" of private lands happened during the early 1970s in the Highlands (San Andrés Larráinzar), the North (Huitiupán, Simojovel and Sabanilla), and the Central Valleys (La Frailesca). But during that period, San Juan Chamula was also shaken by violent clashes between community members and indigenous caciques, which resulted in many dissident families being banished from the town. These incidents, among others, marked the beginning of social mobilizations that extended into the 1980s. At first, local groups acted spontaneously.

Gradually, as peasant groups became involved with organizations of national scope and other social actors became involved, the agrarian movement became stronger and more unified. Peasants sought shelter in the organizations, and the organizations themselves changed to suit regional differences.

Women were present at key moments and whenever they were needed. They participated in marches and demonstrations, occupied land, and lent their support in keeping with the guidelines set by their groups and organizations. However, once the moment of a land invasion, a march, or another action had passed, women went back to their daily chores, and it was the men who dominated the political sphere. Women did not even take part in local assemblies, where a male member represented the family group[2]—and they were a long way from representing their communities at larger gatherings.

One of the features of this period was the violent climate that engulfed those regions where the state and federal government and local power groups were unable to find a political solution to conflicts and opted instead for repression. The drawn-out agrarian struggle and the radical character it assumed in some regions can be explained to some extent in relation to these responses, which allowed and even encouraged violent, often armed clashes between peasants and landowners backed by armed forces.

These long years of disputes profoundly altered the state's social spaces, the placement of individuals within them, and their ways of life and representation. As a result of the numerous land invasions that took place, many of the regions where private property had been the norm were modified to become rural spaces dominated by community property. In some areas of the state where landless rural workers had become essentially an indentured labor force, when they gained access to land and began to lobby for more, plantation workers and day workers experienced a process of "peasantization" and became immersed in new kinds of social relations. Conflict also increased as newly emboldened rural workers continued to pressure for land reform (Villafuerte et al. 1999:86–100). On the other hand, the rural indigenous and mestizo population that could not find a foothold in an *ejido* (agrarian reform community granted land through petitioning the state), a community, or ranches or plantations, emigrated to the bigger towns and cities in Chiapas and beyond.

This intense and violent period of agrarian transformation was accompanied by new social discourses and relations and resulted in the re-creation of a peasant identity. Many other groups in Chiapas, coming

from different situations and conflicts, were mobilized under the umbrella of the peasant struggle. Peasant identity had been metaphorically
and actually re-created during these two decades, but at the same time,
although more gradually and less visibly, the ground was prepared for
building other identities, such as ethnic and gender identities.

Along with the intense confrontations over land in Chiapas, the idea
began to develop in social movement organizations—full of contradictions and hesitations—that "conscious" participation on the part of
women could strengthen the group, the organization, and the community. Independent as well as government-linked official organizations—
and the vast spectrum of positions in between—attempted to win the
support of peasant women for their causes. Thus women's political action became increasingly strong after the Zapatista uprising and was at
the center of heated debate—developed in close relation to peasant
movements in Chiapas in the 1970s and 1980s.

The San Cristóbal Diocese led by Bishop Samuel Ruiz had adopted a
new vision in the late 1960s and 1970s in which oppression and exploitation were the two main social evils that the church should target in its
outreach and education efforts aimed at the rural population of Chiapas,
called the "Option for the Poor." The church's action was certainly important in changing the ideas of the rural population, but the rural men
and women who participated in this evangelizing work were far from
being passive receivers. In fact, one important process that remains unexplored is how the local population adapted and reinterpreted the various discourses of the Catholic Church and other institutions according
to its own interests and perceptions. Those who went on to join peasant
organizations created discourses about their political choice that were
inspired by "the Word of God," but Catholicism also supplied the arguments for those who decided not to join independent organizations.

The diocese's own contribution to the creation of women's new gender identity within the agrarian struggle should not be overlooked. In
fact, the church has always been involved in formulating ideas about
women and their role in different social settings. During that time, the
"Women's Doctrine" of the pastoral team of Bishop Ruiz that was working in rural areas sought to promote women within their families, communities, and organizations according to a socially committed understanding of piety. During the early 1980s, the doctrine taught appreciation
of women's role in accordance with "God's plan" for the family, so that
women could take a more active part in the struggle against exploitative
conditions in general. With this in mind, female religious workers set up
workshops to improve women's literacy and health, to support co-ops,

and to foster groups that would "reflect on and analyze reality." Very soon after that the notion of "women's subordination" began to be debated, and Catholic women began a long process that led to the creation of the Diocesan Council of Women (Coordinadora Diocesana de Mujeres, CODIMUJ) in 1994.

At least in part, this theology shared its interpretation of the situation in Chiapas with other actors who arrived in the state with ideas about social transformation; and all of them together contributed to the creation of new discourses and practices in relation to the local population. Some were associated with government institutions and arrived with the objective of strengthening official plans and projects; others were militant members of opposition political parties or Marxist or Maoist consultants for social organizations. During the administrations of Luis Echeverría (1970–1976) and José López Portillo (1976–1982), the government launched a "modernizing" plan (which centered on oil extraction and hydroelectric projects) and at the same time extended institutional action. To counter the toll of modernization on the poor and to stay social unrest, the government created social and productive support programs for rural areas, such as INMECAFE (Mexican Coffee Institute), TABAMEX (Mexican Tobacco Institute), CONASUPO (National Company of Popular Subsistence), and COPLAMAR (National Social Security Institute, General Council of the National Plan for Deprived Zones and Marginalized Groups). The growth and strengthening of government institutions such as these in Chiapas did not automatically translate into absolute state control over dissident movements— the agrarian struggle continued—but, inadvertently, it opened channels of communication that favored change and the formation of new identities. The jobs that were created in institutions and government agencies attracted civil servants, technicians, and college-educated workers, and as these people came in contact with men and women from the countryside, they brought and were given ideas, points of view, beliefs, and knowledge, often of a contradictory and varied nature, but which nevertheless helped to rehearse and validate other forms of political participation with organizations other than the official government ones. The meetings between all these actors created new forms of interaction, and in different ways favored the social movements that were gestating in rural Chiapas.

Government institutions had also begun to make special policies for indigenous and peasant women, with the objective of widening their support base at a time when their legitimacy was threatened. These initiatives, combined with the indigenist policy (offering assistance to indigenous communities to help them "mainstream") that was a tradition of the Mexican state, ushered in a host of programs that targeted the rural "female sector." The ruling government party, the PRI (Institutional Revolutionary Party), had experience organizing women within the party, but by the early 1980s, they had targeted rural women as well. The government created co-ops and organizations for women artisans, midwives, and traditional healers and offered services such as harvesting and arranging for the sale of vegetables from women's gardens. The female leaders of local PRI organizations, those who directed artisan or merchant associations, became the interlocutors between their communities and the government. Although these spaces followed the policies of the local and federal institutions, they helped to spread the notion that organizing of women was possible and legitimate.

Just as the paths people followed to build organizations were very diverse, so were their actions and the impact they had on the changing conditions in Chiapas. In spite of the different political action guidelines of the independent organizations, and even admitting, as some analysts point out, that the actions and the networks these independent organizations and parties built also reproduced old practices (see García et al. 1998; Villafuerte et al. 1999), their presence meant the opening of new channels of political participation (Garza Caligaris and Toledo 2004).

MARCHING FOR INDIGENOUS DIGNITY: THE CIOAC IN 1983 AND THE EZLN IN 2001

The women who participated in peasant movements acquired important organizational experience; they widened their networks with men and women from different places and with different languages and lifestyles, and they participated in a variety of actions. These experiences in different parts of Chiapas slowly transformed relations between men and women (often in contradictory ways)—their interactions, values, and perceptions—and affected the way in which women's political participation was regarded.

By the beginning of the 1980s, Chiapas had undergone almost ten years of violent land disputes without resolution but with accumulated demands, anger, and bitterness among landowners, peasants, and agricultural workers. Absalón Castellanos Domínguez, governor of Chiapas, began his administration in 1982 with an openly repressive policy that targeted independent opposition organizations, including regional peasant organizations in Chiapas. In this context, the peasants radicalized and intensified their protests. A march from Chiapas to Mexico City in 1983 that included approximately six hundred representatives of municipal areas (Simojovel, Bochil, Jitotol, Las Margaritas, La Trinitaria, La Independencia, Villa de Las Rosas, and Venustiano Carranza) was especially effective in publicizing the demands of the Chiapas peasant movement. All of the participants in this march were members of the peasant organization CIOAC (Independent Organization of Agricultural Workers and Peasants). The twenty-seven-day march was covered by the national press, which made the public aware of CIOAC's demands: end repression and violence, make land available, provide credits, and provide better marketing and working conditions. The public's main impression of the march, however, was the extreme poverty of the participants. Photographs showed bare feet, rubber boots, and broken sandals and always emphasized the women, marching at the front, carrying the national flag.

Large-scale public support for the march with a heavily indigenous component and headed by poor women was to a great extent responsible for its success. However, though there was poverty and suffering, not all participants were equally poor, nor were they all exposed to the same extreme violence; not everyone marching was indigenous, nor did everyone need land. Some peasants who cultivated sugarcane in Pujiltik supported the march by joining in their trucks. Despite the differences among the participants—some were protesting their lack of land; others sought to obtain credits and market their products—the march was characterized as an indigenous march for land rights; it was called the "March of Indigenous Dignity." The homogenizing image of indigenous and particularly of poor women as the key actors served as a cover for a variety of demands originating in different social relationships and giving strength and unity to the event.

Public acceptance of the march's dominant representations of poor, indigenous women was based on historical stereotypes closely related to postrevolutionary nationalism.[3] People's consumption and validation of these images as "legitimate" and "authentic" at the time of the march and even today operates almost as if by consensus. Behind this common notion, however, were, and still are, very different conceptions of the origins of and solutions for inequality.

One decade after the march of the CIOAC, the Zapatista National Liberation Army (EZLN) rose up in arms and caught the world's attention because of the originality of their demands and their strategies. Although the Zapatistas employed new forms of political action, their language, images, and symbols were based on the history of peasant organizing in Mexico. This can be seen in the EZLN march to Mexico City in 2001, seven years after the organization emerged publicly. The march's objective was to defend before the Mexican Congress the reform initiatives to the Mexican Constitution that had been elaborated by legislators of a previous period, based on the signed agreements of the Zapatista army and representatives of the federal government in February 1996. These signed agreements are known as the San Andrés Accords on Indigenous Rights and Culture. These reforms had not been accepted by the government of President Ernesto Zedillo (1994–2000) and had not been discussed by the Congress of that period.

Just as the members of CIOAC had done in 1983, the Zapatistas organized political events in some villages and towns prior to their arrival in Mexico City. In these events, the presentation of the national flag, the national anthem, and the clothing and indigenous languages of the march's participants were an important part of the ritual and part of their political strategy.[4] Their spectacular objective, the symbolic taking of Congress, raised political expectations and elicited the support of various national and international groups.

In 2001 the Zapatistas used symbols similar to those the CIOAC used in 1983. It is interesting to note that the 2001 EZLN mobilization was called the "March for Indigenous Dignity, March for the Color of the Earth." We do not suppose that the Zapatistas made direct reference to the 1983 "March of Indigenous Dignity." Both marches, and their names, are better considered as a continuation of the organized struggle against oppression and discrimination in Chiapas. Both the CIOAC and the EZLN used Mexican national symbols; however, in the 2001 march, the national emblems were mixed with those created in international arenas.

In the 2001 Zapatista march, traditional political symbols were reformulated to relate to democracy, human rights, and affirmative politics. And of course the Zapatistas incorporated other symbols, such as the ski mask and the cloth covering their faces and, most particularly, an emphasis on being indigenous and Mexican. The following speech by EZLN commander Moisés emphasizes this point.

> We will talk and make our other brothers and sisters from many states and from Mexico City understand. We will invite them to join us in our pacific struggle to demand compliance with the San Andrés Accords. We want to include in the Constitution that we as indigenous people are Mexicans but with different cultures and traditions. Before 1994, to be indigenous meant to be looked down on, to be badly treated and humili-

ated, but now, with our struggle, to be indigenous means looking straight ahead with your head held high and with pride. The great Mexico that we have today, we have thanks to our forefathers. We—as indigenous people—have our own way of understanding the world that surrounds us, and we have been resisting for more than 509 years. That is why we still have our musical instruments, our languages, and our customs; they have not been able to erase them despite all their efforts. (Quoted in "Palabras de la Delegación Zapatista a la ciudad de México," www.Ezlnaldf.org/static/delegacion.htm)

The role that the press has played in the construction and reproduction of these images cannot be ignored. After 1994, the Mexican mass media has taken different positions and battled ferociously for and against the social movements, turning into active political participants themselves. This process, however, actually began many years earlier, in the social conflicts of the 1970s and 1980s.[5]

INDIGENOUS WOMEN BETWEEN CONSCIOUSNESS AND BEING LEFT OUT

Essentializing images of "the indigene" or "the peasant" have been strategies of political struggle that have sometimes been successful. In 1983, after their march from Chiapas to Mexico City, members of the peasant organization CIOAC obtained part of the disputed land they had struggled for. In 1984, the Program for Agrarian Rehabilitation was created. This federal program provided funds for CIOAC members and some others to buy properties that had been the object of invasions. The intensity of the confrontations over land lessened in some areas, the land became social property, and private ownership practically disappeared. But the 1983 CIOAC march along with other marches and actions legitimized the agrarian struggle and facilitated a whole program of social transformation.

During the 1983 CIOAC march, journalists, advisers, and leaders stressed the class-consciousness of the indigenous women, understood as the commitment to fight for economic equality. Women's determination to continue marching despite the burden of carrying their children, their food, and the clothes that supporters gave them as they passed, proved—so was the reasoning—their great devotion to the peasant struggle. The indigenous women, carrying the national flag and representing poverty and the extreme fringes of society, became a powerful symbol that included, paradoxically, the contradictory images of consciousness and marginalization.

Women themselves expressed their participation in other terms at the time. Paying attention to these viewpoints allows us to better understand the contradictory space that this march and the larger peasant movement opened for the women. In Carmen's words:

> Seven years ago my husband died, I became a widow and fought on. I am in the struggle for my children, and for them I also participated in the march. I will continue as long as I can. ("Chiapas 84: La guerra de acá," *La Jornada,* October 20, 1984, 15–18)

All CIOAC member families had to participate in an equal way in the actions of the movement, just as they had to in other collective duties in indigenous villages. In general, men represented their families in the march, but widowed women with small children had no choice but to march to gain the land rights for their children. If the organization were to be successful, by Rosa's reasoning, her children would have a small piece of land, and she, even as a woman without any right to land, would have a better life:

> I am the poorest of all, that's how my parents lived, in poverty. Unfortunately, God didn't send me as a man, but as a woman, that's why I have no land, I have nothing. If I was a man, I would still have the right to a piece of land. . . . Even though I realize that I am so poor, what else is there for me to do? Sometimes I leave to work, but often they don't pay me well, what can I do? (Interview, 1984; quoted in Toledo Tello 1986:84)

Widows, at least in the beginning, experienced their situation as a double curse: their poverty and the fact that they had no men to represent them in the struggle. Some of them said that if their husbands were alive, they would not have to suffer the physical hardship of the long march, the fear that leaving for a place so far away implied, or the shame of doing "male" activities. The women who participated in the march did not represent the women of their village; on the contrary, they participated because they lived in less favorable conditions than those women who did not march. In fact, the women who stayed in the villages referred to the widows with profound pity and never felt represented by them.

The participation of women in the marches of 1983 and 2001 has many similarities but also notable differences. While CIOAC widows marched because they were obliged to do so by their circumstances, the Zapatista women had high political and military standing and were carefully selected as spokespersons for indigenous women. In this respect, Comandanta Susana pointed out: "We will represent the Zapatista women, and we will talk to Congress to ask them to include indigenous rights and culture in the constitution. That's why we march and that's why we go to Mexico City" ("Discursos de la Delegación Zapatista a la ciudad de México," www.ezlnaldf.org/static/delegación.htm).

The Zapatistas and the peasants of the CIOAC use similar words and expressions that are part of regional culture. Especially interesting are the words *poverty, poor,* and *suffering,* which have different meanings in both contexts. Rosa, the widow from Simojovel, speaks with compassion about her own living conditions; Zapatista leaders, on the other hand, show a very sophisticated political use of the terms:

> To be indigenous women means that we have thoughts, that we have dignity, and that we need rights. To be an indigenous woman makes us proud, but it is also difficult; it is very difficult because there is suffering and discrimination and poverty. Therefore, as indigenous women, we want that to be recognized in the laws of the Constitution and our dignity to be respected, as it is written in the Cocopa Law. (Comandanta Susana, "Discursos de la Delegación Zapatista a la ciudad de México, 2001," www.Ezlnaldf.org/static/delegacion.htm)

In the 2001 march, the women claimed their gender and ethnicity to become political actors and symbols of a political struggle, colored by nationalism:

> Our trip to Mexico City is very important and very great for the nation and for the world, because we will spread our word as Zapatistas and we will defend our rights as women and as indigenous people. We will personally appear before Congress and we will show how all that was when we signed the San Andrés Accords, about the rights and the culture of the indigenous people, on February 16, 1996. On our way we will be talking to thousands of honest men and women in Mexico. As an indigenous woman, I feel important as a Mexican woman, because we have the history of our first fathers, and they were indigenous too, and they also fought like us not to disappear. Their struggles were different from ours, but we have the same idea of fighting and living. As indigenous women we will not stop fighting while we are not recognized in the Constitution and we will not let

others treat us as animals. (Comandanta Yolanda, "Discursos de la Delegación Zapatista a la ciudad de México, 2001," www.Ezlnaldf.org/static/delegacion.htm)

Twenty years ago the situation was different. Women participated in the CIOAC in the context of the peasant organizations. At the end of each day, the organization leaders, all of whom were men, and their advisers came together for an evaluation meeting. There are many reasons that the rest of the people (men and women) did not participate in these meetings. Exhaustion and the difficulty of understanding the long discussions in Spanish and in Tzotzil and Tojola'bal are certainly one reason. Another was their lack of experience and confidence in their right to express their opinions. But for women, the primary reason was the fact that they realized that their concerns had no place in the meetings.[6]

Social organizations reproduced the inequality that was already present in Mexican society and created their own forms of subordination. Political leadership fell to small groups of individuals and advisers with a broad perspective, supposedly, of social change. They had the capacity, given and legitimized, to organize strategies, to negotiate, and to represent poor peasants. This vertical organization expressed and strengthened the leadership of those who had political experience. The women, who had only a limited knowledge of the Spanish language, little formal schooling, and no experience in participation in assemblies or representing their villages had few possibilities or an interest in participating in the discussions. These asymmetries, given as natural, were recreated and took on their own form in these organizations. If the main objective was to gain land for "the poorest," it was difficult to have discussions about inequality that were not directly related to the lack of means of production. It is not surprising, then, that it was generally assumed that the interests of these women were the same as those of the rest of the people. In this way, the agrarian movement opened up the possibility of participation for peasant women, but there was no space to question politically the differences and inequalities between them and the others, nor did their presence allow for the recognition of other asymmetries within the scope of the organizational projects.

When the Zapatista movement appeared, indigenous and peasant women had already gone through an organizational process, first within mixed (male and female) social movement organizations and then within their own organizations. This process revealed inequalities that had been seen previously as natural by peasant men and women and also by other political actors who worked with them. The participation of the female commanders in the 2001 Zapatista march reflected changes in the social participation of women; however, these changes were are not without contradictions. R. Aída Hernández Castillo and Violeta Zylberberg (2004) document the tensions in the daily life of the indigenous Zapatista women and in social organizations close to the Zapatistas. They analyze how the organization recovers gender demands, encourages the participation of women, and creates specific spaces for women (e.g., the National Congress of Indigenous Women) and, at the same time, how it reproduces obstacles to their actions and to the discussion of women's agendas.

IN DEFENSE OF THE LAND

In the 1983 CIOAC march, the prevalent female image was that of the submissive woman. But at other moments in CIOAC actions during the same period, the image could be exactly the opposite. In Simojovel (a CIOAC stronghold), for example, organized peasants took lands that had belonged for many years to private owners. The peasant discourse was about the recuperation of what was once theirs; the landowners and authorities, however, backed by national agrarian legislation, saw it as an illegal invasion. A lack of negotiated solutions to the conflict brought about confrontations, and the peasant organization in this municipality concentrated its efforts on defending and claiming land they viewed as theirs. Women played a significant role in the ten-year conflict as they stood with their children and the elderly to confront the police and the private army of the landowners, which frequently arrived, led by the owners themselves, to expel "the invaders." This popular strategy consisted in what were considered the passive and defenseless people of a community stopping armed groups usually tied to angry landowners or the state police, under the supposition that they would not be the direct targets of the repression. The men, especially young men, hid in the mountains; they had to be protected, as they led the movement. This form of self-defense—which we can also find in other places and moments—is based on the common image of the nonviolent "nature" of women and their inability to assume leadership. The authorities and local power groups shared these notions, so that sometimes this image was effective and the aggressors retreated. Proof of the acceptance of these ideas is that during these confrontations, arrest warrants were issued only for men even though the whole population participated in the land takeovers.

At other times, despite the inequalities that existed between the self-defense groups and the groups that arrived to remove them in terms of arms and the ability to use them, the results were not always favorable to just one of the factions. The confrontations showed that women were not passive, weak, or incapable; on several occasions, with stones, sticks, insults, and prayers they were able to repel the police, gunmen, and landowners. Many of the confrontations also resulted in removals, rapes, beatings, jailing, and murders. When there was a public outcry against these assaults, gender stereotypes again became prevalent: women again appeared only as defenseless victims of powerful men.

The other side of the coin was represented by local men in power. The landowners of the Simojovel and Huitiupán areas had maintained their dominance until the end of the 1970s. In the taking and defending of the land, the physical confrontations of owners and peasants (who had been the landless workers of the landowners) carried a symbolic significance and implied a break of loyalties that had existed in the midst of contradictory feelings of hate, admiration, tenderness, respect, deceit, and love. In this region, where servile relationships prevailed, women workers frequently had sexual relations with the landowners (Olivera Bustamante 1979), either by physical force or by agreement forged in this context of power. Some of the workers were children of the owner. These linkages, and the resulting relationships, generated ambiguous emotions that were never erased, not even in the most violent moments of the conflict (Toledo Tello 2002). In these confrontations, women had acquired the strength to face the landowners, despite their gender and class and despite being indigenous. Their attitude, the way they held their bodies, and their language constituted a counterhegemonic language. For the landowners, this language was an additional affront to the already existing bitterness over loss of their land. The reaction of the landowners was thus violent.

In the interplay of images and experiences within the agrarian movement of the 1970s and 1980s, the limitations imposed on women by mixed social organizations became more and more obvious. During the next decade, these fractures in traditional gender inequality in Chiapas permitted the rewriting of discourses and gender demands that had by then started to have nationwide importance (see chapters 1 and 4, this volume). In the 1990s women created new organizational forms as part of a gender-centered movement and both used and reformulated the dominant representations of indigenous and peasant women. Many of these images came alive in confrontations between indigenous peoples and the police and federal army after 1994.

One of those moments is captured by a famous photograph of displaced women and children of the Las Abejas organization in the municipality of Chenalhó (by Pedro Valtierra, *La Jornada,* January 4, 1998, front page). This organization—founded in 1992 by Catholic indigenous people linked with the diocese of San Cristóbal—has been close to the Zapatistas in their demands while at the same time maintaining their autonomy and their peaceful struggle. In 1997 hundreds of members of Las Abejas were driven from their homes by militant extremists of the PRI and paramilitary groups. They took refuge in nearby towns such as Acteal and X'oyep. On December 27, 1997, forty-five people died—most of them women and children—in the refugee camp at Acteal at the hands of paramilitary forces.[7] A few days later, military camps were set up in in Chenalhó and other municipalities and road checkpoints and mobile patrols increased. In the refugee camp at X'oyep, some military personnel tried to set up camp next to the spring that provided water to the refugees. At this point, Las Abejas started employing a strategy very similar to that which the peasants of Simojovel had used in defense of their land.

On January 3, 1998, about one hundred women, some carrying babies, surrounded about four hundred soldiers and pushed and screamed at them to leave the camp. Behind them, the men and children formed a second front. Just like the peasants of CIOAC in 1983, Las Abejas faced heavily armed groups in X'oyep in 1997. The image of the weak and pacific woman pushing back the police and soldiers again dominated the organizational strategy and the press images. Valtierra's photograph showing indigenous women repelling the Mexican army bears the caption: "These little, tiny ones, armed with these arms, with these hands, stopped them in X'oyep." Based on the emphasis on their religiosity and their mediating role in municipal conflicts, the members of Las Abejas were identified as pacifists. The killing of their companions in Acteal made them feel and seem vulnerable, though public repudiation of the Acteal massacre and media attention also protected them from further violence. Thus, while the men of the CIOAC, considered by a double discourse to be violent and manipulated by dark interests (First Report of the Government of Juan Sabines, 1980, Governmental Reports of Absalón Castellanos, 1983–1986), had to flee to the mountains, leaving the women to confront the armed groups in Simojovel in the early 1980s, the members of Las Abejas, both men and women, protected themselves with the image of pacifism, vulnerability, and Christian sacrifice (Garza Caligaris 2002).

In the beginning of January 1997, the Mexican army had set up military checkpoints in various places that had a Zapatista presence. This began a strategy aimed at dissolution of the autonomous municipalities of the Zapatistas (see preface). The response of the inhabitants frequently involved mobilizing the women to prevent the military from entering and occupying a community. Journalists, important actors in this conflict, also noted these violent encounters and, though they represented these indigenous Zapatista women as courageous defenders of their territories, the image of women as naturally weak and nonviolent persisted. The gender of those involved in the confrontation highlighted the message Zapatistas wanted to send: unarmed, peaceful, and brave people (represented by their women) challenging a powerful and unjust government (represented by the military, men specializing in violence). An image of Zapatista men facing the same military would not have been as effective.

These images are also taken up by academics of different political viewpoints. A paper by Adriana López Monjardín, for example, uses a contradictory image of Zapatista women—simultaneously brave protectors of their villages and nonviolent victims of aggression:

> After the massacre at Acteal, when the government proposed to "take up the initiative" again, the military incursions against the Zapatista communities found an almost insurmountable obstacle in the women and children. The women faced with bare hands the insults, the sexual harassment, the beatings, and the raids of their homes. The destruction of their villages by the Mexican army has been photographed frequently, and the images went around the world. (López Monjardín and Millán 1999)

The ambiguity of this representation is the reason for its effectiveness. Contradictory representations turn indigenous people, especially women, into actors and symbols in a political game. Adolfo Gilly, in an article that accompanies photographs of women confronting the military—Tojola'bal Zapatistas as well as Tzotziles from Las Abejas—glorifies the indigenous people and alludes to this peasant strategy throughout history:

> They repeat classic gestures: the spear of the nightly round of Rembrandt or of the medieval battle in Paolo Usello. They do not know it, but the memory of their bodies does, because it was always peasants who have done all the armed gestures in all wars in history. (La Jornada, January 4, 1998, 9)

FINAL REFLECTIONS

The social movements that have developed in Chiapas in the past three decades share many elements but also have significant differences. Changes in the political identities and in the priorities of rural social movement organizations, particularly after the public appearance of the EZLN, are notable. While in the 1970s and 1980s land struggles dominated the agendas of rural peasant organizations, in the 1990s collective identity and organizational strategies shifted to indigenous rights and autonomy. Our comparison of the 1983 CIOAC march and the 2001 EZLN march and of the early 1980s struggle for land in Simojovel and the defense of Zapatista autonomous communities in 1997 and 1998 have suggested the central importance of women to all of these struggles. The images of them as political actors are often contradictory—as both passive and nonviolent and as politically conscious, bold women not afraid to take part in armed conflict or confront violence and government authorities. Public images of rural women in Chiapas acquire different connotations depending on the political climate, the social, cultural, and political space within which they function, and the nature of the collective identities that are being strategically deployed. As we have demonstrated, women may be regarded simultaneously as conscious/marginal, as agents/victims, and as strong/vulnerable.

The influence of Mexican postrevolutionary nationalism is evident in both the production and the public consumption of representations of women, peasants, and indigenous people. Many different individuals and institutions take part in the production of these images: social organizations, the Mexican state, churches, academics, the press, police and military corps, local power groups, among others. We have been especially interested in the presence and the positioning of the mass media in relation to these images. During the 1970s and 1980s, a major part of peasant organizations' actions went unnoticed by the public. However, the incipient and selective coverage of the press of peasant actions in the 1980s began to influence social movements themselves as well as government policy. After 1994, the role of the media in the conflicts in Chiapas has been decisive; the media has disseminated and legitimated the images of peasants and indigenous peoples. Used as a negotiation tool, stereotypes of indigenous peoples—in particular, of women—have been politically useful and have had great symbolic power. Despite their efficacy, however, and because of their links with deeply rooted and naturalized social relations historically, these images may contribute to reinforcing relations of subordination between genders and classes, leaders and common folk, peasants and power groups.

NOTES

1. Among the many studies written about the Chiapas peasant movement, the following are noteworthy: Paniagua 1983; Pérez Castro 1988; Rojas 1995; Harvey [1998] 2000.

2. Even today, only widows who have no grown sons to represent them take part in general assemblies in most of rural Chiapas, and this includes women who define themselves as Zapatistas. During the assemblies, however, the few women who attend are unlikely to express their opinions. Breaking the inertia established by years of unequal gender relations will take more time and effort.

3. With regard to the representations of indigenous people and peasants in the construction of the nation, there exists an abundant literature: Villoro 1984; Stavenhagen 1968; Bonfil Batalla 1972, [1986] 1990; Palacios 1999. With respect to the changes in the representations of indigenous people in the past three decades, see Hvostoff 2000. There have been few attempts to explore the gender image with respect to the state, but Hernández Castillo 2001 offers important elements to stimulate further investigation.

4. Many of the representatives of the indigenous organizations that accompanied the commanders of the EZLN in the 2001 march no longer used indigenous languages on a daily basis, nor did they wear their traditional clothing. However, the symbolic importance of the march and its supporters being perceived as "indigenous" led to the political use of these elements in some of the most important actions during the mobilization.

5. Hvostoff (2000) has analyzed the transformations of the public image of the indigenous Mexican between the 1970s and the year of the Zapatista uprising, 1994. With respect to the images reproduced in the national media, she notes: "While in the beginning of the 1970s the press still represented them as being poor, primitive, and unworldly—in the best of cases, like children, we see from 1994 on combative, authentic, and emancipated indigenous people" (57). In our view, the process has been more complex, as the press has taken different positions and presented diverse and contradictory images.

6. Surely, the daily worries of the majority of the men were also left unaddressed in the meetings. An analysis of the reasons for their political participation and their interests would open a heretofore unexplored field for analysis.

7. There is an abundant literature on the massacre in Acteal, for example, Hernández Castillo 1998c; Centro de Derechos Humanos "Fray Bartolomé de Las Casas" 1998.

*Older women have played important roles
in the processes of political organizing.*

*Age and gender marked the ways in which women
experienced militarization and displacement.*

*Religion has been a significant channel
for women's organizing.*

*Women begin engaging in domestic labor
at a very early age.*

This Tzeltal girl carries her younger sibling in a sling on her back, as many young girls do.

Many children displaced by paramilitary violence have lived more of their lives in refugee camps than in their home communities.

*Girls born in Zapatista regions after 1994
grow up in a social context marked by shifting
gender norms, though how much roles have
changed differs from region to region.*

*Coffee is a vital cash crop. Unlike many other crops, such as corn, which
is generally sown and harvested by the male members of the community,
women and girls actively participate in coffee harvesting.*

*After paramilitaries stole a coffee harvest belonging
to Las Abejas, the Fray Bartolomé Human Rights Center
organized a brigade to observe the harvest.*

*The life expectancy of indigenous women is significantly lower
than that of non-indigenous women.*

The average age of marriage for young women, once as low as fourteen, has increased in recent years.

Engaging in organized struggle entails a triple workday for many women.

*Women have been at the forefront of confronting the federal army and resist-
ing military incursion into their communities, particularly
in the aftermath of the massacre at Acteal.*

*Women often bear the burden of reconstructing homes and families
devastated by "natural" disasters.*

Women demanded justice for the deaths of their friends and families in the massacre of Acteal.

Zapatista base supporters organized to accompany displaced people returning to their homes.

Women organized to demand aid from the government following Hurricane Mitch.

The militarization of the conflict region brought prostitution into the communities.

Women in Acteal march and pray on International Women's Day.

Dissident women.

FOUR

WEAVING IN THE SPACES

Indigenous Women's Organizing and the Politics of Scale in Mexico

MAYLEI BLACKWELL

This chapter widens the lens of gender and cultural politics in Chiapas by tracing how the presence of women in the Zapatista National Liberation Army (EZLN) has had an impact on local community organizations, reshaped indigenous women's politics throughout Mexico, contributed to the formation of the national indigenous women's network, and created new opportunities for transnational organizing. In chronicling the emergence of a national indigenous women's movement in the 1990s in Mexico, I focus on the Coordinadora Nacional de Mujeres Indígenas de México (National Council of Indigenous Women, CONAMI [formerly CNMI]), the first national indigenous women's organization in Mexico's history, to illustrate how indigenous women activists have developed a strategy of weaving in and between local, national, and transnational scales of power to create new spaces of participation as well as new forms of consciousness, identities, and discourse. My discussion here is based on oral histories of members of the CONAMI, ethnographic data gathered at several (trans)national gatherings, and an analysis of movement documents. I examine how the Chiapas uprising opened new political spaces for indigenous women and increased social movement networking between what feminist geographers call scales of power.

INDIGENOUS WOMEN AND THE POLITICS OF SCALE

Indigenous women, as one of the most marginalized sectors of Mexican society, have effectively moved within the limited social and political spaces allowed them, creating new forms of identity and social meaning in the crevices of discourses that exclude them and building new forms of political subjectivity and new spaces of political engagement. Out of the most restrictive locations, indigenous women have developed a form of differential consciousness, which is a political skill gained by moving in and between different scales of power or arenas of representation at all levels. To understand the full national impact and the transnational implications of the uprising in Chiapas for indigenous women, it is critical to understand more precisely how organizers developed this strategy.

In my search for conceptual language to express this movement in and between sites of power, I have found the ways in which geographers understand scale in the social construction of space especially helpful. In naming these levels of political representation and new sites of struggle, I have turned to the rich literature on scale elaborated by feminist geographers (Braman 1996; Marston 2000; Smith 1992; Staheli 1994). Scale is "the embodiment of social relations of empowerment and disempowerment and the arena through which they operate" (Swyngedouw 1997:169, cited in Marston 2000).[1] Lynn Staheli (1994:388) argues, "To the extent that oppositional movements can move across scales—that is, the extent that they can take advantage of the resources at one scale to overcome the constraints encountered at different scales (in the way that more powerful actors do)—they may have greater potential for processing their claims."

With limited access to cultural capital and material resources, indigenous women move in and between scales of power to gather and produce knowledge and political learning as well as to create solidarity and new forms of consciousness, thereby using gains in one scale of power to open spaces or leverage demands in others. For example, they have deployed national indigenous claims for autonomy to press for the democratization of local gendered practices. Organizers have used the momentum of local movements to build a women's network within the national indigenous movement and even demand women's formal leadership in national organizations. In turn, they have leveraged their participation in transnational organizing and continental networks to create an autonomous indigenous women's network on the national level as well as to develop strategies for using international law or the discourse on the globalization of rights to reorient entrenched and racist state policies. This strategy has multiplied the places in which indigenous women's demands are engaged and has helped them to create new organizational spaces for themselves. I map how the linkages between these scales of power shape the way in which indigenous women articulate themselves as political subjects and influence the discursive strategies they employ. By weaving in and between local, national, and transnational spaces, indigenous women have forged their own forms of differential consciousness and political subjectivity based on a fusion of experiences and discourses from those multiple locales. Effectively using these interstitial spaces to create new sites for participation, modalities of organizing and discursive strategies, indigenous women have transformed various scales of power or instances of governance and authority into scales of resistance. By documenting women's struggle for participation within the national indigenous movement, within their own communities, and at the transnational and international levels, I weave an analysis of how the impact of women's involvement in the Chiapas uprising has reverberated along three threads of indigenous women's political organizing.

The first thread of analysis draws from oral histories of indigenous women activists who narrate the symbolic and material consequences of the Women's Revolutionary Law and the way in which the presence of female leaders helped to create a new indigenous women's political subjectivity. Inspired by figures such as Comandanta Ramona, who was instrumental in the process that led to the Women's Revolutionary Law, and Comandanta Esthér, who spoke to the Mexican Congress in March 2001 after the Zapatista March, women activists have created alternative political imaginaries in which their voices can be heard, and they have translated this new visibility translocally to validate women's new community organizing and leadership roles. These oral histories give testimony to how organized indigenous women have used developments in Chiapas to leverage rights and create new spaces of empowerment on the local, community level. Using the impact of the EZLN model of grassroots women's leadership, indigenous women organizers have forged new forms of gendered subjectivity by moving in and between numerous organizational and political arenas and creating translocal symbols, models of leadership, and tools of empowerment.

The second analytical thread explores the national scale of organizing by chronicling the formation of the first national indigenous women's social movement network, the Coordinadora National de Mujeres Indígenas in 1997. The roots of indigenous women's organizing in the 1980s came to the surface in the 1990s as indigenous organizers, building on longer regional histories of indigenous community mobilization and resistance, used the momentum created by the Zapatista uprising in Chiapas to form a national movement. Forums, workshops, and national meetings held throughout Mexico became the foundation of the national indigenous movement and provided vital spaces in which to build the ideological and organizational impulse for indigenous women to form a national network. As a formal articulation of the national indigenous women's movement in Mexico, the CONAMI functions as a plural, autonomous coordinator of organized indigenous women in Mexico that brings together representatives from approximately one hundred indigenous, peasant, community, or regional organizations. While CONAMI members participate actively in both major independent national indigenous networks, the Congreso Nacional Indígena (National Indigenous Congress, CNI) and the Asamblea Nacional Indígena Plural por la Autonomía (National Plural Indigenous Assembly for Autonomy, ANIPA), they have also established their autonomy as women by forming their own independent organization.

The third and last thread of analysis traces how the transnational scale of organizing has been used to avert roadblocks to women's participation in the national indigenous movement. I examine the formation of the Enlace Continental de Mujeres Indígenas (Continental Network of Indigenous Women) as a transnational space for developing strategies for indigenous women's organizing in the formal international arena such as the UN Decade of Indigenous People. Together, these three threads of analysis demonstrate that indigenous women have created new political subjectivities and discursive strategies not only by trafficking narrative frames, symbols, images, strategies, and stories between scales of power but also by reshaping and translating them locally.

REBELLION AT THE ROOTS:
INDIGENOUS WOMEN'S INSURGENCY
AND THE CHIAPAS REBELLION

While January 1, 1994, is known as the date when the EZLN initiated an armed uprising, International Women's Day, March 8, 1993, has been called the First Uprising. Subcomandante Marcos has historicized this watershed moment as the First Uprising because of the significance of the grassroots consultation process through which the community approved the Women's Revolutionary Law. While the law guarantees a broad range of women's rights and responsibilities, it is just one of the sources of inspiration other indigenous women identify as important. That 30 percent of the EZLN's forces are women and women serve visibly in the leadership of the Indigenous Revolutionary Clandestine Committee (Comité Clandestino Revolucionario Indígena, CCRI) is not only a political reality; they serve as powerful and meaningful symbols of struggle for organizers who work at the intersection of indigenous autonomy and gender equality.

The Mexican government's response to women's participation in the Chiapas uprising illustrates the profoundly gendered nature of racial discrimination in Mexico and the state's dual and contradictory logic of racism. On the one hand, the Women's Revolutionary Law, specifically, the claims to reproductive health and the right to decide when and how many children to bear, is given as clear evidence of outside influence on the indigenous uprising. On the other hand, claims to indigenous autonomy have been denied by the government because indigenous cultures are dismissed as not being advanced (read civilized) enough to protect the rights of women in their cultures. While the legitimacy of the Mexican state's claim to be a defender of women's rights is certainly arguable, what is revealed is how the question of indigenous women's rights has been caught up in an externally imposed, state-defined binary of indigenous tradition and change. Indigenous women have not only had to create new spaces for political participation, their resistance has relied on their ability to counter state discourses of *indigenismo* that has silenced their historical agency (Blackwell 2004; Hernández Castillo 1994b, 1997, 2001a). Yet indigenous women's activism has been characterized not only by their efforts to combat decades of political corruption, violence, and oppression inflicted on them from outside their own communities but also by their efforts to democratize their own homes, communities, and traditional governance structures.

Todas Somos Ramona: Local Empowerment, Women's Leadership, and la Palabra de la Mujer Indígena

The Women's Revolutionary Law had an impact on women in the EZLN and the Zapatista base communities. But it also marked a turning point for women working in mixed-gender organizations to create new spaces for women to gain a voice, to demand their own rights as indigenous women, and to spark new processes of empowerment. The visibility of women's demands and the central role of women in the EZLN empowered other women to create new forms of gender consciousness, articulate their own gendered demands, and develop a new political language for expressing their agency and sense of cultural belonging. In this sense, the mask of Ramona has reflected indigenous women's political subjectivity back to local organizers and made grassroots women's leadership visible to the broader indigenous movement and to Mexican society in general. For example, "Lorena," a Tzotzil weaver from Chiapas, described how, though she had participated in weavers' cooperatives for a decade prior to the uprising, the uprising resulted in a shift in how women saw themselves:

> Then we began to participate in politics in '94, when we began to change the theme because we realized that in a cooperative we [women] were not taken into account and were ignored by the men. We had a cooperative, but we did not get to manage it. It was the men who decided, the men who gave their opinions on how they wanted the cooperative to function. Now we are beginning to participate since '94, since we have begun to take on more strength and valor. It's not just in the cooperative; it is in different events that we have attended as women. Now we can make the decisions, we can also be in the decision-making process that only men had ruled. After '94 various organizations emerged, the women organized, began to work collectively in ways they had not before. We always had had a lot of fear. . . . We were always dependents of our fathers, or our husbands. . . . We were not able to speak of things that we felt. Now we feel a bit more free, because we can think, and it was this [organizing] that gave us courage so that we could express our feelings too. (Interview, April 1, 2000)

In Chiapas, the Women's Revolutionary Law gave rise to many independent women's organizations (Hernández Castillo 1994b; Olivera Bustamante 1994; Palomo and Lovera 1999:65) and also transformed the local scale of power. For example, women in community groups throughout the country bagan to discuss demands human and civil rights in rural areas and held workshops to discuss Article 4 of the Constitution and the issue of *usos y costumbres* (customs and practices).[2] Through these grassroots meetings and workshops, indigenous women came together to discuss the role of women in indigenous cultures and deliberate about what they like and dislike and what they find empowering and disempowering with respect to their dignity as women. As early as May 19–20, 1994, a workshop titled "The Rights of Women in Our Cultures and Traditions" was held in San Cristóbal de las Casas, Chiapas, to prepare for the National Democratic Convention. Approximately twenty-four women's organizations from throughout Chiapas met in August 1994; the second session, in October 1994, brought together five hundred women from one hundred organizations (Palomo, Castro, and Orci 1999). In September 1994 the State Convention of Ciapanecan Women brought together urban mestizas, members of NGOs, feminists and nonfeminists, members of ecclesiatical base communitites (CEBs), as well as Tzeltal and

Tzotzil women from the highlands, members of weavers' and artisans' cooperatives, midwives, and Tojola'bal, Chol, Mam, and mestiza women from the jungle and the coast (Hernández Castillo 1998a:131). It provided an important space for women working in mixed organizations to reflect on the way in which the issues they deal with in peasant and indigenous organizations are gendered or specific to women.[3]

Numerous workshops and meetings of this nature served as consciousness-raising sessions in which indigenous women drew from their daily lived experience to analyze the structures that oppress them and the cultural, economic, and political processes that exclude them. Specifically, these early workshops began the conversations that would spread across the nation in relation to the consultation process of the San Andres Accords and at national and regional meetings organized to discuss *usos y costumbres* and the role of women's rights in the fight for indigenous autonomy. Women began to assess and engage cultural practices that had been seen as "tradition" and to reaffirm that indigenous cultures are lived traditions that change. In Chiapas, many women began to question forced marriage, the lack of access to reproductive health care, and the lack of control over reproduction. They agreed that autonomy for indigenous women includes bodily autonomy and that women themselves must make decisions about life partners and when, if, and how many children to bear. These early local meetings, moreover, became the catalyst for consensus among women nationally and regionally that indigenous customs and practices should be honored when they respect "the human rights of indigenous women" and when they do not "threaten their dignity."[4]

Many women also reaffirmed indigenous cultural practices that empower them as women and their collective self-determination and autonomy as indigenous peoples, for example, traditional dress, knowledge of traditional medicine, juridical systems, and spiritual practices (or relationships with people or nature that respect their worldview). They assessed their role in the social, cultural, economic, and political life of their communities and came to a new gender consciousness about those roles and their desires for more equitable participation. This process helped to shape a new sense of collective identity as indigenous women, which empowered women in their own communities.

Translocal Organizing

Because the historical impact of the EZLN uprising draws on prior organizing of indigenous women across Mexico, the reverberations of the gendered demands of women in Chiapas in turn helped to empower women on other local levels of organizing (Harvey [1998] 2000; Stephen 2002). The mobilization of indigenous women in Chiapas has created a wider conversation that has legitimated organizers in other regions who had been participating in political and community organizing for decades. The visibility of women's leadership and the demands of indigenous women also helped local organizers to leverage greater participation in their own communities throughout Mexico. Indigenous women organizers have developed a translocal strategy to open up new spaces for other women's participation, community leadership, and empowerment.

The oral histories narrated by CONAMI women illustrate that indigenous women had walked many paths of insurgency before coming together to build a national movement. Their early organizing revolved around liberation theology and community-based organizing; campesino or rural peasant organizations; economic collectives and productive projects developed out of the economic crisis in Mexico; and traditional indigenous governing structures and early indigenous rights organizations.[5] While indigenous women emerged as new political subjects in the 1990s by using the political learning that they had gained from those organizing experiences, the gendered insurgency of indigenous women in Chiapas was a catalyst for building a national indigenous women's movement. It was not until 1994 that women's mass participation and leadership within the EZLN made indigenous women visible as political subjects and provided other indigenous women with the powerful image that emphasized the importance of gender equity as a crucial component in the struggle for indigenous rights and autonomy (Hernández Castillo 2001a).

The majority of the CONAMI women I interviewed began organizing in the 1980s. Yet what the oral histories reveal is that there are two distinct generations of activists with two sets of generational experiences. One generation began to participate as married women with families who either responded to the severe economic crisis of the 1980s by joining women's community-based productive projects aimed at increasing their family income or began organizing through the church. The younger generation of activists began to participate in indigenous and peasant organizing as young girls with their fathers or other relatives and quickly became organizers in their own right.

Although married or widowed women negotiated their activism with partners and family members, they had some degree of social legitimacy and mobility in terms of social and cultural gendered expectations because of their married status. The organization of women in Chiapas and the mobilization of women at national indigenous meetings gave visibility and legitimacy to many women of this generation who moved into the leadership of the national indigenous movement. Among these women are Sofia Robles, a longtime organizer of Servicios del Pueblo Mixe (SER) in Oaxaca; Doña Rufina Villa of Mesevalsivamej, one of the oldest women's organization in Mexico (founded in 1985); Margarita Gutiérrez, a Ñha-Ñhu activist from Hidaldo; and María Jesús Patricio, a Nahautl leader from Jalisco. All of the younger generation of women's leadership resisted the conventional gendered expectations of parents and community members to become "capacitadas" (trained organizers) and began working in weaver's cooperatives, indigenous rights organizations, and traditional indigenous communal structures. From there, the women of that generation went on to become human rights and community leaders, community educators, or promoters of indigenous cultural recovery, indigenous women's reproductive health, and women's rights within the struggle for indigenous autonomy.

One thread that unified all their testimonies is the challenges they faced as young women community leaders who, because of their work and their new roles as community leaders, had chosen not to marry or conform to gendered norms and community expectations. Because they had followed a nontraditional path (i.e., they did not marry at the traditional age or follow the path expected of them), their families often did not support them and their political work was a source of conflict. For example, a powerful young organizer, Hermalinda Tiburcio, who is a member of 500 Years of Indigenous Resistance and the CONAMI, related that she had to run away from home and learn to survive on her own in order to attend school because her father had refused to allow her to pursue an education and wanted her to marry. She made her way on her own, taking in wash to survive, and lived in virtual exile until she began working to document human rights abuses by the military—which involved rape, murder, and incarceration of leadership—after the community she worked for declared itself an autonomous municipality.

> I left the house very young. We lived . . . well, my father was very poor. I had to run away from my house in order to go study because my father did not want to allow me to go study. He told me, "No, you have to marry, all your sisters already married." Then, one day, I had to escape . . . it was the 9th of June . . . and I went like a guy [*un tipo*] to study in the city. I arrived and began to search for work . . . I became trained as a technician of community development. . . . I had to run away from my

house. . . . I did not return to my house because my father wanted me to marry. I had to seek out a living not knowing how to live and where, but I enjoyed my autonomy because I was not dependent on my parents, or anyone, I just worked and studied. I never really knew what autonomy meant or if daughters were allowed to study. I thought it was only my father who did not allow me to study, but when I traveled in the communities [later working as an organizer] I saw that nobody studied.

It was very difficult. We women live a very difficult life because many times we are afraid to leave. We don't know what we'll find, how we'll eat or what we'll encounter. So we are always afraid, but when I left, I lost this fear. Even though I felt very, very alone . . . little by little I recovered and after a while saw that I had a future and had to seek out that future. I worked at a market, and I washed people's clothes and later I learned to iron. . . . So my work and my autonomy has cost me a lot, but thank God I learned so many things. It's as if I have lived eighty years and really I have barely lived twenty-three. I learned many things about how to take care of myself. (Tiburcio 2000)

Cándida Jiménez, a community educator, travels through different pueblos of the highlands of Oaxaca, but when she reaches her hometown, she often confronts physical threats, sexual harassment, and unwanted, aggressive proposals of marriage.

It was the same with my father who wanted me to marry at thirteen years old. I said, "I will not marry at the age of thirteen," and this meant disobedience. . . . For five years, my father did not speak to me. I wrote to him and asked his pardon, "Ay, but no, forgive me, I do not want to marry." He told me, "You are not my daughter. I don't know you. I don't want to see you." And he wouldn't see me. I went anyways because I had to see them . . . and see my mother.

And it's the same with men when they saw that I was free, right? . . . They were always bothering me to marry them. Two, three men following along behind me, [taunting] "Why don't you get married? Let's get married," and whatever else they would say. I would say, "I don't want to marry, and I don't love you, I don't want to." They would try to make me there in the community . . . before I was not as capable as I am now . . . when a woman says no, it's another thing. Because then they feel the authority to beat you, to obligate you, and to tell you that by force you have to be their girlfriend, that you have to marry him. They have stopped me, grabbed my hands so that I would say yes, I'll be yours. But I say, no, I will never be yours, or crazy. If I say no, it's no. (Jiménez 1999)

While many pueblos have traditions of women's leadership and political participation, some communities in resistance are undergoing cultural, social, and political revitalization and community structures are changing due to economic, labor, and migratory patterns. The transformation of gender roles can be a source of conflict (Hernández Castillo 1994a). Yet the visibility of women's participation and leadership in Chiapas helped to normalize these changes and even put them in a positive light. The Women's Revolutionary Law as well as the growth of a national movement helped activists to create solidarity among themselves and with activists from other regions. Crucially, it helped families to accept the kinds of gender and cultural transformation that the younger women represent. While female organizers still face sexual harassment and have to negotiate their roles with family members, parents are beginning to see their daughters in a different light. For example, Hermalinda discusses the changes in her parents' attitudes:

My family has come to respect me very much. They feel proud of me. I have achieved and earned a space that before they did not value. And now they see that I have walked with [accompanied] this movement and I have helped other people. I tell them, "No, I don't want what happened to me to happen to other women, I had to run away to study and I don't want others to have to leave to study. I want them to know there is another way of life." (Tiburcio 2000)

Still, while some parents still fear for the lives and personal safety of their daughters, especially in zones that are increasingly militarized, others have come to respect the work their daughters are doing, and some daughters increasingly feel that they have other choices than to live in community exile to be part of the struggle for indigenous rights.

A CHANGE IN THE WIND: INDIGENOUS WOMEN BUILDING A NATIONAL MOVEMENT

Each day we are closer to lifting our faces . . . to recovering our dignity.

MARGARITA GUTIÉRREZ, 2001

In the ten years after the uprising in Chiapas, the EZLN convened many sectors of civil society, creating a political opening in which to build a

national network of indigenous social movement organizations throughout Mexico. The political force of the Chiapas uprising allowed other
regional indigenous movements to become visible and generated the
momentum to build national indigenous networks. This vibrant national movement draws from diverse political sectors, and women have
accompanied this process at each step of its construction, from the surge
in regional-based women's meetings to the women's caucuses and committees at national gatherings. In fact, these two levels of participation,
or scales of power, became intertwined and mutually reinforcing. Indigenous women used regional structures to call more women to participate; and as they gained a voice and articulated a national agenda, they
used those developments to encourage local organizations and indigenous municipal structures to become more open to women.

Building on the foundation provided by regional-based women's
meetings, new sites of convergence and dialogue occurred at the National Democratic Convention, the National Indigenous Forum, the
Seminar on Reforms to Article 4 of the Constitution, and, in more distant ways, in response to preparations for the Fourth World Conference
on Women and the UN Decade of Indigenous Peoples. In each national
political formation within the indigenous movement, women constructed internal structures of participation and representation such as
the Women's Commissions of ANIPA and the CNI. As the indigenous
movement grew at the national level, women also created a parallel
structure of political participation when they began convening, organizing and attending national indigenous women's meetings as early as
1995, which served as the organizational stepping-stones to build their
own network, the Coordinadora Nacional de Mujeres Indígenas de
México, in 1997.

In the years following the uprising in Chiapas, the mobilization of
indigenous peoples continued, spread, and coalesced on the national
level and women have made themselves much more visible as actors in
the indigenous movement by constructing a specific space to articulate
their own demands, denunciations, hopes, and projects as fully participating members of their communities (Bonfil Sánchez and del Pont Lalli
1999:239). Moreover, they have effectively shifted indigenous political
demands by adding their own analyses of how political and cultural
power is organized through the intersections of gender, indigeneity, and
class and have made a space for themselves by weaving in and between
multiscaled relations of power.

A political identity as indigenous women has been constructed
through women's participation in a larger civil society mobilization ini-

tiated by the EZLN, which is unique in Latin American insurgency because its negotiations with the government have not focused just on their own demands but have involved a larger consultation with diverse social sectors throughout Mexico. Recognizing that a change in the regime would not be enough to initiate a process of democratization, the EZLN has attempted to bring together sectors that have previously found little commonality and to involve them in the larger project of building a democratic civil society in Mexico. I want to briefly unweave various strands of this mobilization of civil society to show how they have converged into a space for indigenous women's organizing that eventually led to the formation of the CONAMI.

Women's participation in indigenous organizing after 1994 paralleled the growing power of the indigenous movements as it sought to create spaces within it for dialogue about gendering the demand for the "right to have rights." One step in creating a space for women nationally was the *sexta pregunta* (sixth question) of the Zapatistas' first Consulta Nacional, which asked whether women should have parity in participation and within all *cargos* (positions of responsibility). It received a resounding "Yes!" The National Democratic Convention in Aguascalientes, Chiapas, August 6–9, 1994, was a historic moment. Another was the National Indigenous Convention in December 1994, where the final declaration of the convention, "Declaración de la Montaña de Guerrero," greeted and congratulated the large number of female delegates, acknowledging women's already pivotal role in the indigenous movement of Mexico. These meetings signaled the growing convergence and *acercamiento* (coming together) of indigenous organizations that began meeting to discuss various proposals for indigenous autonomy.

The San Andrés Accords

Initiated in February 1994, the San Andrés Accords were the first in a set of negotiations between the EZLN and the federal government in what was supposed to be several rounds of talks addressing different aspects of indigenous demands.[6] The accords were eventually signed on February 16, 1996, in San Andrés Larrainzar, renamed by the Zapatistas San Andés Sacam ch'en (San Andrés of the Poor in Tzotzil), but the government has yet to fulfill its side of the negotiations. The Accords on Indigenous Rights and Culture are historically important because they recognize *pueblos indios* as legal subjects and legitimate the concepts of self-determination and autonomy, thus laying the groundwork for cultural and political autonomy, greater self-determination, and legal claims to indigenous rights.[7] The accords not only guarantee access to political representation within governing state structures but also guarantee the validity of internal structures of indigenous self-government.

"Situation, Rights, and Culture of Indigenous Women" was one of the working sessions in the dialogues between the EZLN and the government in which indigenous women, nineteen invited guests, and twelve advisers from Indian communities and women's organizations throughout Mexico participated in the first session of the Peace dialogues "Indigenous Rights and Culture." Consensus among the invited advisers of both the government and the EZLN was reached recognizing the triple oppression of indigenous women, as well as their marginalization both inside and outside the community; the urgent need for greater participation on the part of women under conditions of equality with men; and the need to have access to different levels of representation and power both in and outside of their pueblos (Gutiérrez and Palomo 1999:65). Although the Comisión de Concordia y Pacificación (Commission of Concord and Peace, COCOPA) did not ratify the women's session document, the call for autonomy was echoed in several other important seminars and women's meetings.

Asamblea Nacional Indígena Plural por la Autonomía

One turning point in creating new spaces of participation occurred in August 1995 at the third ANIPA, held in the city of Oaxaca, where Josefa González Ventura, a Ñu Savi women well respected for her long history of struggle, was successful in calling for a working session on the rights of women. ANIPA was formally established after the second National Indigenous Convention in Juchitán, Oaxaca, and after the dissolution of the National Democratic Convention, which was marked by tensions in its efforts to unite indigenous organizations as a sector.[8]

It was during the working session at the third national assembly that women's spaces within the national scale of power began to be forged. Yet it is also clear that the transnational scale of power facilitated the process in which indigenous women in Mexico would organize and articulate themselves politically at the national level. For example, at the first national meeting, the Mexican delegates who had just returned from the First Continental Encuentro of Indigenous Women of the First Nations of Abya Yala, held in Quito, Ecuador, July 30–August 4, discussed their commitment to hold the Second Continental Encuentro in Mexico City in 1997. In addition to recognizing the need for a space for indigenous women to meet nationally, the meeting focused on the problematic circumstances of indigenous women and their lack of access to decision-making processes both within and outside of their pueblos. In one of the first statements of women to emerge from the indigenous movement outside of Chiapas, participants at the women's meeting held at the third ANIPA found that indigenous women's political participation should be guaranteed "in the home, the community, the municipalities, in autonomous regions, and at the national level." Further, "it was in this assembly that the fulfillment of a national meeting of indigenous women was proposed in order to have more in-depth discussion and analysis of the initiative for a law of autonomous regions" (Gutiérrez and Palomo 1999:64).

Encuentro Nacional de Mujeres de la ANIPA

Indigenous women committed to take the San Andrés Accords to their own pueblos to generate national discussion and meet again to discuss indigenous autonomy from a gendered perspective. Two hundred seventy women from different parts of the country and diverse pueblos came together at the Encuentro Nacional de Mujeres de la ANIPA in December 1995 in San Cristóbal de las Casas, Chiapas, two days before the fourth assembly. The first national Women's Conference of ANIPA helped to clarify women's demands in relation to the call for indigenous autonomy. Indigenous women activists recognized that forms of self-governance and recognition of cultural and traditional norms are positive, but they broke with the uncritical celebrations of tradition to identify both good and bad customs. There "are customs that can be counter productive or contrary to the dignity or liberty of women," remarked Juliana Gómez, a Mixteca representative of the Editorial Center of Indigenous Literature in Oaxaca (quoted in Santamaria 1996:7).

In their consideration of ANIPA's proposal for Autonomous Pluriethnic Regions (RAP) at the Women's Conference, indigenous women organizers demanded a better definition of ANIPA's legislative initiative in terms of guaranteeing women's rights in RAPs and the issues of autonomy and gender rights:

> Autonomy for us women implies the right to autonomy, [where] we as women can make ourselves capable to look for spaces and mechanisms to be heard in community assemblies and to have positions of responsibility [cargos]. Similarly it implies facing our own fears and daring to make decisions and to participate, to seek out economic independence, to have

independence in the family, to continue informing ourselves, because knowledge gives us autonomy. To spread women's experiences in order to encourage others to participate, to be able to participate in this type of meeting.[9]

To continue building a larger space of participation for indigenous women, they agreed to search for forms of organization that they hoped would grow into a national network.

The National Indigenous Congress

The National Indigenous Congress convened by the EZLN as a way to forge dialogue on the San Andrés Accords held its first working session, "Indigenous Culture and Rights," on January 3–8, 1996. This forum took on growing urgency in the midst of increased government military harassment of Zapatista base communities in the highlands and the jungle at the end of 1995. The National Indigenous Congress signaled the existence of a broad spectrum of indigenous actors among multiple sectors of indigenous society (Vera Herrera 1998:35).[10]

In the next six months, three hundred delegates met in Oaxaca, Jalisco, Veracruz, San Luis Potosí, Puebla, Tabasco, Campeche, Quintana Roo, and Michoacán. In July 1966 the delegates met again in Chiapas, but on August 29 the EZLN left the negotiations with the federal government to demand the release of Zapatistas who were detained in northern Chiapas as well as the release of other political prisoners. However, they made it clear that they were not breaking off the negotiations, only demanding minimal conditions before they would continue.

It was in the context of increasing militarization that organizations within the Permanent National Indigenous Forum convened an urgent meeting in Mexico City in October 1996 to plan a large encuentro of all indigenous organizations in the country (Hernández Navarro 1999). Although there was a stalemate between the EZLN and the government, which would not grant the right of free transit, the EZLN selected Comandanta Ramona, a respected member of the EZLN, to be their representative at the meeting. Comandanta Ramona and one thousand delegates came to the meeting, where the National Indigenous Congress was formalized. The CNI was a unifying moment in the indigenous movement. One of the leaders of what would later become the Coordinadora Nacional de Mujeres Indígenas, María de Jesús Patricio, read the final declaration. During this period, the indigenous women's movement was also growing and consolidating. In the Women's Commission of the National Indigenous Forum in January 1996 the accords that were discussed and approved in San Andrés were further considered. Through the Women's Commission of the CNI and a national meeting of indigenous women, the First National Encuentro of Indigenous Women was planned.

COORDINADORA NACIONAL DE MUJERES INDÍGENAS DE MÉXICO

The First National Encuentro of Indigenous Women, aptly titled "Constructing Our Own History," was held in Oaxaca in 1997. With attendance by more than seven hundred indigenous women from diverse states, organizations, and the majority of Mexico's fifty-six pueblos, as well as Comandanta Ramona and a women's delegation from the EZLN, the formation of the CONAMI was seen as a historic mandate. Cándida Jimenez, Mixe *promotora* (promoter) from Oaxaca, stated, "In this great event we agreed that it was the moment to unite forces and to work together towards the respect of our rights that have been violated. The Coordinadora Nacional de Mujeres Indígenas was given formality and a representative from each state was chosen."

This organization focuses on human rights, reproductive health, stopping family and military violence, and collective self-education on international and national treaties, pacts, accords, and conventions concerning the rights of indigenous peoples, specifically from the perspective of indigenous women. The organization is an inclusive, politicallypluralistic and participatory space that engages in dialogue through seminars, workshops, and meetings to discuss women's rights in indigenous cultures, cultural demands, the demands against the state, women's participation in the UN Decade of Indigenous Peoples, and ways to guarantee indigenous women's rights in the movement for the Mexican Constitutional Recognition of the Rights of Indigenous Peoples.[11] The stated objectives of the CONAMI are to construct a space for analysis and reflection on the problems confronting indigenous women in Mexico; to sensitize indigenous pueblos and national society to have respect for the human rights of indigenous women, including a vision of gender; to influence in an organized manner the political, social, and cultural processes that affect indigenous women; to fortify and consolidate the CONAMI as the coordinator of all organizations, networks, and projects as a plural and inclusive space of indigenous women throughout the country;

and to strengthen the processes of autonomy and self-determination of indigenous pueblos, with conscious and true participation of women.

The CONAMI mirrors the diversity of mobilized sectors within the indigenous movement. It includes representatives of local and regional organizations that represent a geographic range and broad spectrum of kinds of organizations. Operating as a representative coordinating body of the organized indigenous women's movement in Mexico consisting of approximately one hundred organizations, members participate as representatives of their own pueblos' traditional governing structures and community or regional organizations. Others participate as members of peasant organizations, rural associations, or collectives.[12] While a good number of the participants belong to independent indigenous women's groups, the majority belong to mixed gender organizations, so the CONAMI functions as a vital space of participation and reflection on how to address their political, economic, cultural, and social problems and devise strategies that address their lived conditions as indigenous peoples, women, and members of the most economically marginalized communities in the nation.

Three representatives of the CONAMI from each state attend national meetings and distribute information to those who cannot travel. The circulation and distribution of information is crucial since many indigenous women are unable to leave their daily responsibilities to travel to the capital every two months. The bimonthly meetings of an elected coordinating team ensures continuity and organizational coherence, and representatives often serve on the six commissions that have been set up to address financing, human rights, international organizing, and training and capacity building.

The CONAMI has held several national workshops and has begun training *promotoras* in areas ranging from reproductive health and human rights to the prevention of violence against women and indigenous women's autonomy. The focus of the national workshops are twofold: on the internal community level, indigenous women have made demands for reproductive health, campaigns to prevent violence against women and interfamilial violence, a call for greater participation of women in the decision-making structures of their pueblos, a reconsideration of *usos y costumbres* so that they are respected only when they do not violate women's dignity, and the right for women to inherit land. Training and discussion of issues external to the pueblos in which indigenous women reside include demands for human, cultural, collective, and territorial rights of *pueblos indios;* violence against indigenous women carried out by police and military forces as well as state agencies; and international conventions on labor, discrimination against women, intellectual property rights, and biological diversity.

While most women in the CONAMI come from their local or regional organizations, they represent the ideological diversity or various approaches and organizational sites of the national indigenous movement. Several women participate in both ANIPA and the CNI, in which ANIPA participates. Margarita Gutiérrez has been a member of ANIPA since its founding and has served as executive president. Martha Sánchez, current president of ANIPA, is an Amuzgo from Guerrero, former secretary of 500 Años de Resistencia Indígena, and a leader of the CONAMI. Many women, including María de Jesús Patricio, Sofía Robles, and Cándida Jimenez, have been on the coordinating team of the CONAMI and are active in the CNI. The CONAMI has established and maintains its autonomy from both the CNI and ANIPA. With respect to this history and the importance of indigenous women's organizational autonomy as well as indigenous women's strategies of moving in and between organizational spaces to create new modes of articulation for themselves, Sofia Robles, a Mixe-Zapotec from Oaxaca, explains:

> Well, the CNI named a women's commission, and I am part of this CNI women's commission with other women. But then we continued, in addition to the CNI commission, parallel to this, we continued to maintain a small women's space. This was where we talked and we gained strength. It was like being in dialogue with the CNI. And this is where the Coordinadora originated. . . . [It] was born after the First National Encuentro of Indigenous Women, already the most inclusive encuentro where several organizations participated.
>
> The CNI has had its lows, it has had its difficult times. . . . But the important part is that women's issues are maintained, right? Independently from the CNI. . . . And I think that this was a good thing because if the CNI falls, the women are still there. It's like a CNI working group, but it is not the CNI, nor is it because of the CNI that we meet, but rather it is because of the desire to maintain a Coordinadora Nacional, to make it possible for women. (Robles 1999)

Building a National Movement: Weaving Local Participation

National mobilization has been key for indigenous women organizers in gaining new spaces at the local level. Initially active within local movements and indigenous community radio, Margarita Gutiérrez went on to participate as a member of the early indigenous national organization, the Frente Independiente de Pueblos Indios (FIPI), served in the executive leadership of the Secretaría de Pueblos Indígenas of the PRD on the national level, and provided key leadership for the indigenous women's movement. Although she has served as a representative in international work such as the UN Permanent Forum for Indigenous People, Margarita believes that the construction of a national indigenous women's movement is important:

> It was the collective space of coming together that allowed us to clarify our consciousness as indigenous women and the profound historical knowledge of our pueblos. We suffer double discrimination as indigenous people and women outside of our communities, in addition to being denied full participation in our own pueblos and the right to speak in community forums. It was our common history that brought us together to consider a proposal for indigenous autonomy from the voice of women. (Gutiérrez 2001)

Participating in the national mobilization of indigenous women has given local activists important political tools for promoting gender equality and a respect for women's human rights within indigenous cultures. Local groups have not only been inspired by the increased visibility of women leaders; the mobilization of women and the development of a gendered critique within the national movement have given women new leverage in pressing for women's participation in local indigenous assemblies, where traditionally women had not participated. They have used the presence of the women at the national level and their own experiences and political learning within those structures to call for a range of demands such as an increase of women's leadership in political organizations, the addition of a women's rights agenda to the claims of indigenous autonomy, and the development of women's health and reproductive education within their own communities. They have brought home the declarations from the various national congresses of ANIPA and the CNI, as well as the declarations from the women's meetings, to teach other men and women of their communities and to press for gender equality within local organizations or indigenous structures of representation.

The shared strategies and empowerment they gained from other women in those spaces has helped them to increase the spaces of indigenous women's political participation within local organizations and to create new venues where their gendered political demands can be addressed. For example, organizers and activists used the occasion of the

Second National Encuentro of Indigenous Women, held March 31– April 2, 2000, in Chilpancingo, Guerrero, to gender existing political claims to indigenous autonomy, bring attention to the gendered implications of the increased militarization of Chiapas, Oaxaca, and Guerrero, as well as critique government anti-poverty programs that promote the sterilization of indigenous women. Organized and convened by the CONAMI, five hundred participants from twelve states with delegates representing more than fifty organizations, a wide array of indigenous women's groups, and mixed indigenous organizations gathered to discuss the theme "¡Construyendo la Equidad, Democracia y Justicia!" (Constructing Equity, Democracy and Justice).

Local activists used the Encuentro to draw media attention to the growing human rights violations and militarization within that state. Although there was a formal meeting with specific themes discussed at length in working sessions, the denunciations of human rights violations were strategically presented to the media and effectively captured the attention of the press as well as officials from various governmental agencies who were present. The documented cases and denunciations centered on violations of human rights in the indigenous zones of Oaxaca and Guerrero as well as forced sterilization (without informed consent) by employees of the Secretariat of Health; women from the municipalities of Ayutla and Acatepec were present to give testimony on their experiences. The four indigenous groups of Guerrero, Amuzgo, Mixteco, Tlapaneco and Nahua joined to denounce the militarization of many of their communities.

While many women gave reports on human rights from the perspective of their communities as a whole, several individual cases, such as two cases of rape the previous year in Barrio Nuevo San José in the municipality of Tlacoachistlahuaca, were also discussed. The women who had suffered these attacks gave their testimonies, as did women from Santíago Mixquetitlán and San Ildefonso, which have been overrun with military and police. Many women noted that the military entered their communities on the pretext of reforestation programs or anti-narcotrafficking activities, but the end result has been political repression and violence against women.

At the Second Encuentro, many of the organizers from Guerrero spoke of the need to find justice for the ongoing human rights violations. For example, Limni Irazema Dircio from the organization Titeke Sihuame Tajome in Chilapa stated, "We have been trying to push for the defense of human rights for indigenous people, and we know above all, it is the woman who is discriminated against, harassed and repressed, and for that reason, we are struggling." Calling for the support of agencies to help guarantee their rights, Cándida Jiménez stated, "There is repression against indigenous pueblos and even more against the poor, where there exist violations of our rights as women, because we have little backing from anyone, let alone from the institutions."

Hermalinda Tiburcio from Rancho Nuevo a la Democracia also spoke of the importance of indigenous women speaking for themselves: "Those [women] with their own voice state what they are experiencing in the indigenous zones because much of the time it is from the desks [those who have the power to write] who say that nothing is occurring in the indigenous zones." A theme of the shared testimonies of human rights violations was that the responsible governmental agencies have consistently denied that such violations exist. Marta Sánchez, an Amuzgo from Xochistlahuaca, stated, "Even though [the government] says that there are no abuses against indigenous women, we say that there are, and for this reason we will present testimonies [from the victims] and included [at this Encuentro] will be women who have been subjected to humiliating situations of having their human rights violated."

Several women gave testimonies about the specific kinds of violations that are occurring in their regions and communities. For example, Lorena, a Tzotzil from Chiapas, reported, "The most grave problem is that of militarization because we can not work tranquilly, nor leave [our communities] from any route because on all sides there are soldiers in our communities." Doña Rufina Villa, from an indigenous women's organization in the Sierra Norte of Puebla, recognized the many kinds of violence that indigenous women face both within and outside their homes, which constituted a violation of their right to bodily integrity. Part of the work of the CONAMI has been to recognize the various forms of violence in their lives. Doña Rufina Villa stated that, in her region of Sierra Norte of Puebla, "There is no violence from the Mexican military, but there is violence from the police who beat and violate the rights of the youth. In addition, there is more interfamilial violence against women and children."

In this way, the work and presence of the CONAMI has been critical in legitimating women community leaders and providing them with a broader forum in which the intersection of indigenous, women's, and economic rights can be analyzed and articulated. For example, Hermalinda Turbicio, a Mixtec from Guerrero, was unexpectedly catapulted into a leadership role as she began coordinating denunciations and calling media attention to the growing human rights violations and militarization that occurred in the sierra of Guerrero after el Rancho Nuevo a la Democracia declared itself an autonomous indigenous region. In the heart of the mountain, the indigenous municipalities of Tlacoachistla-huaca, Metlatonoc, and Xochistlahuca declared themselves autono-mous from the government and formed an indigenous municipality in rebellion on December 16, 1995. This was after approximately one hundred people from thirteen villages walked nearly thirty-five miles to take part in a seven-month occupation of the Municipal Palace in Tlacoachistlahuaca where their demands included the completion of a development plan for the region (to include paved roads, running water, and electricity), as well recognition of elected municipal commissioners from their communities.

After seeing no results from their action, a remote village of approxi-mately seven hundred Mixteco Indians joined together to declare them-selves an autonomous indigenous municipality and change their name from Rancho Viejo (Old Ranch) to Rancho Nuevo a la Democracia (New Ranch for Democracy). Since the initiation of their struggle, Mix-tec activists have witnessed incursions from the Judicial State Police, the Mexican army, and paramilitary groups, and there has been documen-tation of increasing threats, disappearances, torture, and murders. Spe-cifically, human rights activists have decried the murder of at least thir-teen indigenous peasants in the region, Rancho Nuevo witnessed the incarceration of their leaders, and numerous rapes occurred.[13]

Participation in national organizations such as the CONAMI has helped to validate women's local leadership as well as support and deepen the work of leaders like Hermalinda. Hermalinda told the story of how, from her humble beginnings as a secretary, she began to participate in the struggle and provided leadership in the community by organizing the denunciations of the human rights violations and repression. Below she describes how she began, how the community has slowly changed their view of her leadership, and how the CONAMI has played a role in her work.

My name is Hermalinda Tiburcio Cayetano. I am twenty-three years old, I am originally from a community called Yoloxochitl, which means "flower of the heart," and I speak Mixtec [and] I am from [that] indige-nous pueblo. . . . My life, I've dedicated many years of my life to the empowerment capacity building of indigenous women. It cost me a lot to get here, but it has been a space that I have been earning, and . . . well, I am [still] very young in this struggle. In 1998 I came as the secretary in the autonomous [indigenous] municipality of Rancho Nuevo a la Democ-racia. I arrived there as a secretary in the municipal government . . . and

I began to live in another world. I saw the community members' struggle, and then I had to join the struggle. . . . There were many deaths before I arrived. . . . They've been struggling for five years, [but] the municipality has not been recognized yet.

Even though life like this [in the struggle] has been very difficult, in part because I am a woman, and it is very difficult to travel through the communities. The community members have attacked me a lot; those who think that they are the only ones with the moral authority to do things. So during those years I've lived, kind of in that crisis, they tell me, "No, but it's that you're a woman, you can't govern." . . . [During the] six months when one of the community leaders was put in jail,[14] then we did everything we could, thanks to the community members, who supported me a lot. We took several measures and then, well, the people recognized my capacity to resolve issues, to solve problems, to take measures necessary, and to bring in women so that they too are empowered. Joining with the Coordinador helps me to find other ways that women can participate [so that] it won't just be me who comes out to speak, but that in time there will be more and more women [speaking]. . . . Because I would want all of my knowledge and my ideas to be transmitted to other women. (Tiburcio 2000)

The national scale of power is used in tandem with local movements to bring critically needed attention to local struggles. This interweaving of scales of power and resistance is evidenced, for example, in the final declaration from that gathering, which reads:

[We denounce the] trampling and violations of our human rights on the part of the military that, with the pretext of doing a social labor or combating narcotrafficking, has come violating [raping] women, inducing prostitution, destroying the social fabric of the communities, and sowing death in our lands. . . . We denounce the methods that through programs like Progresa, Procampo, and institutions of health, have come to violate our reproductive rights as indigenous women. We have documented cases of women and men who have been sterilized without their consent, and out of those supposed programs to combat poverty we continue to be pressured to have no children. Equally we ratify in this Second Encuentro that we will continue pursuing our denunciations to the national and international levels [in such forums] as the UN and OAS [Organization of American States] about the violations of our human rights, and we will continue to demand the fulfillment and recognition of our rights as indigenous pueblos. And that we do not want to continue to be used as electoral booty in election campaigns that profit from our poverty. We are in soli-darity with the struggle that is being developed by our *compañeras* in the Yalaltecas Union of Women for the respect of their free determination in the election of their own authorities and the defense of communitarian institutions [traditional indigenous communal structures].

The development of indigenous women's political presence and agenda inspired many other women to be more vocal. It helped to legiti-mate those indigenous women who had been active in gender issues be-fore the uprising. It helped to create a different horizon of women's po-litical participation, which put women's concerns and gender oppression as a coordinate within a larger constellation of social justice struggles for indigenous peoples. It helped to legitimate the concerns of many CONAMI women, and especially for the younger generation of activ-ists, it helped to reaffirm the life choices they had made and bring greater understanding by family and community members.

Local organizers also formed translocal strategies to leverage new political spaces and local empowerment. They gained access for greater women's participation in mixed gender organizations or traditional gov-ernance structures by pointing to other local women's participation or drawing attention to a national movement of indigenous women. The CONAMI's work in calling indigenous women to action and articulat-ing a political framework for women within the struggle for indigenous autonomy has been key to linking local groups empowering women's voices in local politics. One critical result of this process of moving in and between national and local structures is that indigenous women have gendered indigenous demands for autonomy by expanding juridi-cal, territorial, and cultural claims to include women's bodily, political, and economic autonomy. The call for autonomy, asserted as a legal claim of collective group rights, forms the larger framework of basic rights for indigenous people that includes the right to be a pueblo, the right to land and protection of territory, the right to self-determination and autonomy, the right to their own cultural traditions and forms of political representation and jurisprudence, and the right to protect and use the natural resources of the land, among others. The sharing of con-versations and strategies between national and local levels of organiza-tion has helped the indigenous women's movement in Mexico to situate their own demands within a *practice* of autonomy aimed at transform-ing the embedded gendered structures that govern the conditions of their daily lives. Moving beyond the shortcomings of rights discourse, indigenous women organizers are not waiting for the state to grant them their rights; they have begun to develop decolonized zones of cultural self-determination.

This national space has helped women to counter the way that legislators have attempted to derail claims to indigenous autonomy in Mexico by asserting that they do not protect women's rights. Indigenous women organizers have pointed out that they cannot have rights as indigenous women if their rights as indigenous people do not exist. They have also stated that within indigenous autonomy, traditions and practices as well as indigenous juridical and political structures should be changed if they do not encourage the full participation of women or if they violate women's human rights in any way. Yet, despite the growth of such a vibrant movement, these new spaces of participation have not been free of conflict and negotiation.

Despite women's participation in every step of building a national indigenous movement in Mexico, their participation has been blocked or contested at the national level at a few critical junctures. For example, to maintain the continuity of all the advances that indigenous women had gained, the Seminar on the Legislation and Women, Article 4 of the Constitution, organized by K'inal Antsetik and SEDEPAC, was held from May to December 1996, with meetings on two days of each month. Specialists in gender, jurisprudence, and indigenous law analyzed the deficiencies in the San Andrés Accords and strategies for implementation.

The results of the seminar were brought to the CNI in Mexico City in October 1996, where the women noted that none of the working sessions were dedicated to discussion of women's issues. They struggled to institutionalize a women's session, but there was opposition. Yet Margarita Gutiérrez claims, "The women won our first battle. Because, even though some leaders supported our proposals and others opposed [them], we had some male allies in favor of our organization as women" (Gutiérrez 2001). The proposal was defeated by fifty votes (there was a total of five hundred delegates). Working quickly, the women came up with an alternative plan, and the resolution that passed established that the document that the women presented would have to be discussed in each of the working sessions. This "defeat" of their initial proposal also led to their success in guaranteeing that women's concerns were taken up in each of the working sessions. Commentors have suggested, "The presence of Comandanta Ramona of the EZLN in that event was an initiative to not fall into pessimism and disillusionment, and it opened our hearts and nourished us to continue, convinced that it was possible that the women organize ourselves" (Gutiérrez 2001). This denial of space for indigenous women's voices and issues was also echoed at the Third National Indigenous Congress held in March 2001, where the proposal to dedicate one of the simultaneous working sessions to women's concerns was contested.[15]

WEAVING IN TRANSNATIONAL SPACES: THE CONTINENTAL INDIGENOUS WOMEN'S NETWORK

Despite the considerable obstacles within the national movement for indigenous rights, women organizers found ways to open up national organizational structures by turning to organizing at the transnational level. In fact, the formation of the first national independent indigenous women's organization, the Coordinadora Nacional de Mujeres Indígenas, was not merely the result of women's participation within a national process but the product of a transnational formation as well. The genesis of that meeting was not at the local or national level; it was at the First Continental Encuentro of Indigenous Women of the First Nations of Abya Yala in 1995.[16] Indigenous women leaders from Mexico, who had attended the First Continental Encuentro in Quito, Ecuador, and helped to found the Continental Network of Indigenous Women, agreed to organize the Second Continental Encuentro two years later. Mexico was selected as the site of the meeting to bring solidarity, support, and critical attention to the Chiapas uprising. The 1997 National Encuentro in Oaxaca, and founding convention of the CONAMI, was organized as the preparatory meeting to convene a national meeting and create a national structure for hosting the Second Continental Encuentro of Indigenous Women that was held later that year in Mexico City. The existence of a transnational network of indigenous women helped to create the need for the formation of an autonomous indigenous women's network in Mexico, which facilitated the linkage of the struggles of indigenous women in different regions of Mexico as well as throughout Latin America.

International indigenous organizing has a long history in which Indian nations have used the international sphere to lobby for their land and treaty rights and to petition against land seizures. While indigenous movements had been growing in number and strength in the Americas, the density of cross-border contacts increased around the numerous events organized to protest the 1992 quincentenary celebration of Columbus's stumble onto the New World. The United Nations declared 1992 "The Year of Indigenous People," and that same year Rigoberta Menchú was awarded the Nobel Peace Prize. Recognizing that a year was perhaps not long enough to address indigenous peoples' struggles for survival worldwide, in 1993 the United Nations announced that the Decade of Indigenous People would take place between 1995 and 2004, and Menchú was named its goodwill ambassador. Two goals of the Decade were to establish a permanent forum for indigenous peoples in the United Nations and pass a draft declaration on the rights of indigenous peoples by the UN General Assembly.[17]

The emergence of the Continental Indigenous Women's Network was, in part, a response to the ways they were excluded from regional organizing for the 1995 Fourth World Conference on Women in Beijing, China. Indigenous women had already been using the UN meetings as a springboard for their own organizing due to the lack of attention to issues important to indigenous women in those international arenas, but the Beijing process provided them with an opportunity to build an alternative transnational network. In the 1990s, Latin America witnessed the blossoming of indigenous movements that built on the experience of 1992 as well as numerous mass mobilizations in Panama, Ecuador, Colombia, and Mexico. When indigenous women came to the Mar de Plata NGO preparatory meeting for the Fourth World Conference on Women in Beijing in 1995, they were unsettled by their lack of representation. They questioned why an adviser on indigenous women's issues, who should have been selected by themselves as indigenous women, had already been assigned (Robles 1999). The Beijing process, in both positive and negative ways, facilitated a space for indigenous women in Latin America to articulate a transnational regional identity and begin to strategize greater participation both at the Fourth World Conference on Women and at the UN Decade of Indigenous People.

Sofía Robles, member of the CONAMI, served as the state of Oaxaca's representative to the Mexican delegation to Beijing and later became the Latin American regional indigenous women's representative in Beijing. Sofia described the Mar de Plata Latin American and Caribbean preparatory meeting:

> There in Mar de Plata we created an indigenous women's session, but from the beginning we had many demands because they gave us the worst space that could possibly be shared with us, and it began from there. . . . We began to talk with the NGOs about having to respect us, support us, and share financing with us. (Robles 1999)

To combat their marginalization within the Beijing process specifically and the international system generally, indigenous women organizers developed a transnational space in which to organize themselves, formulate their strategies, and coordinate their actions on a continental level. The First Continental Encuentro of Indigenous Women of the First Nations of Abya Yala was convened by the Confederación Nacional de Mujeres Indígenas del Ecuador after it was decided at the Mar de Plata meeting that indigenous women needed their own space to deliberate how they would participate and intervene in the Beijing process. One hundred seventy indigenous women from twenty countries from the continent attended the Ecuador meeting with two primary goals: "To analyze [their] proposals in the face of the IV World Conference of Women and to initiate projects and strategies of action for the long term under the framework of the International Decade of Indigenous Peoples."[18] While their proposals were accepted too late to affect the preparatory discussion of the Platform for Action, indigenous women organizers felt they still had made important strides.[19] Sofia reported:

> For us, it was important to meet because we firmly believe that we deserve our own space to discuss our problems and points of view, without closing ourselves off to alliances with other sectors. Since Mar de Plata we felt the necessity to seek a preparatory space before arriving at Beijing, [although] we recognize . . . the document of the Platform for Action had already been discussed in the Prepcom [preparatory meeting]. Nevertheless there were some points that we were able to push for such as the ratification and application of Convention 169 of the ILO [International Labor Organization] and in all the points that refer to research carried out in indigenous communities, we demanded that we no longer continue to be objects of study unless such study brings programs for real [community] development.[20]

The documents from the continental meeting show critical discussions and strategy building around their lack of representation and their experience from the NGO forum at Mar de Plata that suggested that if they did not organize and represent their own voice, somebody else would speak for them. They resolved to work on a document to represent the women of the "first nations of Abya Yala," which was produced in their final declaration, *Declaración del Sol*.[21] This regional meeting helped women to prepare for the Fourth World Conference on Women where the "Beijing Declaration of Indigenous Women" was drafted to include a fifty-point platform on a diverse range of issues confronting indigenous women.[22]

Abya Yala: The Continental Network of Indigenous Women

It is crucial that the experiences of indigenous women in the Chiapas uprising led them to create new forms of political consciousness, articulate a new collective identity, and create new transnational spaces, but it is also crucial that indigenous women have accomplished this by weaving in and between scales of power. Indigenous women have increasingly accessed the international system and have learned to use the various UN conventions effectively. Yet these overarching international structures rely on and reaffirm the power of nation-states. Even while some social movement researchers claim that global NGOs will provide a counterbalance to corporate globalization, all these structures are highly institutionalized and often exclusionary. The exclusion of indigenous women from the international forum has led to their creation of transnational networks, which in turn have supported the creation of national organizations, which enable collaboration among local movements.

The First Continental Encuentro of Indigenous Women in Quito, Ecuador, in August 1995 helped to create a collective agenda for indigenous women in relation to the Fourth World Conference on Women in Beijing, but it also facilitated the formation of the Continental Network of Indigenous Women. An initiative of First Nations women of Canada in 1993, the hemispheric organization emerged out of three regional workshops held in Panama, Colombia, and Canada between 1995 and 1996 in which indigenous women leaders from northern, central, and southern countries in the hemisphere created a continental strategy and vision. It is a space where "indigenous women promote linkages, solidarity and exchange of experiences in order to find collective alternatives."[23] Designed to enrich women's political capacity through regional meetings and working commissions, the network supports and forges indigenous women's organizing at the community, national, and international levels. At the Second Continental Encuentro of Indigenous Women, held in Mexico City in December 1997, indigenous women from twenty-two countries came together to create an organizational structure that designated three regions and four working commissions.[24] The Third Encuentro was held in Panama in March 2000, and the Fourth Encuentro was held in Lima, Peru, April 4–7, 2004.

Ranging from questions of intellectual property, land and treaty rights, and gendered meanings of indigenous autonomy, from the United Nations to often remote pueblos, the Continental Network of Indigenous Women has been a space to discuss indigenous women's political subjectivity, discursive strategies, and representation struggles. It is historically important because it spans North, Central, and South America and facilitates critical linkages between regional and national movements, especially needed given the regional economic integration and new conditions engendered by neoliberal economic policies under the guise of free trade. The Continental Network has also helped indigenous women to become more effective actors within international spaces because it has functioned as a parallel transnational network in which indigenous women come together to discuss shared issues, formulate strategies, and share political knowledge. This structure serves as a parallel arena in which to access and engage the formal mechanisms of the international system and the bodies of the United Nations as well as an arena from which to launch their own collective interventions. More than just a parallel arena, the Continental Network has also served as a mediating space between local, national, and international scales of power.

Implications of Transnational Organizing

Weaving in and between various scales of power has led indigenous women organizers not only to negotiate power in those scales but also to transform them into scales of resistance. This strategy is one born of necessity; it is a strategy developed by the most marginalized sectors of society. This movement in and between spaces of political participation has produced what the Chicana feminist theorist Chela Sandoval (1991) has called differential consciousness—a mobile, tactical form of consciousness contingent on reading and responding to multiple, shifting contexts of power. I employ her method and theory of differential consciousness because it describes the ways in which indigenous women in Mexico have moved within and between modes and sites of discourse in the cultural and historical circuits that structure power and meaning in their lives and their movements.[25]

Indigenous women emerged as political subjects in Mexico out of the interstitial spaces between varying scales of power, and this movement between scales is key to how they have created alternative discourses and strategies as new political subjects. As a method, differential consciousness names the way indigenous women decolonize knowledge by revitalizing indigenous epistemologies and forms of knowledge while initiating a broad dialogue among other sectors of civil society about democratic rights and participation.[26] It names how indigenous women have called for indigenous autonomy based on traditional customs and practices, indigenous jurisprudence, and self-governance while at the same time working to transform those practices in relation to gender equality and women's human rights.

Out of the most restrictive locations, indigenous women have developed a form of differential consciousness, which, more than a survival strategy, is a political skill through which they have begun to challenge their marginalization both in society at large and in other social movements. Differential consciousness functions as a method for understanding how, as a response to the very restricted spaces of representation indigenous women are permitted, they have multiplied and transformed the social and political spaces where indigenous women's issues are taken up. Indigenous women traveled through all these sites through decades of political experience and new scales of power and resistance, drawing from diverse elements in order to form their own form of political consciousness. As they have moved through differentiated scales of power, they have developed hybrid discourses and strategies as well as discursive registers where they have constituted new forms as well as transformed old ones.

Moving in and between local, national, and transnational levels of organization has produced new hybrid identities, new forms of consciousness, new strategies, and new frames through which to understand the shared issues of indigenous women, especially in these times of increased globalization. For example, organizers and weavers from Mexico have entered into a transnational conversation with other indigenous women on cultural production and weaving that was formerly understood as a local issue. Because of the global forces of tourism, commercialization, and corporate co-optation of a range of indigenous knowledge, including art and textile, medicinal, herbal, and agricultural sciences, a new conversation about intellectual property law has begun. The Continental Indigenous Women's Network's Commission on Craft Commercialization sponsored research by a Canadian member organization on native women's arts production, commercialization, and the protection of intellectual property rights. Other member organizations carried out similar research in Guatemala. They all came together in April 1999 for the Inter-American Training Workshop on Intellectual Property Rights as applied to indigenous women's art designs.

In working groups on indigenous knowledge, globalization, and Western and indigenous concepts of intellectual property, they found that their designs are the property of intergenerational cultural inheritance. From this, they understood the need to protect the autonomy of their cultural traditions from the forces of commercialization and globalization. Whereas intellectual property law refers to individuals and applies only to marketed goods, their designs collectively belong to the community and there are internal rules and codes of ethics that guide the protection and reproduction of designs. Further, the workshop generated a proposal for action and supported the drafting of a common code of ethics. Lorena described the local empowerment of women's leadership in her weavers' cooperative, but she also discussed the importance of participating with women from pueblos throughout Mexico as well as with indigenous women throughout the hemisphere. These experiences help women to link local and transnational scales of resistance and empowerment and produce new hybrid strategies that allow a blending of traditional knowledge with specificity and tools that women's rights, human rights, and indigenous rights discourses offer.

CONCLUSION

The EZLN uprising, specifically, women's role in the uprising, changed the political opportunity structure of indigenous women's organizing in Mexico and reverberated throughout the hemisphere. The widespread response to and solidarity with the uprising increased the density of transnational networks that helped indigenous women to create horizontal affiliations with other political actors and social movements, among themselves, across local movements in Mexico, and with other indigenous women across the Americas.[27] These affiliations helped to create new linkages and facilitate indigenous women's movements that cross scales of power and create new spaces of resistance. The broad reverberations of the Chiapas uprising are tied to the existence of indigenous networks and histories of organizing prior to the uprising, the new modes of communication and the solidarity it inspired, as well as the new strategies and scales of resistance indigenous movements are devising to confront the shared challenges posed by economic globalization.

The engagement of new scales of power and spaces of participation and resistance are especially important for indigenous women in light of the growth of a neoliberal political and state project. Within Mexico at the national level, the emergence of a neoliberal state has frustrated much of the promise of democratic transition. Whereas new social movements and historical actors such as indigenous peoples, women, gays, and lesbians had previously been successful at creating political identities outside of state corporatism, the state has, in its new neoliberal form, selectively addressed (or some would say, co-opted) indigenous rights within the Constitution with many contradictory consequences. For example, in 1992, as part of the North American Free Trade Agreement negotiations, the Mexican government dismantled the *ejido* system and in the same year amended Article 4 of the Constitution to recognize the pluricultural nature of Mexico, but so far this has been largely a symbolic gesture. In its transformation to neoliberalism, the Mexican state has become increasingly skilled at "international appeasement rather than democratic accountability" (Brysk 1994:45). The recent Indian Rights Bill of 2001, President Vicente Fox's attempt to fulfill his campaign promise to solve the Zapatista problem in twenty minutes, guts the San Andrés Accords and fails to meet the most basic agreements on indigenous rights signed by the government and the EZLN. Fox's new attempt at international appeasement can be seen as paving the way for the Plan Puebla Panamá, which will devastate southern Mexico and undermine not just the territorial base but the environment and labor rights as well. So as the state reacts and selectively co-opts political demands to serve its neoliberal interests, using different scales of power to create new venues of pressure and political organization becomes even more urgent. Indigenous activists have witnessed the intransigence of the state in following through on the San Andrés Accords and realize that relying solely on the federal government would imperil their struggle to guarantee indigenous rights.

What I have found, then, is that indigenous women activists have begun to move in and between scales of power in order to use existing arenas of participation and create new ones. This movement between scales of power has helped them to create new forms of pressure as well as solidarity constituencies.[28] These are new organizational spaces that have produced new discourses, strategies, and modes of organizing as well as new arenas where rights can be claimed. This method of weaving in and between scales of power to broker new spaces for themselves expands and complicates the models of transnational organizing that we have been working with. It gives a more complex and mobile mapping of transnational social movements and their "internalities of power" because indigenous women are social actors who have been marginalized even within their own oppositional national, local, and transnational movements.

Scholars of transnational social movements have theorized that political actors whose demands, interests, and political needs are blocked at the national level by the state often create or participate in transnational advocacy networks. In their influential work, Margaret Keck and Kathryn Sikkink (1998) argue that transnational networks form to avert blockages at the national level and garner support and strength in transnational arenas to form a boomerang effect that comes back around to pressure or leverage demands on nation-states. Indigenous women's strategies of moving in and between scales of power complicates the boomerang effect and names a political method deployed by political actors who are multiply marginalized at each tier of political participation. Weaving between political spaces or scales of power is a strategy of those who do not have power at any given scale of power from which to launch campaigns for their demands or basic rights. Their method of political organizing reflects the complex and multiscaled approach that they have developed as social movement actors who have to negotiate multiple marginalization: gender, ethnicity, and class.[29] They challenge researchers and scholars to examine the forces of power both within and outside of communities that converge to structure the daily lives of indigenous women. The movement between scales of power can produce not only new hybrid identities and strategies but also what Sonia Alvarez (2000) describes as new logics of transnational organizing. It allows us to map the ways in which political actors are negotiating and organizing around what other feminist scholars of transnationalism have called scattered hegemonies (Grewal and Kaplan 1994)—that is, how micro and macro structures of power are complexly organized at each scale of power.

As a movement, indigenous women have strategically created women's spaces within mixed-gender regional organizations. At the same time, they have built networks that parallel the national indigenous movement to bring together women activists and organizers from both mixed-gender organizations and women's groups. These structures provide a critical space of collaboration from which to construct their gender-specific indigenous visions. The CONAMI amplifies women's voices within the national scale of power and creates a structure in which linkages can be to other scales of power, those at the local and transnational levels. Further, these multiscaled strategies of resistance provide spaces of retreat or advancement when there are blockages in one scale or arena of participation. For example, when full women's participation was blocked within the national indigenous movement, they created the Coordinadora Nacional de Mujeres Indígenas through their participation in the Continental Network. When there have been problems or disagreements within the CONAMI, women often have retreated into statewide politics or created statewide indigenous women's conferences and networks, such as was the case in Jalisco, Oaxaca, and Guerrero. In addition, organizers have used contacts in the CONAMI as resources for establishing alliances in already existing statewide organizations that may be male dominated. Negotiating and creating these mobile structures of power and resistance has also helped indigenous women to create new transnational political imaginaries and organizational structures, such as women of the First Nations of Abya Yala. These new imaginaries facilitate new national, transnational, and translocal forms of solidarity, identity, and exchange.

NOTES

This chapter is based on archival research, ethnographic fieldwork, and oral histories collected from more than a dozen women in the leadership of the indigenous women's movement in Mexico between March 1998 and March 2002. In addition, I conducted interviews with government officials, academics, and nongovernmental organizations and attended local, national, regional, continental, and international forums organized by the Coordinadora Nacional de Mujeres Indígenas de México since 1998. I want to thank the UC MEXUS for funding part of the fieldwork on which this chapter is based.

I also want to thank the indigenous women leaders who shared generously their insights and time, as well as the many intellectuals and NGO workers who support the movement and guided me in my fieldwork. I am grateful to Lynn Stephen and the two reviewers for the University of Texas Press for their generous and insightful comments.

1. I thank Lise Nelson for directing me to theorization of scale by feminist geographers.

2. "Mujeres indígenas de Chiapas: Nuestros derechos, costumbres y tradiciones," pamphlet published by K'inal Ansetik and the Unión Regional de los Altos de Chiapas. The pamphlet details the information gathered in a series of indigenous women's workshops and compiled by Nellys Palomo, Yolanda Castro, and Cristina Orci. Republished in Palomo and Lovera 1999:65.

3. For a rich discussion of pre-1994 women's organizing in Chiapas, the impact of the Zapatista uprising, and women's organizing after 1994, including the National Convention of Women, see Stephen 1988.

4. This wording comes from an early national indigenous women's meeting in August 1995 at the third Asamblea Nacional Indígena Plural por la Autonomía. For examples of these discussions, see Lagarde 1999; Palomo n.d.; Palomo, Castro, and Orci 1999; and *Propuestas de las mujeres indígenas al Congreso Nacional Indígena: Seminario Legislación y Mujer: Reformas al artículo 4 constitucional*. These discussions took place in many arenas, including Encuentro con Mujeres Zapatistas during the Consulta nacional por el respeto de los derechos indígenas y para el termino de la guerra de exterminación, Foro Cultural Azcapotzalco, March 16, 1999; Taller Nacional: Las Mujeres Indíge-

nas en el Proceso Autonómico, organized by the CONAMI, August 20 and 21, 1999, México, D.F.; Segundo Encuentro Nacional de Mujeres Indígenas, organized by the CONAMI, Chilpancingo, Guerrero, March 31–April 2, 2000.

5. For fuller analysis of the organizational roots of indigenous women's organizing, see Blackwell 2000.

6. The dialogues on indigenous rights and culture were divided into the following categories: (1) autonomy; (2) justice; (3) political representation and participation; (4) situation, rights, and culture of indigenous women; (5) means of communication; and (6) promotion and development of indigenous culture.

7. The San Andrés documents, communiqués, accords, testimonies, and analyses are gathered in Hernández Navarro and Vera Herra 1998.

8. ANIPA held its first assembly on April 8, 1995, and is a result of the attempts to construct internal consensus among indigenous pueblos in relation to the legislative proposals surrounding autonomy. It was convened by indigenous deputies and senators (Auldárico Hernández Gerónimo, Chontal senator from the state of Tabasco, and Antonio Hernández Cruz, Maya-Tojala'bal deputy from Chiapas); the Commission on Human Rights and Indigenous Peoples of the PRD; indigenous organizations and NGOs such as RAP, el Grupo de Apoyo al Autonomía Regional Indígena (GAARI), and the Comisión Mexicana de Defensa y Promoción de los Derechos Humanos.

9. See Palomo 1996, which includes the "Conclusiones de Encuentro Nacional de las Mujeres de ANIPA," "El Mesa de Mujeres del Foro Nacional Indígena (convocado por los Zapatistas y la COCOPA)," and "La Mesa del Diálogo." See also "Encuentro Nacional de Mujeres de la Asamblea Nacional Indígena para la Autonomía (ANIPA)," in Lovera and Palomo 1999:363.

10. After the success of the first meeting, the CCRI announced that it considered each of the organizations present at the first National Indigenous Congress part of a Comisión Promotora (Advisory Commission). Each organization was to elect a representative to sit on the commission, whose charge it was to establish a permanent indigenous national forum according to the EZLN philosophy, *mandar obedeciendo*—to rule by obeying. After the commission's first meeting, it was decided that there would be two representatives per organization, so that women would have an equal opportunity to participate. The idea was to prevent the accumulation of power in the hands of a few and to create a space for open dialogue in a lasting national independent structure of the indigenous movement. In the words of Comandante David, "In accordance with the proposals of the communiqué by which all were invited to this meeting (that we meet under the philosophy to rule by obeying), we have avoided the creation of a hierarchy and a bureaucracy. We are practicing a new organizational and political culture that originates from the proposals of indigenous pueblos that they have practiced in their communities for centuries" (quoted in Vera Herrera 1998:41–42).

11. Plenary on the Plan of Action for the CNMI, II Encuentro Nacional de Mujeres Indígenas.

12. Many women come from indigenous councils, unions, and assemblies, some from traditional indigenous structures or councils comprising several in-

digenous organizations and others more focused on indigenous rights and political mobilization, such as the Unión de Comunidades Indígenas de la Zona Norte del Istmo. (UCIZONI) and Servicios del Pueblo Mixe (SER) from Oaxaca or the Consejo Guerrerense 500 Años de Resistenica Indígena, as well as the Consejo de Pueblos Nahuas del Alto Balsas from Guerrero, Consejo de la Nacionalidad Nahautl from the state of Mexico, or the Nación Purhépecha Zapatista from Michoacán. There are also an impressive number of indigenous women's organizations such as Grupo de Mujeres Indígenas and Masehaulcihuame (meaning women who work together and support one another) from Puebla, Mujeres Indígenas en Lucha and Mujeres Independientes, both from Guerrero, Mujeres Olvidadas del Rincón Mixe from Oaxaca, Grupo Erandi (Erandi means "dawn" in Purhépecha) from Michoacán, and Grupo de Mujeres de San Cristóbal de las Casas Chiapas. A large cross section come to the CNMI from peasant organizations, both mixed and women's groups, such as the Consejo Estatal de Organizaciones Indígenas y Campesinas (CEOIC), the Asociación Rural de Interés Colectivo (ARIC-Democrático), and the Central Independiente de Obreros Agrícolas y Campesinos (CIOAC), all from Chiapas—as well as women's rural and peasant organizations such as the Unión de Mujeres Campesinas de Xilitla from San Luis Potosí, the S.S.S. Titekititoketaome Sihuame from Guerrero, and the S.S.S. Maseual Siuamej Mosenyolchicauani from Puebla. There are also women participating from groups organized around productive projects such as small coffee producers from Vera Cruz and Puebla, and women's weaving collectives such as J'Pas Lumetik and Jolom Mayaetik of Chiapas that have a close relationship to K'inal Antsetik, a women's NGO in Chiapas.

13. La Liga Mexicana por la Defensa de los Derechos Humanos, "La actuación de paramilitares en el Estado de Guerrero agrave la situación de derechos humanos en esa región," communiqué of December 27, 1998. For a history of indigenous struggle in Guerrero, see Matias Alonso 1997.

14. The leader she refers to here was the president of the Indigenous Municipality in Rebellion, Marcelino Isidro de los Santos, who was arrested on December 5, 1998.

15. At the third National Indigenous Council that I attended in Cinurio, Michoacán, March 2–4, 2002, indigenous women asked that one of the sessions be designated a women's session (mesa de mujeres) where they could discuss their specific concerns and develop some strategies. Although there were many sectors of the indigenous movement, such as the EZLN, that supported the idea, there was also considerable resistance. The would-be mesa de mujeres ended up being a four-hour session the first half of which was taken up by debate about whether or not women should have their own space. While the resistance, articulated by the men at the session, seemed to dwindle with the passage of time, the tide of the session turned when woman after woman got up to speak. Although the space was not formally granted and much of the focus and momentum was lost, the session became a defacto women's space in which women of the EZLN delegation spoke and listened. The leader of the Indigenous Movement of Ecuador, Blanca Chancoso, also spoke of solidarity and the growing continental movement of indigenous peoples in the region.

16. Abya Yala means "Continent of Life" in the language of the Kuna peoples of Panama and Colombia. Abya Yala, as a concept, is shared with other indigenous rights organizations that bridge North and South America.

17. While indigenous peoples have historically sought out the United Nations as a forum for their grievances with governments, there has been no formal mechanism through which to represent their interests to any UN body. Although compromises had to be made, the Permanent Forum on Indigenous Issues was formally established on July 28, 2000, by the Economic and Social Council, on the recommendation of the Commission on Human Rights. For histories of indigenous organizing and the international system, see Brysk 2000; Dunbar Ortiz 1984; Washinawatok 1998.

18. Press release sent by Sofía Robles H., Women's Commission of SER to Mexico from the First Continental Encuentro. Document available at CIMAC, Communicación y Información de la Mujer, Mexico City.

19. With financial support from the UN Population Fund of Ecuador, the Encuentro worked for five days to present their petition to Virginia Vargas, NGO coordinator of Latin America and the Caribbean. See Vargas 1998 for further information on the Beijing process in Latin America.

20. Press release, 1995.

21. The delegation from Mexico included Sofía Robles from SER, Margarita Gutiérrez from the Frente Independiente de Pueblos Indígenas, Martha Sánchez from the Consejo Guerrerense 500 Años de Resistencia Indígena y Popular, and Beatriz Gutiérrez from the Red Nacional de Mujeres Indígenas. For full discussion of results, see *Declaración del Sol*.

22. Beijing Declaration of Indigenous Women, NGO Forum, UN Fourth World Conference on Women, Huairou, Beijing, Peoples Republic of China.

23. Pamphlet, Enlace Continental de Mujeres Indígenas.

24. The regional networks are North, Central, and South, chaired respectively by the Coordinator of Indigenous Women (CNMI) in Mexico, the Association of Indigenous Women of the Atlantic Coast (AMICA) in Nicaragua, and the Confederation of Indigenous Nationalities of Ecuador (CONAIE). The working commissions are Central Commission, Commission on Commercialization and Intellectual Property, Commission on International Instruments (which works on conventions and treaties that affect indigenous women), and the Communications Secretariat.

25. In my deployment of differential consciousness, because the fifth mode of consciousness overrides and reconstructs the other modes it moves between, the tactical shifts in consciousness theorized by Sandoval do not need to remain stuck in the modes of consciousness and discourses of liberation handed down by the narrow view of U.S. feminism (limited to liberal, radical, cultural, separatist) that she critiques. The importance of her model is that it articulates how multiply situated political actors (i.e., actors situated by multiple forms of oppression) read power in diverse contexts. For example, Sandoval argues that differential consciousness is not inextricably bound to gender, nation, race, sex, or class. "It is rather *a theory and method of oppositional consciousness* that rose out of a specific deployment, that is, out of a particular *tactical* expression

of U.S. third world feminist politics that more and more became its overriding strategy" (Sandoval 1998:361; original emphasis).

26. For an important discussion of what she theorizes as third space feminisms, see Emma Pérez's (1999) examination of the archaeology of identities produced in the interstitial or "in between" spaces.

27. The concept of horizontal affiliations is theorized by Lowe (1996).

28. A drawback of this kind of organizing is the risk of becoming the "outsider within" as any gendered demands are susceptible to the claim that they are "foreign" feminist imports, especially in the translation of discursive frames from the transnational or international scale of organization back to the local scale or through processes of localization. Several organizers have commented on how their challenge to gender inequality has been met with claims of cultural inauthenticity. Also, if they work in the national or international scale, they are often challenged when they return to their communities as being inauthentic or somehow no longer homegrown. On the other hand, it is also sometimes difficult to make and sustain connections; if one segment of the movement at one scale of power becomes fragmented or divided, the relationships that are mediated between other scales have to be reestablished or renegotiated. Sometimes actors do not effectively move in and between the politics of scale; for example, they get stuck in participation at the international level and become divorced from other levels of organization and representation. There is also the critique of "International Indians" who have made their political careers at the United Nation, thereby calling into question the issue of representativeness. The CON-AMI sees attendance at international meetings as part of capacity building of organizers. Therefore, nomination to an international committee is for a specific term, after which other persons are given the opportunity to serve.

29. Other researchers working with indigenous women's movements in Mexico have also mentioned the simultaneous struggles against racial/ethnic, gender, and class oppression that have been theorized by U.S. women of color. See the important article by Hernández Castillo (2001), which uses Rushin's poem that provided the imagery for the historic and groundbreaking work by U.S. women of color, *This Bridge Called My Back: Writings by Radical Women of Color,* edited by Cherríe Moraga and Gloria Anzaldúa.

RIGHTS AND GENDER
IN ETHNOGRAPHIC CONTEXT

FIVE

INDIGENOUS WOMEN'S ACTIVISM IN OAXACA AND CHIAPAS

LYNN M. STEPHEN

When Zapatista Comandanta Esther addressed the Mexican Congress in March 2001 in a special session on indigenous rights, a key symbolic boundary had been crossed. In Teotitlán del Valle, Oaxaca, Aurora Bazán López was keeping track of the Zapatista march to Mexico City and Comandanta Esther's address to Congress. Aurora served as a federal indigenous representative (*diputada federal indígena*) from the state of Oaxaca from 1997 to 2000 on behalf of the Ecological Green Party of Mexico (Partido Verde Ecologista de México). She was also the first indigenous woman to serve on the National Commission of Concord and Pacification (Comisión de Concordia y Pacificación, COCOPA) in resolving the conflict between the Zapatista National Liberation Army (EZLN) and the Mexican government. Aurora, like Esther, had also occupied a position of unique symbolic importance for indigenous women.

Aurora and I became friends in summer 2001. She told me her personal history and of some of the great contradictions in her life. The one she highlighted most frequently was the contrast between her life as a federal representative traveling extensively around Mexico and life in her Zapotec hometown where social custom obliges her to ask her husband's permission to go on an errand or visit a friend. Her insight captures a key dimension of the complexity of indigenous women's struggles to gain access, power, and leadership roles in the formal and informal political spaces and organizations that govern their lives: local gendered customs of appropriate male and female behavior and the possibility of more egalitarian roles for men and women in regional movements and sometimes in national politics create a contradictory terrain for women activists who are attempting to empower their ethnic groups and themselves as women.

Much recent scholarship has focused on how the Zapatista uprising and movement have allowed indigenous women to move into new roles and positions of authority. However, while the events of the uprising and since have been important, it was several decades of prior experience in Chiapas and elsewhere that was key to facilitating some of the changes in indigenous gender roles that many attribute to the Zapatista movement. In this chapter I explore the factors that influence the challenges and contradictions faced by indigenous women activists, primarily at the local level. I draw my observations from researching women's political participation in Tojola'bal Zapatista base communities in Chiapas and Zapotec women's participation in community politics and the development of craft production for export in Oaxaca. I focus on the interaction between what are often mistakenly labeled "traditional" ethnic-based forms of local social and political organization such as *ejido* governance structures and civil and religious *cargo* systems and newer forms of organizing such as religious groups, peasant organizations, political-military movements, cooperatives, and cooperative federations. I argue that a combination of women's local, ethnic-based skills and leadership knowledge and their experiences in newer forms of local and regional organization permits them to broaden their participation in local politics and to create more egalitarian gender relations of power.

GENDER AND "TRADITIONAL" FORMS OF INDIGENOUS GOVERNANCE IN TOJOLA'BAL AND ZAPOTEC COMMUNITIES

What are often reported as "traditional" forms of government in indigenous communities have a particular history, as do forms of government everywhere. Before talking about the specific ways that gender roles in community politics have begun to shift in Tojola'bal and Zapotec communities and why, I want to digress briefly into what is meant by "traditional" forms of governance, what their gender roles are, and why some women are interested in challenging them.

Anthropologists working in southern Mexico in the states of Oaxaca and Chiapas often reported that "traditional" indigenous forms of government are based on what they called the civil-religious *cargo* system. Such systems were described as intertwining hierarchies of civil and religious office that allowed individual men to advance their civil political careers as they took on religious sponsorship of cult celebrations for saints and virgins. More recent ethnohistorical and ethnographic work has shown that where civil-religious *cargo* systems were intertwined, this was a historically and place-specific occurrence (see Chance 1990). In Chiapas, where several generations of anthropologists focused on the civil-religious hierarchy as the core of indigenous communities, the work of Robert Wasserstrom (1983), Frank Cancian (1990, 1992), and Jan Rus (1994) was fundamental in showing how local political forces such as caciques and economic forces, including economic stratification and entrepreneurial activities, have undermined the sponsorship of religious *cargos*.

In other areas of Chiapas, such as the Tojola'bal region in the extreme south-center of the state, local systems of governance were strongly affected by recruitment of the Tojola'bales as sharecroppers and indentured servants by nineteenth-century mestizo landowners. The ethnohistorians Antonio Gómez Hernández and Mario Humberto Ruz (1992) suggest that Tojola'bal identity and community institutions were significantly reorganized on the large ranches and plantations where the Tojola'bales labored as sharecroppers bound by debt peonage. As confirmed in the research of Shannon Mattiace (2001:74–77) carried out in the Tojola'bal region in the mid-1990s, while in some cases traditions such as *romerias* (pilgrimages to other ethnic Mayan communities in Chiapas and Guatemala) encouraged interethnic contact in the mid-1900s, local emphasis at that time and into the present has been on the *ejido* form of governance.[1] In the Lacandon jungle where Tojola'bales who were sharecroppers on *fincas* migrated to begin again in *ejido* communities, the *ejido* form of government as proscribed in the Mexican Constitution became the new "traditional" structure for local politics. The *ejido* structure has three parts: (a) the collectivity of individual voting *ejidatarios* (those who have use rights to *ejido* land), who constitute the decision-making *asamblea ejidal* (assembly); (b) the *comisariado ejidal* (ejidal commission with elected authorities), including the *presidente* or *comisariado* (president), *secretario* (secretary), *tesorero* (treasurer), and *vocales* (commission members); and (c) the *comité de vigilancia* (vigilance committee), composed of president, secretary, treasurer, and members.

The original *ejido* law, unchanged until 1971, allowed women use rights only if they were mothers or widows maintaining their families. Single men over twenty-one or younger who lacked legal guardians could be given land, but women could not. The result of this federal regulation and its implementation in Tojola'bal Lacandon communities was a male-dominated government. A few women (usually widows) participated historically as voting members of *ejido* assemblies in most communities, but by and large local assemblies were dominated by men. In the historical *ejido* documents I have examined from five Tojola'bal communities, I have yet to find any mention of women being elected as *ejido* authorities. The *ejido* structure, its assembly and strong identification with male authority and voting and speaking privileges (with some exceptions), became the "traditional" form of Tojola'bal governance until the 1970s, at which time it began to compete with other forms of governance such as that offered by Catholic liberation theology organizations and *ejido* unions. As summarized by Mattiace (2001:75), "Many Tojolabales . . . , especially in areas of traditional settlement, have come to identify closely with localized ejido communities. In some cases this 'new' identification is now several decades old."

In Zapotec communities in the Tlacolula Valley of Oaxaca, as in Chiapas, "traditional" forms of local indigenous governance were also often classified by anthropologists as civil-religious *cargo* systems. As among researchers in Chiapas, ethnohistorical work has revealed (Chance 1990; Chance and Taylor 1985) that during the early colonial period, local governance in indigenous communities was structured only as a civil hierarchy. Religious activities were centered in *cofradías*, religious corporations founded to pay for the cult of local saints. *Cofradías* owned land and herds, and the proceeds paid for local cult celebrations. Only after *cofradía* property was expropriated, first by the church and later by state sanctions against collective property (1856), did individual households begin to sponsor cult celebrations for local saints. Individual sponsorship of cult celebrations for saints probably began during the mid- to late eighteenth century when *cofradía* land finally disappeared after the 1856 Ley Lerdo that abolished the property rights of all corporate organizations. Soon after the announcement of the Ley Lerdo, according to the historian Charles Berry (1981:176), there were villages in the central valleys of Oaxaca that quickly sold some of the common lands dedicated to the support of the *cofradías* or divided these lands among community members.

From the mid- to late 1800s until the 1960s, the religious *cargo* system bound up in the celebration of *mayordomías* (sponsorship of cult celebrations for local saints and virgins) was both the primary focus of community ceremonial life and a major arena for the development of prestige, respect, and local political authority in many Zapotec communities. In contrast to the *ejido* form of government that became "traditional" in many Tojola'bal communities, in Zapotec communities in the Tlacolula Valley, both men and women actively participated in the *mayordomías* of the religious hierarchy and received authority and prestige for doing so. During the same period, the civil *cargo* system (volunteer offices and positions within the community governance system) was linked to the religious *cargo* system. While offices of the civil *cargo* system were and are held by men, the *mayordomía* sponsorships of the religious *cargo* system were held by pairs of men and women both of whom received authority and prestige (see Stephen 2005:234–243). The contributions of women to the civil *cargo* system were and continue to be recognized informally as supporting the community through the work they do when their husbands are absent doing *cargos*. Men and a few women served as mayor, police, judges, school committee members, members of committees that oversee firefighting, education, irrigation, communal land, and more.

The decoupling of civil and religious *cargo* systems in Oaxaca and elsewhere since the 1950s is related to the increasing integration of community political structures with those of state and national governments (see Chance 1990). Slowly, beginning in the 1920s and 1930s, civil *cargo* positions have been elected as specified by the 1917 Mexican Constitution.[2] The *asamblea municipal* replaced council of elders' (*štič bəngul* in Zapotec) meetings. Some people say that these were the basis for community meetings in the past; others, that the council of elders gave advice to the municipal president. One of the consequences of the divorce of religious hierarchies from civil ones in Zapotec communities was that women lost their most formal remaining link to institutional community politics. In Teotitlán del Valle *asambleas* historically were attended only by men; in the mid-1990s women began to participate in small numbers as members of women's weaving cooperatives. Nevertheless, women continued to use the authority and prestige they accrued through their roles as *mayordomas* (see Stephen 1991:160–177) and *madrinas* in the ritual kinship system of *compadrazco* (see Sault 2001) to increase their influence in community politics and in other spheres of life.

Thus while Zapotec community political life came to resemble that of Tojola'bal *ejidos* in the 1960s and 1970s in terms of male-only assemblies and male officials, women had a deep and sustained history through their role as *mayordomas* in accruing prestige, respect, and authority that allowed them to have an impact on community politics. In both contexts, the social custom and perceived historical, local "tradition" was an almost exclusively male system of formal governance. In both contexts, women have challenged this tradition through their incorporation into competing forms of local organizing but have also relied on their historical skills and experience to create forms of governance and social organization that more fully include them.

CHALLENGES TO "TRADITION": NEW FORMS OF LOCAL ORGANIZING

La Realidad and Guadalupe Tepeyac, Chiapas

One of the most frequently asked questions about women in Chiapas is, how have women's roles changed significantly in Zapatista communities? This question assumes, of course, that there is one consistent set of roles for women across indigenous communities in Chiapas in different regions, from different cultural and ethnic traditions, and with differing histories of engagement with a wide range of religious, political, and state institutions. My own research (Stephen 2000, 2002) and that of Christine Eber (1999, 2000, 2001), Aída Hernández Castillo (1998a, 2001), June Nash (2001), Guiomar Rovira (1994, 1997), Shannon Speed (chapter 7, this volume), Melissa Forbis (chapter 6, this volume), Violeta Zylberberg Panebianco (chapter 8, this volume) and Sara Lovera and Nellys Palomo (1997) suggest the range of gender roles assumed by women who are a part of Zapatista base communities and in the regular armed units of the EZLN. While there are significant differences between women who live away from their communities as *insurgentas* in military camps and those who remain in their home communities, there are also important differences between the experiences of women in differing base communities. Some of these may be tied to long-standing historical differences such as those between Tojola'bal communities where local governance structures and political cultures are strongly linked to the *ejido* as a form of organization (see Mattiace 1998:178; 2001) versus, for example, Tzotzil communities where civil-religious *cargo* systems and ties to the long-dominating PRI strongly influenced political participation and organization (Eber 2001). Such differences can also be linked to catechist education and regional peasant organizations such as the ARIC-Unión de Uniones in the Tzeltal region studied by Xóchitl Leyva Solano (1994, 2001), which has undergone significant political factionalism. The ARIC was dominant before 1994 but has been replaced by a wide range of local factions (Leyva Solano 2001:25). In each of these instances, the regional and ethnic context in which a particular community exists can have a significant impact on local gender roles.

The Tojola'bal communities of Guadalupe Tepeyac and La Realidad were formally constituted as *ejidos* in 1956 and 1966 respectively. Each had petitioned for land one to three years before and had populations that migrated to the area as many as eighteen years earlier. Most of the founders of these *ejidos* had worked as sharecroppers for ranchers who lived at the outer edges of the Lacandon jungle. In hopes of a new beginning, they moved onto what were national lands in the expectation of being able to make an independent living raising cattle, corn, beans, and coffee.

Although women were among the pioneers who cleared the land, built houses, and harvested coffee (Stephen 2002:110–11; Rovira 1997:58), very few were named *ejidatarias*. Records of *ejido* assemblies indicate that women were seldom present during local government meetings.[3] However, they developed other skills that proved important in the roles they took on in the 1970s, 1980s, and 1990s as community leaders and participants in new forms of governance. Because women and men often spent their days apart—men worked in the corn and coffee fields; women gathered firewood, delivered food to the men, and attended domestic animals and children—women were often alone in their communities and on the roads and paths leading to the fields. They developed a keen awareness of one another's daily routines, shared news and information while joined in common bathing and clothes-washing areas, and often worked together when gathering firewood. As they walked to and from their homes to outlying places, they kept close track of any unusual occurrences such as strangers, stray animals, damaged crops, and impending bad weather (interviews Guadalupe Tepeyac 1994; La Realidad 1995, 1996, 1997). When coffee harvests began, often women worked alongside men. They were keenly aware of the economics of coffee production and often sold small lots of coffee beans to outside merchants and bargained with merchants to buy basic necessities that were not produced in their communities.

As Marist priests and several Protestant sects began to work in the area and cultivated women's participation through meetings and Bible study groups in the 1960s and 1970s, women became more literate, had opportunities to meet with others outside their homes, and developed public speaking skills. When regional peasant organizations such as Lucha Campesina (formed in 1979) and later the Unión de Ejidos de la Selva (formed in 1983) began to work in these two communities, the political culture they brought did not encourage the active participation of women. Because they were structured as regional *ejido* organizations, they essentially continued the male-dominated political culture of the *ejidos*. The educational and inspirational meetings of the Catholic and Protestant groups did more to nourish women's participation.

When Guadalupe Tepeyac and La Realidad became central to the building of both the military and civilian base movements of the EZLN in the 1980s and 1990s, women were among the first incorporated into clandestine committees and later into armed militia groups. Norma, a Zapatista recruit from Guadalupe Tepeyac, explained this to me in 1994 when she was eighteen:

> When our struggle started, it was clandestine. They told us not to tell anyone except our parents. . . . Because if the government arrived . . . [her gestures suggest that people would be caught and punished]. We decided that women could join the struggle. We women don't have everything that we need. We need a good place to live, we need food. Women didn't have that. We didn't have anything. So we decided to integrate ourselves with the [Zapatista] army to fight with the men.

As the governance structure of these communities changed to accommodate the secret presence of the EZLN, the local political culture began to change: women were encouraged to speak up at secret meetings, to meet on their own, and to take on important leadership roles. By the time the EZLN went public in 1994, the local political structure in La Realidad and Guadalupe Tepeyac had already been transformed with regard to local gender and age roles. All men, women, and children were strongly encouraged to attend community meetings, and the meetings did not end until everyone had spoken. Women organized around specific tasks, including health, education, community defense, and food procurement. After the communities came under attack from the Mexican Army, and in the case of Guadalupe Tepeyac relocated for almost eight years, local gender roles for women came to include front-line confrontations with soldiers, communicating with reporters and foreigners about the urgent needs of the community, and traveling to San Andrés Larraínzar and San Cristóbal de las Casas and elsewhere to support and protect EZLN delegations during peace talks, forums, and other events (see Stephen 2000:235–236; 2002:207–209). The following extract from my interview with Ruth, from La Realidad, illustrates how women were instrumental in keeping the Mexican Army from moving in to La Realidad when they invaded Guadalupe Tepeyac in 1995.

> Ruth: We don't want the Mexican Army to come here and offer us a few things because they don't even give out the little amount of what they

bring. Because of this, we organized ourselves, the women. We don't want them here. We aren't in agreement to receive things from the army.

LS: How were the women organized?

Ruth: We organized ourselves. We said that we don't want them here. We shoved the soldiers away and told them to retreat because our children get frightened when they see the weapons, when they see their vehicles. They come with tanks, with machine guns, this is what we don't accept. So we shouted, "We don't want you to come here." The whole town was shouting. We had to shout at them.

Some women from these communities eventually traveled throughout Mexico with Zapatista caravans in 1997 and 2001 (Stephen 2000: 235–236).

Thus, in Guadalupe Tepeyac and La Realidad, what were quite limited roles for women in local political structures expanded through the educational work of the Catholic and Protestant churches and through the conscious and active recruitment of women—often before men—into the secret structure of the EZLN. As the EZLN prepared to go public and participating communities voted on whether to go to war at the end of 1992, the political culture of the EZLN seems to have become dominant in La Realidad and Guadalupe Tepeyac. Those members of the community who did not support the effort to go to war left, probably under considerable pressure. Those who remained were a solid core committed to the struggle of the EZLN. Although the *ejido* continued to meet in 1992 and 1993, the alternative political structure of the EZLN clearly took precedence. Here, everyone in the community participated in organized activities, could speak at meetings, and was involved in votes and decision making. A significant transformation had occurred in the participation of women in local politics and their incorporation into a wide range of community planning, decision making, and activities. I suspect that the change in gender roles for women in local politics shifted to a greater degree in these two communities than in many others.

The Zapatistas' Women's Revolutionary Law was also discussed at great length in these two *ejidos* much earlier than, for example, in the highland communities around Chenalhó (see Section One for the Women's Revolutionary Law). While the level of gendered democracy called for by the law was somewhat utopian in terms of women's right to full political participation and control over all decisions that affect their sexuality, their responsibilities in raising children, their health, education, and conditions of work, in La Realidad and Guadalupe Tepeyac there were serious discussions and attempts to implement the law. After the invasions and forced relocation of Guadalupe Tepeyac in 1995 and the militarization of the region around La Realidad, such efforts became less of a priority. Local defense and organizing efforts took precedence, as did the structuring and maintenance of autonomous municipalities. Nevertheless, the gendered changes in local political culture and the ongoing presence of female spokespersons and leaders in these communities were notable.

The contrast between the apparently significant degree of change in local gender roles in the community political culture in these two *ejidos* versus the continued constraints on women's local participation as noted by Eber (1999) in Tzotzil Zapatista base communities in San Pedro Chenalhó confirms the importance of examining the variance between gender roles at the local level as well as how differing local experiences with nonlocal forms of organizing (e.g., church groups, peasant organizations, and military-political movements like the EZLN) may or may not generate greater political participation by women at the local level. An analysis of gender roles in local politics in a Zapotec community in Oaxaca underscores this point.

Teotitlán del Valle, Oaxaca

Unlike the Tojola'bal communities of La Realidad and Guadalupe Tepeyac, the Zapotec community of Teotitlán has a long history. It has probably been a population center for at least two thousand years. Teotitlán is not an *ejido;* its lands passed from a communal regime with some private property under indigenous rulers to a modified property scheme under Spanish colonialism that conserved a vast part of its communal land and created a sector of privately owned and inherited land that has slowly expanded since Mexican independence. During the colonial period, the primary system of local governance in Teotitlán was a civil *cargo* system that was coordinated with local *cofradías* that took on responsibility for cult celebrations for the local pantheon of saints. From the mid- to late 1800s to about 1960, sponsorship was taken up by individual *mayordomos* who were responsible for cult celebrations for some twenty saints and virgins (see Stephen 2005:235–246). When I lived in Teotitlán del Valle in the mid-1980s, the civil *cargo* system was completely separate from the religious *cargo* system, and only two or three *mayordomías* were being celebrated on a regular basis. Women were still active in those that continued to exist but were completely excluded from attending community assemblies and holding positions in the civil *cargo* system.

The de facto exclusion of women from assemblies and *cargo* posts, however, did not receive support from everyone. In 1986 a slight majority of both men and women surveyed believed that assemblies would be better if women attended and that women were qualified to hold posts in the civil *cargo* system—even though they did not at the time. When divided by their class position in the community as merchants (who purchased textiles from others and contracted them as workers) and weavers (who worked for merchants indirectly or directly as contracted labor), significantly more male weavers (78 percent) than merchants (56 percent) believed that assemblies would be better if women attended (Stephen 2005:297–298). In a similar pattern, more male weavers (85 percent) than merchants (68 percent) believed that women were qualified to hold posts in the civil *cargo* system. At the time, male weavers seemed to have a higher level of confidence in the abilities of women to organize, to get things done, and to keep things running smoothly. The merchants felt that more education and experience dealing with outsiders were the most important qualifications for attending assemblies and taking on civil *cargo* posts.

Among women, slightly more merchants (60 percent) than weavers (56 percent) believed assemblies would be better if women attended. Also among women, significantly more merchants (80 percent) than weavers (56 percent) believed that women were qualified to hold posts in the civil *cargo* system (Stephen 2005:298). These differences seem to be related to the belief on the part of both groups of women that higher levels of education, fluency in Spanish, and experience outside the community were important for contributing to community assemblies and serving in civil *cargo* posts. Female merchants were more fluent in Spanish and had more contacts with outsiders than did female weavers. Among the women I surveyed in 1986, there was a higher rate of monolingualism among weavers (45 percent) than merchants (33 percent) (Stephen 2005:302).

In the mid-1980s women served in a minimal capacity in the civil *cargo* system through the government-mandated women's health committee and in the local branch of the Sistema Nacional para el Desarollo Integral de la Familia (DIF) and as secretaries of kindergarten and primary school parents' committees. The primary reason for women's absence from community assemblies and civil *cargo* posts given to me in interviews in the 1980s and recently was "costumbre" (custom):

"Se hizo costumbre" (It became the custom), "Costum shte re" (It's the custom here). When I asked about the reasons for opposing having women in these roles, they often had to do with gender-based codes of respect based on a tradition of strict gender segregation in most spaces outside the household compound (and even there when that area is converted into ritual space for ceremonies). Respect for men and women is demonstrated during ritual occasions by spatial segregation by gender whereby men and women eat, work, and often dance in separate areas. In ceremonial spaces in front of the church and the municipal building, men and women also occupy separate spaces. Since the municipal assembly has "traditionally" been a male space, some thought it would be disrespectful to both men and women for women to occupy that space. Women who wanted to go to assemblies and felt qualified to hold *cargo* posts commented in 2002 and 2003 that it was not only "costumbre" but also "machismo" (their word) and a lack of confidence in women that prevented their participation.

In the mid-1980s a group of younger women, many of whom sold textiles for their families in the local artisan market, launched a vocal critique of their exclusion from the committee that regulated the market as well as from community assemblies. This group of women and their public critique were pivotal in beginning what is an ongoing change in local gender roles in the political arena in Teotitlán. In 1986 some aspects of their critique were taken up by several local women who had returned to the community after living in places such as Mexico City and Oaxaca where their roles as women were not so restricted.

In 1986 organizing for the first women's weaving cooperative in Teotitlán got under way, driven largely by the energies of one woman. Aurora Contreras Lazo had returned from living for ten years in Mexico City and was struck by some of the major differences between life for women there and in Teotitlán. She commented in summer 2001:

> The idea behind the group was to find a way for women and girls to leave. In the city you can leave, do what you like. Even though you have to ask permission, you can go. Here, it was different. A woman alone can't leave the community or go out at all. They say, "What is she going to do? What is she looking for?" Women didn't have the possibility of leaving this community to sell their textiles. The idea was to look for exhibits and expositions. We started getting women together for a group. We started with about fifty women and girls and we were able to officially constitute ourselves and start to get support. We were called Te Gunaa Ruinchi Laadi [Women Who Weave]. This group still exists.

Women Who Weave not only aspired to help women to sell their own goods but also collectively set out to try to circumvent the control that local merchants had and still have over the sale of textiles. While everyone in Teotitlán has benefited from the successful commercialization and export of textiles since the late 1970s, some have benefited much more than others. About six to seven extended merchant families still control the bulk of the business, either buying finished pieces from independent weavers looking for a market or contracting weavers directly as labor, giving them materials, designs, and dimensions of textiles to produce. The increased ability of people in Teotitlán to export since the initiation of the North American Free Trade Agreement in 1994 has primarily benefited these merchant families.

The initial members of Women Who Weave modeled alternative gender roles for women in Teotitlán in terms of increased mobility within and outside the community (often as far away as Mexico City), renegotiations of the household division of labor so that husbands and children took on some domestic responsibilities when women left to go to meetings or exhibitions, establishing a women's presence in community assemblies, and getting the community accustomed to women having a presence at public events as an organized group. Women Who Weave dissolved in 1988 as a result of internal disagreements. However, one part of the initial group formed a second cooperative that was active from 1988 to 1990, and by the mid-1990s there were five women's cooperatives founded by women who were active in Women Who Weave. These women artisan leaders have gone on to assume key roles in their community: the only female secretary named by municipal presidents to work in community government, a federal representative, and roles in a variety of offices linking the community to other parts of Oaxaca and Mexico.

With five women's cooperatives active in the mid-1990s involving up to seventy-five women and their families, both the cooperatives and the women became more visible in the community. It was no longer unusual for unaccompanied women to travel to Oaxaca and stay overnight to sell the wares of their group. Women from the cooperatives marched in local parades marking national holidays, met weekly or biweekly in one another's homes, and developed extended support networks.

The second incarnation of Women Who Weave began to attend community assemblies at the invitation of the municipal president in 1989. These women were the first to set foot in the all-male assemblies. They remember it as very difficult. Cristina Ruiz[4] commented, "We received a lot of criticism. They said, 'What are you doing? You would be better off going back to your kitchens.' We even got this kind of comment from the men in the *municipio* who were the elected authorities. . . . We had to be really tough to go back." The women of the cooperative entered the meetings as a group and sat together on a bench in the front. Dozens of women I interviewed acknowledged the importance of this breakthrough. When Women Who Weave split up, their attendance at community assemblies dropped off. It was not until the second and third cooperatives were formed that women began to attend the meetings again in small groups of five to ten. Many found it difficult to continue, however, because of gossip and pressure from older men and women in the community. For almost eight years, until 2001, women's attendance at assemblies was sporadic. The women in cooperatives decided instead to concentrate their energies on promoting their groups. Many established a regular presence in Oaxaca with their wares and also began to participate in federations of craft co-ops from other parts of the state. For women who managed to stay active in the co-ops for several years, another area of significant change was in their relationships with their husbands, in-laws, and children. For substantial numbers of married women in the cooperatives, the most difficult battle was getting family members to understand what they were trying to accomplish. For women such as Marcelina Ruiz, who was a member of the original cooperative and has led another one for the past ten years, having her husband help her and work with the group has been an important gain:

> It was a huge battle with our husbands. We had to break our chains with them there in the community. Thanks to all our struggle, now they help us. Our husbands understand us. They understand that what we are doing isn't just for women but for the whole family. When we first started, it was a huge battle. The fact that we were leaving the community was really looked down upon. . . . Later when our husbands saw what we were doing, that in fact we sold more than the men who came to Oaxaca did, they let us alone. . . . Now they are happy to help us.

The presence and activities of the women's cooperatives seemed to have an impact elsewhere as well. Sometime in the early 1990s, women became a part of the municipal marketing committee and by the mid-1990s began to serve as elected officers. The cooperatives also were able to compete with local merchants during the periods when members were actively selling their goods in Oaxaca directly to tourists and occasionally to a larger U.S. clientele.

From 2000 to 2004, another six cooperatives were formed, three of them involving both men and women and one of them involving men only. With more than 150 individuals and their families now involved in cooperatives, the groups constitute a significant presence in the community. They are invited as groups to attend community assemblies, and women's participation in community meetings has increased. In fall 2001, at a meeting where the new municipal president was elected, more than 250 women attended, invited by the outgoing municipal president. A significant bloc of the women who attended were in cooperative groups. Others were affiliated with government programs such as PROGRESA (now called Oportunidades). The municipal president elected for the 2000–2004 term was referred to by some as "el presidente de las mujeres" (the women's president) because they all voted for him. Women who attended the meeting recalled that it was "impressive" to see that about 25 percent of those present were women and that they all voted. Although attendance has not remained as high, women have established a consistent presence at community assemblies since that time. In addition, in the politicizing that goes on at the market, at fiestas, and other sites, a few women have been actively proposed—by men and women—as candidates for civil *cargo* positions in the future, something that I never heard fifteen years ago.

THE INFLUENCE OF NEWER AND "TRADITIONAL" FORMS OF ORGANIZING ON SHIFTING LOCAL GENDER ROLES

The previous discussion of changes in gender roles in relation to indigenous women's participation in community politics, freedom of movement, and ability to meet independently and initiate their own projects underscores the importance of the interaction of local, ethnic-based forms of social and political organization that come to define the norm with other forms of organizing that also take place at the local level. While it might be tempting to state that "outside" influences are the primary reason for the expansion in women's roles and participation in local political and social institutions in both cases discussed, this is far too simple an explanation. It does not take into account the political and social skills and leadership abilities indigenous women had before the arrival of religious groups and the EZLN in Chiapas and before the cooperatives in Teotitlán. In both cases, women possessed skills and experiences related to what I have called local ethnic-based forms of social and political organization that also served their capacity to move into more flexible and expanded gender roles in the 1980s and 1990s with the influence of new institutions and ways of organizing in their communities.

In the Tojola'bal communities of Chiapas, older and middle-aged women had significant experience in creating whole new communities through their roles in founding their *ejidos* and literally carving communities and fields out of the jungles. They had no infrastructure to support them in terms of medical services, schools, markets, or even basic transportation until only a few years before the Zapatista uprising. Although excluded from *ejido* assemblies and governance, women developed a range of local skills and experience tied to their physical isolation and need to communicate with one another in what was often a gender-segregated world. Maintenance of extensive communication networks with other women, daily accounting of important events and unusual or dangerous occurrences, collaboration in gathering firewood and harvesting coffee, and knowledge and ability to travel through extended stretches of jungle pathways to and from their homes to the fields—all of this cultivated important skills in women that when joined with the literacy, public speaking, and other organizing skills learned through participation in liberation theology study groups and the EZLN gave women in Guadalupe Tepeyac and La Realidad formidable tools to use in defending their communities from the Mexican Army and in becoming valued participants and leaders in the new vision of community they are working to create. Without their prior experience, women in La Realidad and Guadalupe Tepeyac would not have been able, interested, or willing to take hold of the new opportunities offered to them by organizers from the Catholic church, various Protestant sects and mainline churches, and the EZLN.

In Teotitlán del Valle, women's ability to successfully organize into a significant number of weaving cooperatives and to use these cooperatives as a platform for opening up political space for women in the formal system of governance was based on skills and leadership styles tied to their roles in *mayordomías, compadrazgo,* and migration to Mexico City and elsewhere. Women's influence on public opinion by virtue of their status as *mayordomas* or as experienced participants in other rituals, their extensive connections to others through kin and *compadrazgo* networks, and their ability to organize and lobby during fiestas, in the market, and at community bathing and laundry sites were all important in organizing the cooperatives initially and in helping women to maintain positions of solidarity and support with one another when their behavior was criticized. The experience of others outside of the community as domestic workers in Mexico City and elsewhere provided them with a different set of norms for measuring community customs that restricted women's freedom of movement and forbade them from selling their textiles outside of their community. Thus both "traditional" gender roles for women within the community as well as the influence of living elsewhere were important in allowing them to organize at the local level in new ways.

CONCLUSION

In this ethnographically based chapter, I have emphasized the importance of looking at community-specific gender roles for women in what have often been called "traditional" forms of local governance and looking at how women's roles in such institutions interact with other forms of organizing that take place at the local level. I have maintained that the capacity for indigenous women to be successful in opening up local political systems to their participation and leadership is predicated on the recognition of specific skills and experience they develop in local, ethnic-linked forms of governance—even if such systems formally exclude women—and other forms of organization that may offer more egalitarian forms of organizing for women. Women who emerge as local leaders in the context of weaving cooperatives in Teotitlán or in the community council of La Realidad have developed a unique set of skills and abilities that not only gives them credibility in their own communities, but also the capacity to translate their leadership to broader regional and national forums for indigenous rights. This capacity is rooted in their ability to articulate local gendered contests over political power and ethnic and cultural rights with regional and national forms of association that offer a different set of gendered political roles and often emphasize a specific ethnic identity or a pan-indigenous form of identity as a basis for organization. The examples offered here are illustrations of the politics of scale discussed by Blackwell (chapter 4, this volume). Here, Tojola'bal and Zapotec women have been able to scale up and adapt local, ethnic-based skills to other forms of organization and association.

Indigenous women leaders such as Comandanta Esther and Aurora Bazán López are involved in the crafting of indigenous nationalism in Mexico, and their work requires gendered behavior that facilitates national and sometimes international communication, agreements, and travel. While they are certainly unique individuals with strong organizing talents and personal charisma, their ability to work the borders of community, nation, and the world can be linked to the kind of experiences and skills they share with local women activists in Chiapas and Oaxaca. Through combining local, ethnic-based skills and identity with nonethnic forms of organization and communication, they can serve as translators and bridges between different constituencies in the nation. As Mexican indigenous women continue to promote and enlarge their share of national and international political space, we have much to learn from them in how to negotiate cultural difference in processes of globalization.

NOTES

This chapter is based on research carried out in Chiapas from 1994 to 2000 and in Oaxaca from 2001 to 2004. I gratefully acknowledge support from the Wenner-Gren Foundation for Anthropological Research, the Center for U.S.-Mexican Studies, a Summer Research Award for Faculty from the University of Oregon, and a grant from the Center for the Study of Women in Society at the University of Oregon.

1. *Ejidos* were created after the Mexican Revolution to satisfy the demands of landless peasants who had seen their communal village lands eaten up by large agricultural estates and/or who had served as laborers on those estates. The term *ejido* refers to a specific area of land as well. For many communities, *ejido* refers to territory tied to the community. The formation of *ejidos* since the Mexican Revolution (until 1992) has involved the transference of over 70 million hectares from large estates to slightly more than three million peasant beneficiaries. The term *ejidatario* refers to those people who have land rights in the *ejido*. This right was either granted through petitioning the government as part of a group of people in order to receive access to land or through inheritance. No new *ejidos* have been formed since 1992 when the Mexican government implemented a reform to Article 27 of the Mexican Constitution that eliminated the government's obligation to redistribute land (Stephen 2002:6–7, 62–88).

2. "Elected" can have a range of meanings. In some cases it involves a slate of competing candidates for whom assembly members vote by stating the name of their preferred candidate; the verbal votes for each are then tallied. In other cases it can mean an unopposed slate of candidates named by outgoing community authorities that is confirmed by verbal vote.

3. Even when La Realidad was under EZLN control in the 1990s, the rights of women to *ejido* land were no different from the pre-1971 government criteria,

according to several *ejidatarios* I spoke with in 1996. They stated that in the *ejido* of La Realidad, women gained rights to *ejido* land as widows if their husbands had been *ejidatarios* or as single mothers. While all men over the age of eighteen whether single or married could have access to *ejido* land, married women and single women without children could not.

4. A pseudonym at her request. I have used pseudonyms when the women requested them.

SIX

AUTONOMY AND A HANDFUL OF HERBS

Contesting Gender and Ethnic Identities through Healing

MELISSA M. FORBIS

This chapter is dedicated to Compañera Guadalupe
of Altamirano, Chiapas. Lupe was a tireless health promoter
and community organizer who died in 2003 of uterine cancer,
which went undetected until too late.

The struggle of the Zapatista National Liberation Army (EZLN) has been notable for the large number of indigenous women in leadership roles and its continued discursive commitment to gender equity. Although there has been considerable debate about what this commitment has meant in terms of actual change in gender relations and practices on the ground, it is undeniable that moves toward gender equity have been made and that they are frequently tied to contestations surrounding ethnicity and class. On March 28, 2001, Comandanta Esther became not only the first member of the EZLN but also the first indigenous woman to address the Mexican Congress. This chapter analyzes these changes in gender relations and practices through an ethnographic consideration of a women's herbal medicine training project in a *municipio autónomo,* or autonomous township, of the area known as the Cañadas, the canyons leading to the Lacandon jungle. The EZLN announced the formation of these autonomous townships at the end of 1994, and approximately thirty-three exist to date. I focus on how this health work has empowered Zapatista women to confront and renegotiate gender, ethnic, and class relations within their families, communities, and region—processes that are not without personal consequences. I show how this health work relates to the Zapatista movement's larger goals, the demands for rights and resources in the context of Mexico's neoliberal reforms and state decentralization.[1]

In this chapter I use the term "ethnicity," which has been most commonly associated in Latin America with indigenous peoples, rather than "race," which usually denotes peoples of African descent; however, I employ the term "racism" when describing discrimination based on ethnic status.[2] The conceptual relationships between the terms "ethnicity" and "race," as well as the place of indigenous peoples and Afro-descent peoples in the nation, have not received much attention or analysis in Mexico.

This chapter is based on data and interviews collected between 1997 and 2001 and in 2003 for a project, proposed by township authorities in late 1996, investigating the feasibility of a health program focused on medicinal plants, with community women as the participants. I worked as an adviser on this project for three and a half years. For the first two years, I collaborated with a Mexican colleague, who worked independently of her job at the nongovernmental organization (NGO) Chiltak, based in San Cristóbal de las Casas. After the first year, my colleague returned full-time to Chiltak, dedicating herself to women's reproductive health. Many civil society and solidarity volunteers assisted the project over the years; two Basque women in particular volunteered for extended periods. The resulting program and courses were coordinated closely with regional authorities and the participants and their communities.

The women who participated in this project, called *promotoras de salud* (lay health workers/promoters), began a process of recuperating local medical knowledge as part of a movement toward community self-sufficiency. They characterize themselves as healers who are working collectively and using local natural resources in service to their communities. The valorization of this work by the autonomous township has strengthened indigenous identities through a link to "ancestral knowledge" and cultural practices. Community members describe how these important knowledges and practices fell into disuse (*se perdió*) when they migrated to new ecological regions in search of land and as a result of their overreliance on government health programs. This process implies a critique of the local hegemony of Western medicine, viewed both as a necessity and as a symbol of the mistreatment and oppression of indigenous and poor peoples.

I do not examine the specific local medical practices of the *promotoras* in this zone, although those practices are significant in the context of current debates about biopiracy, traditional medicine, and authenticity. Instead, I focus on women's participation in this project as a transformative process that contributed to the strengthening of women's organizing and altered relations of power at the local and regional levels.

This health work responds directly to the larger goals of the Zapatista movement for indigenous rights and autonomy. In the EZLN's Declaration of War in 1994, health care was one of the main demands. The declaration, written by Subcomandante Marcos in 1992 and published in January 1994 under the title "Chiapas: The Southeast in Two Winds," states:

> Government agencies made some horrifying statistics known: in Chiapas 14,500 people die every year, the highest mortality rate in the country. The causes? Curable diseases such as respiratory infections, enteritis, parasites, amoebas, malaria, salmonella, scabies, dengue, pulmonary tuberculosis, trachoma, typhus, cholera, and measles. Many say that this figure is actually over 15,000 because deaths in the marginalized zones, the majority of the state, are not reported. (Marcos and Ponce de León 2001:31)

"THE MOST VULNERABLE CHILDREN OF THE STATE": MODERNIZATION AND NEOLIBERAL REFORMS

Marcos's statement, meant to show the depths of government disregard, captures the abysmal state of health care in Chiapas. Although statistics vary from source to source, the general situation in Chiapas is alarming. The rate of maternal mortality is 15 to 18 deaths per 10,000 women in the Selva (greater Lacandon jungle) region. In the central and coastal parts of the state, areas with a small indigenous population, the rate is only 3 for every 10,000 women. The rate of infant mortality is 37.6 for every 1,000 births in the Selva region, with prebirth infections and gastrointestinal diseases the leading causes (Tuñon Pablos, Rojas Wiesner, and Sánchez Ramírez 1998). In areas with high indigenous populations, there are elevated incidences of digestive and respiratory illnesses. These preventable and curable diseases are the leading causes of death, despite decades of official policies and programs aimed at improving the health of the indigenous peoples of Chiapas.

During the presidency of Lázaro Cárdenas in the 1930s, fostering an *estado de bienestar* (state of well-being) became a national project. This initiative was coupled with another national project—the targeting of indigenous groups in Mexico for assimilation. The Instituto Nacional Indigenista's (National Indigenist Institute, INI) health program began in highland Chiapas in 1951 with the intention of "bringing the benefits of modern medicine to the indigenous" (Holland 1963:211).[3] This health program, part of a larger INI project, exposes federal efforts that used improvement in health as a hook to assimilate indigenous peoples to mestizo modernity. The concept of *mestizaje,* or race mixing, was critical to the construction of a postrevolution unitary Mexican national identity (see Brading 1973; Gamio 1916; Hewitt de Alcántara 1984).

Highland communities and state government officials[4] initially were opposed the INI project, but its eventual acceptance assured replication in other parts of the state. INI staff efforts to bring locals into their teams accelerated the project's success. However, the aim of this collaboration was not to share medical practices but to aid in the process of assimilation. "The [indigenous] medical promoter plays an important intercultural role in the contact between indigenous patients and the INI doctors, in that the position of the former is to interpret the concepts of one cultural system in those of the other" (Holland 1963:223). INI doctors characterized most local healers, or *curanderos,* as operating in the magico-religious realm and thus as charlatans.

That the INI health program began in Chiapas is not a surprise; the state fulfilled a key role in nurturing the image of the indigenous Other in the national imagination. The two defining historical political elements in Chiapas were paternalism and patriarchy. In the 1970s politicians publicly referred to indigenous groups as the "most vulnerable children of the state" (París Pombo 1993:106). Treated as children (and as the failed objects of modernization), the population was deemed by the majority of physicians as responsible for their own ill health because of their ignorance. Emphasis was placed on the importance of education and prevention programs, and the socioeconomic conditions were overlooked. In the 1970s and 1980s, government programs took an intercultural turn, building on the work of the INI and leading to a program of "parallel medicine" that incorporated traditional medicine and plant medicine (Freyermuth Enciso 1993:79–85).

This turn to parallel medicine dovetails with the neoliberal reforms that accompanied Mexico's economic crisis in the early 1980s. It is also part of a broader pairing of neoliberalism and multiculturalism. Over the past few decades, these reforms have ushered in processes of decentralization, with an emphasis on civil society associations, citizen participation, and the increased presence of multilateral organizations. In terms of health, these changes translated into a displacement of state responsibility for health care onto individuals or groups, with an attendant drop in economic resources available for these services. A drive to modernize the institutions of the Cárdenas era by privatizing

MELISSA M. FORBIS

services accompanied this displacement (López Arellano and Blanco Gil 1993:25–26).

In the 1990s, these reforms were augmented by a policy of self-help that emphasized individual responsibility for health (López Arellano and Blanco Gil:67). A faith in modernity and progress as cures to all social ills lingers behind these policies; the decentralization of services is championed as the democratization of health care. Dr. Jaime Page Pliego notes:

> What has been said is concretized: on the one hand, in the actions that are directed at the urban and rural marginalized, [toward] mainly self-help and individual and family responsibility in health and the prevention of illness; and on the other, in terms of finances, as year after year they [the federal government] reduce the economic resources for the operation of government and parastate health institutions. Both measures result in the deterioration of the quality of medical attention. (2000:183–184)

Cloaked in a discourse that celebrates indigenous culture, local indigenous healers are a crucial element in the official neoliberal strategy. "The ethnic pluralism of the eighties was curiously like an escape valve in the face of the budgetary pressures of the assistential programs" (París Pombo 200:114). Thus, these programs simultaneously moved the risks and responsibilities of health to local sites and promoted resource-empty multiculturalism.

In this move to decentralization, indigenous women were frequently characterized as the most vulnerable sector. As Nahela Becerril Albarrán and colleagues (2000:369) state, "According to development theory, the woman represents a wasted human resource that should be 'integrated' into production and the market." Indigenous women were also regarded as the most culturally distinct and "backward" of the nation, and as hindrances to progress. Many governmental anti-poverty assistance programs, such as Programa Nacional de Solidaridad (PRONASOL), Programa de Educación, Salud y Alimentación (PROGRESA), and, most recently, Oportunidades, focus on women as their target population. Indeed, the members of the family who are selected to participate in Oportunidades[5] and receive compensation are generally the mothers, "in order to strengthen their position in the family and community." [6] There is a built-in oversight mechanism with a list of conditions for "recertification," a prerequisite for women's continuing participation. Women are required to complete a series of tasks and to maintain certain standards in the home in areas such as hygiene and child care. The overseers are

180

volunteers, other poor women from the same communities or neighborhoods. This is one of the ways in which the program undermines women's solidarity.

In Chiapas, where rhetoric of the family dominated official political ideology, these programs could be characterized as fulfilling a social welfare mission. However, as París Pombo (1993:103) notes, paternalism and patriarchy "translate into a devaluation of some sociopolitical actors—in particular, Indians and women—contributing to the creation of situations of marginalization and discrimination." In the end, these programs reinforce the socioeconomic inequalities they intend to improve. Rather than focus on and change the underlying reasons for the marginalization and extreme poverty of certain communities in Mexico, the programs imagine individual solutions that still create dependencies and undermine collective social relations.

MIGRATION, AGITATION, AND THE EMERGENCE OF INDIGENOUS MOVEMENTS

The medicinal plant health project took place in the Cañadas, one of the most marginalized regions of Mexico whose historical trajectory has been different from that of the highlands. It is also the region where the EZLN began to organize. In the 1950s, looking for arable land or work on plantations, people from the central highlands and nearby towns, such as Comitán and Altamirano, began to settle in the sparsely populated Cañadas. There was a second wave of migration in the 1960s and 1970s spurred by a nationwide government program that brought mestizos to settle the jungle (De Vos 2000). Families indeed were able to gain land and resources. However, the new settlements also precipitated transformations in community and family structures, including the nature of gendered work as women worked side-by-side with men to clear land and establish their new communities (Garza Caligaris et al. 1993; Leyva Solano and Franco 1996).

These changes served families well after the Zapatista uprising. The Zapatistas took over former plantation and ranch lands, formed Nuevo Centros de Población (New Population Centers), and began rebuilding their lives. The Cañadas area was home to the largest number of *tierras recuperadas,* or "recovered" lands. The newly constructed communities were exclusively Zapatista, although not necessarily composed of people from the same community of origin or ethnic group. For example, the residents of one large community near the town of Altamirano were

Tzeltal and Tojola'bal-speaking peoples from five communities and *ejidos*. Several of the new communities built on recovered lands in the Patihuitz canyon became home to Tzotzil highlander refugees after the Acteal massacre.[7]

Significant shifts in the Catholic Church ran parallel to the process of migration. In the 1960s the diocese of San Cristóbal, under the leadership of Bishop Samuel Ruiz, began to develop a local form of Catholicism influenced by liberation theology and indigenous traditions. The church began to ordain indigenous catechists. Married men's ordainments were often joint appointments, with their wives also agreeing to serve. Later, the Diocesan Council of Women (CODIMUJ) and the Palabra de Dios (Word of God) organized individual women. This evangelizing work was highly successful in the Cañadas, often complementing other organizing around agrarian issues. Women from a variety of rural and urban areas participated in these groups and learned skills such as public speaking, reading, writing, and mathematics.

Migration coupled with the government's assimilationist policies aided in the transformation of the migrants into campesinos (peasants), stripped of their ethnic identities. I am not suggesting that people fully embraced the government's policy of "indigeneity"; however, certain official criteria were internalized and naturalized. Once, when I referred to Aurora[8] as indigenous, she quickly replied, "No, I'm not indigenous. My family used to be Tzeltal, but they moved and I can't really speak [Tzeltal] anymore." Organizing struggles took the form of peasant movements (see Harvey 1998; Mattiace 1998). Many women's first experiences of agitation centered on agrarian demands in organizations such as the Unión de Uniones, although they did not generally serve leadership roles. Many women also joined the EZLN in the 1980s when it was still a clandestine organization, viewing it as a more militant option (pers. com., June 1, 2003).

In terms of healing practices, these migrations often meant moving to a new bioregion with different plant species. In addition to the migrants' diminished knowledge of their immediate environments, government health programs encouraged their attachment to the social welfare system. In repeated conversations, community members charge that participating in these processes of modernization made them lose ancestral knowledge (*se perdió el costumbre*). This expression of "loss" refers not to a permanent erasure but rather to a state of disuse and devaluation of previous practices and traditions.

It was not just migration and changes in community-state relations that caused the "loss" of this aspect of local indigenous culture. Despite their benefits, religious groups had a deleterious effect on indigenous healing practices. The labeling of these practices as witchcraft (*brujería*) aided in the replacement of local medicines (Ayora Díaz 2000). Lupe, a health promoter and member of the Palabra de Dios who is in her fifties, told me, "Yes, there are still some old ones around who know the customs, but they don't tell many people because . . . they don't want to be called *brujos* [witches]. I help people, but only if they come to talk to me here [at my house]." When I asked her who would call them *brujos,* she told me that years ago it was the Catholic Church, but, she added, "things are changing, people don't remember anymore." Rosalva Aída Hernández Castillo (1996:38) observes that "the migrations, organizational experiences, religious groups and even the government programs have equally influenced the way in which indigenous men and women conceive of and define their identities."

IDENTITY, AUTONOMY, AND RIGHTS

The character of political opposition has shifted with the introduction of neoliberal reforms and has emerged as a cultural politics of indigenous identity, often transcending regional and national boundaries. Many early mobilizations focused on the "right to have rights" (Álvarez, Dagnino, and Escobar 1998). Lisa Lowe and David Lloyd (1997) point to the nature of state changes as aiding in the opening of spaces that allowed for these kinds of cultural-political struggles to come forward. In the 1990s demands focused on the right to difference, on contesting the nature of national identity, and on resources based on identity.

Many saw the failure of class in the rise of these identity-based movements. Yet the EZLN emerged as a movement that combined ethnic demands with class and gender demands for both rights and resources. Previous peasant movements organized exclusively around class did not speak to the power of racism to structure life in Mexico; race is a lived category of experience and contributes to the force of indigenous movements. Reducing these struggles to an essential class contestation is precisely the type of mistake that feminist scholars have been writing against, pointing out that identities are multiple and that while they may be expressed more strongly through certain categories at certain moments, they are always lived simultaneously (Alexander and Mohanty 1997; Anzaldúa 1991; McClaurin 2001).

In its initial communiqués, the EZLN highlighted concerns such as land rights, structural poverty, and racism and rejected the role of transnational capital in Mexican social life through privatization and treaties like the North American Free Trade Agreement. These concerns expose the importance of relations outside the community for building identity. Akhil Gupta and James Ferguson (1997:13–14) note, "At issue is not simply that one is located in a certain place but that the particular place is set apart from and opposed to other places. The 'global' relations that we have argued are constitutive of locality are therefore centrally involved in the production of 'local' identities too."

Thus, the EZLN's struggle over regional and national spaces is also a struggle in a global context, drawing from international movements for indigenous rights and treaties (such as the International Labor Organization Convention 169)[9] and contributing to those contestations. Chela Sandoval (2000) refers to this as an "oppositional consciousness" in which the colonized are continually aware of the constructedness of their identities and shift their subjectivities in order to position themselves differently within structures of power. In addition to forging a struggle around indigenous identity at the national and international levels, EZLN demands for territorial autonomy signal a return to the local as a strategic space: autonomy is not just an oppositional form; it also signifies the creation of a new social and political practice.

The EZLN's autonomy project requires the transformation of the relationship of communities to the state. On August 9, 2003, the EZLN took another concrete step toward political self-determination by creating five Caracoles, homes of the Juntas de Buen Gobierno (Good Governance Councils).[10] This change implies the territorial consolidation of an autonomous form of governance, complete with health services and educational and justice systems for the autonomous townships and regions. The juntas are also attempting to create an open and direct relationship with national and international civil society. These new relationships affect the conceptualization of gender relations and identities. As people transform gender relations, new meanings of autonomy emerge, which in turn affect the nature of the project. Collective autonomy does not sacrifice the personal but draws from it. "In this sense, the Zapatista struggle considers the woman part of this project [of transformation] and also the subject of transformation" (Olivera and Ramírez Méndez 2001:37).

Although Zapatista women are distinguished by their participation in their own political movement, they share concerns with other indigenous women. Their struggles resonate across political affiliations and spaces. Some of these predated and contributed to the Zapatista uprising, and others emerged out of or gained new impetus from the struggle. Examples are the first Indigenous Congress (1974), CODIMUJ, the Congreso Nacional Indígena (founded 1996), and the Coordinadora Nacional de Mujeres Indígenas (founded 1997). The discourses of the EZLN *comandantas* also mention these other relations and are frequently addressed to other indigenous women.

Within the webs of power and "multiple networks of collective obligations and solidarities" (Chatterjee 1998:282) that constitute them as subjects, Zapatista women discuss their identities specifically as indigenous women and call attention to the triple oppression of racism, sexism, and classism. Central to understanding how indigenous women are forging new identities is understanding how one becomes a "woman" through race and class (Mohanty 1991), which is also a geographically constructed process (de la Cadena 2000). This geographic construction is itself also gendered and racialized: the local is configured as a natural "feminine" indigenous space as opposed to a "masculine" white global space (Massey 1994).

Understanding identities as multiple forces us to break from dichotomous characterizations of the local and the global, as well as the community and the state, and to recognize these as mutually constitutive. This relationship is apparent; community identities emerge from the local geographic space and from the global discursive space of belonging to a pueblo or people. As Martha Sánchez Nestor (2003:20), an Amuzga woman who is the general coordinator of the Asamblea Nacional Indígena Plural por la Autonomía (Pluralistic Indigenous National Assembly in Support of Autonomy, ANIPA) and a member of the National Council of Indigenous Women, notes, "Just like self-determination and autonomy, which cannot be put into practice if they do not have a territory, we women cannot put into practice our rights if indigenous peoples (pueblos) don't exist. . . . [The pueblos] will form the basis of these deep changes, since our sons also deserve, as our legacy, a new form of relating to their sisters."

This new form of relating is frequently phrased and understood as "women's rights." These rights include the right to difference; to *dignidad* (dignity), to being respected for who they are; and the right to participate, *caminando parejo*.[11] Accepted internally in March 1993 and made public on January 1, 1994, the EZLN's Women's Revolutionary Law codified many of their demands. These rights grow out of women's day-to-day experiences in combination with reference to abstract laws, such as universal human rights. What is at stake is not just gaining these rights but being able to practice them in the context of their communities. This other sense of "rights" shows that the creation of spaces is as important as attaining legal recognition. As Margarita Gutiérrez and Nellys Palomo note:

> The spaces that we are constructing at the individual and collective levels try to make visible and define our place as women. In some pueblos, there are specific women's spaces and in others, they exist inside of mixed organizations, where there are women's commissions or women elders' councils. In any of these experiences, we have kept present the notion that our struggle cannot be divorced from the community or from the struggle of our peoples and our brothers. (1999:59)

The process of struggling for these rights contributes to the shaping of women's identities. "Without neglecting other rights, they put emphasis on their political rights, since these encompass their right to have opinions, to decide, to direct, to choose, and to participate in decision making in all areas and levels" (Sánchez 2003:15). The right of indigenous women to participate does not just imply the presence of women in councils, assemblies, or commissions but also the right to make decisions that affect themselves and their communities. The report of a 1993 INI gathering of indigenous women from across Mexico who worked on INI projects emphasized the right to participate throughout the proceedings: "In the community our lives are centered on the respect of our customs, beliefs and how we have the obligation to serve the indigenous community" (INI 1997:30).

When limits are placed on these rights in the name of culture, they are criticized by indigenous women, not to divide their communities, but to make them more cohesive. Female Zapatista leaders have said publicly that they reserve the right to transform the traditions that oppress them as women; they are struggling for liberation. This agency undermines the image of the indigenous woman as merely the transmitter of culture, a view that discounts the continual processes of (re-)creation of both indigenous culture and their own identities. As Consuelo Sánchez notes:

> In this way, far from weakening the ethnic identity of the indigenous women who make critiques, they are more and more conscious of their ethnic belonging and clearly express their desire to reaffirm and strengthen their ethnic identity. However, they add that the capacity of their peoples to mold their identities, with the end of constructing more equitable and tolerant relations, should be promoted. (2003:13)

ORGANIZING FOR HEALTH

Declaration of Moisés Gandhi, February 1997

Health is the well-being of the people [*pueblo*] and the individual, who have the capacity and motivation for all types of activities whether social or political. Health is living without humiliation; being able to develop ourselves as women and men; it is being able to struggle for a new country [*patria*] where the poor and particularly the indigenous peoples can make decisions autonomously. Poverty, militarization and war destroy health. (Moisés Gandhi Relator@s 1997:229)

At the time of the 1994 uprising, EZLN demands for health care centered on access and availability to Western medicine,[12] which had supplanted many traditional healing practices in the Cañadas. In this region, adequate health care often depends on how close one lives to towns with medical services, whether specialized treatment is available, and who is in charge. Complicating access to health services are health providers' racist attitudes toward their patients, especially at intake: "It is common that these professionals [medical residents] have theoretical deficiencies about cultural aspects, which give place to an insensitive medical practice toward the beliefs and customs of the population" (CONAPO 1994:46).

After the uprising, government health officials began to offer myriad programs to Zapatista communities to combat the idea that the lack of adequate services was one of the factors that had fueled the struggle. However, the EZLN had implemented a policy of refusing all government aid until that aid is distributed equally to all Mexicans. Zapatista communities characterize themselves as being "in resistance." In the autonomous township of 17 de Noviembre (official township of Altamirano), desires for training programs in the use of medicinal plants coalesced after the Mexican Federal Army offensive of February 1995, when people had to flee from their communities into the mountains. Under extreme conditions, without much food or medicine, many became ill. After returning home, community members and regional leaders evaluated the experience and identified the need for the training of local herbalists. Carmen, the women's regional authority organizing the health project, described the feelings of shame that many shared: "So many children were sick and we were in the mountains and knew that there were remedies around us. But we didn't know what they were, so we were afraid to try them."

Government, Catholic Church, and NGO projects had for decades been providing some health promoter training. The EZLN had also been doing clandestine health work since the 1980s, preparing a military sanitary corps. Although a few projects included elements of plant medicine and even acupuncture, health promoters who participated in these projects assert that the emphasis was on mastering the basics of Western medicine. During a meeting (*encuentro*) of ninety-one health promoters and advisers from sixteen different organizations held in the Zapatista community of Moisés Gandhi in 1997, an indigenous participant remarked:

> The old ones used only plants, right now, we are losing this, we're using [pharmaceutical] medicines. But up until now, the old ones still have this knowledge, because it's better. It is necessary that we know the plants that will cure illnesses; suddenly the problems could start again because the government doesn't understand. If the problem of war comes again and we don't know the plants, what are we going to use to cure ourselves [*los indígenas*]? (Moisés Gandhi Relator@s 1997:51)

Although lay health promoter training preceded the uprising, health demands and training projects were now articulating the desire to foster self-determination so as to bolster a regional autonomy project and an emergent indigenous cultural identity. Women, perceived by many as crucial to the preservation and promotion of cultural identities in the home, were also recognized as important to the success of transforming—locally and nationally—these cultural identities.

The project in 17 de Noviembre was earmarked for women participants. In this region, gender-exclusive projects for women were not unheard of, but they were usually in the area of production, such as collectives formed to raise chickens for eggs and meat. Health and education projects were typically male groups; the few women who were involved tended to participate less and to defer to men in discussions. In the first round of our courses, there were about twenty participants; in the second, the number fluctuated between thirty-four and forty. The women were mainly Tzeltal and Tojola'bal and came from a mixture of urban Altamirano neighborhoods, established *ejidos* and communities, and Nuevo Centros. Community and neighborhood assemblies selected two women and named them to be *promotoras de salud*. Thus, their work as promotoras was a *cargo*.

The *cargo* system is part of an indigenous form of governance whose positions of responsibility carry obligations to the community and the autonomous township. Generally, community assemblies name members to a position. In some communities, generally *ejidos,* assembly attendance is exclusively male. One of the changes instituted by the EZLN was incorporating women into the assemblies. Although this is not always the case, any issue involving women, such as the naming of *promotoras,* will happen at an assembly with all members of the community present. Once named, the person is expected to accept the position. It is also difficult to voluntarily renounce a *cargo.* Indeed, people who do their jobs well are often "promoted" to positions of higher responsibility—whether they want the change or not.

At its inception, this health project was one of many in the region, including an allopathic health-training project (almost exclusively male), an education project, production projects (agrarian and artisanal), and human rights training. Carmen, the women's authority for the region, worked to organize this particular project "because it can help bring the women together, so they can begin to participate and learn many things and not be ashamed." She said that one of the reasons for the selection of women was that it would complement the work of the other health promoters, almost all of whom were men. She explained:

> During the day, the men go to their *milpas* [fields], which are far away from the community, and they don't return until the afternoon. Even the promoters must go to their *milpas.* Sometimes the women leave to gather firewood or to help in the *milpa* when it's time to weed. But their *mero* [real] work is in the home. If someone got injured or became ill in the community, the *promotoras* would be there.

She also voiced the complaint that "men get all the projects" and that this hurts communities because women are important; they take care of the house, raise children, make sure the family is well nourished, and work in collectives and the church, and they have been responsible for decreasing men's drinking and domestic violence. Although some projects begin as women's projects, she noted that men sometimes advocate for inclusion, or if there are problems with a collective, she said, "rather than help the women solve the problems, men intervene and take it over." Women's right to participate, part of the Women's Revolutionary Law,[13] was an underlying reason for developing projects for women. Becoming a *promotora* is a way for women to organize and contest gender hierarchies publicly—by demanding their right to work for the good of the community through health, just as men have done.

Finally, Carmen told me that the autonomous townships needed to foster self-sufficiency, since "the government programs are only for the rich." "We poor people are left begging for help when we are sick. Right now, there is another hospital run by the nuns [Hospital San Carlos in Altamirano] and they help us, but what will happen if they go? Or stop helping us?" In this area, limited access, high costs, and the availability of privately run charity hospitals led the government to shift the responsibilities and risks for health to local communities. Although the Hospital San Carlos had provided many services free or at minimal cost, at the time of this writing, it had been forced to raise patient fees, and fewer people were able to use its services. Without diminishing the EZLN demands for adequate health coverage for all, regional authorities supported plant-based medicine as a natural resource that anyone could access and use, without having to pay money. In addition to harvesting wild plants, there was a proposal to create medicinal plant gardens, especially in communities with existing women's collective vegetable gardens, making medicinal plants affordable and accessible. Thus, this work brings together issues of gender, class, and ethnicity under the umbrella of autonomy.

My colleague and I began the first course by asking the question, "What do you know already about medicinal plants?" The answer was a resounding silence, which we attributed initially to women's fear of speaking in public. Then we asked, "If someone is sick in your family, what do you do?" Tere, one of the most outspoken women in the course, replied first: "It depends on what the sickness is. If my little son is vomiting, then I go out and get a handful of *mirto* and I boil it with water. Then when it cools, I give it to him, bit by bit." After Tere spoke, more women joined in and related their plant remedies for nausea and vomiting and other illnesses. The resulting discussion and exchange of practical knowledge of medicinal plants and home remedies lasted several hours. Several of the women revealed that they were also *curanderas* and treated illness through religious means, a gift they had received in dreams. A number of others had learned about medicinal plants from family members who were considered skilled herbalists in their areas. Yet others were midwives who used plants in their practice.

What became clear was that the *promotoras* did not view this knowledge of healing as "medicine"; medicine is something done in clinics and hospitals. As one woman protested, "But this is just something we do at home." Although home remedies are frequently the first stage of medical treatment for illness, as mentioned by the *promotoras* and others (see CONAPO 1994), they are not considered actual "medicine" because they are not done by anyone with specialized knowledge. Even those women who had specialized knowledge were hesitant to see their work as medicine.[14] Building on this discussion, the *promotoras* talked about the nature of health, why their work is important, and their goals for the project, which included the following:

1. Improve health conditions.

2. Regain their traditions.

3. Support women's organizing and participation.

4. Support community self-sufficiency, which leads to autonomy and not dependency.

5. Fight against the *mal gobierno*[15] and its policies.

For many of these women, participation in a course like this was a considerable change, although it was not always recognized as such. Clara, a forty-three-year-old Tzeltal woman who had participated in a previous project, became one of the first *promotoras* in the township. Leaving her home to organize in the region was so significant that she clearly remembered the day she began her work: "I began *caminando*[16] on October 12, 1994." This was a common occurrence.

When the *promotoras* discussed how they could participate to improve community health, most of them emphasized the recuperation of traditional knowledge. Rosa understood this lack of knowledge as colonial subversion: "The *mal gobierno* took this away from us. They convinced us that it was no good. We stopped believing in it. But we know our ancestors knew how to take care of themselves before others came here." The recuperation of this knowledge is also the (re-)creation of indigenous culture. Part of the recuperation involves reaffirming its value and finding ways to treat the illnesses that affect many people—such as *aire* (illness carried by the wind), *susto* (fright), and *ojo* (evil eye)—that are not within the scope of Western medicine. Even if health providers understood these spiritual ailments, hospitals would not have appropriate treatments.

When indigenous women are organizing, they are often at a disadvantage because they are more likely to be monolingual or illiterate (Rojas 1994) and live mainly in rural areas, although in this case, many older women from Altamirano were also illiterate. The *promotoras* recognized that improving these skills would help them to organize more effectively and not feel "left outside." This process unfolded as skills sharing. The communities would name at least one woman, usually a younger woman, who was literate. In this way, women who were already skilled could participate even if they were unable to speak Spanish or read and write—such as Ana, who spoke only Tzeltal but could identify most of the plants in the area.

Although nineteen-year-old Lucinda was one of the few women to complete primary schooling, she hardly participated in the course at the beginning. Knowing that she had been excited to start the course, I asked her, "Why aren't you speaking up?" She responded, "I'm afraid to say something wrong . . . people will laugh." Women without much experience speaking in public felt ashamed to voice their opinions. Often older women served as an important bridge between women, facilitating communication and setting an example. Alejandra and Hermelinda are both in their sixties and trilingual (Tzeltal, Tojola'bal, and Spanish), and neither could read or write. They had no fear of speaking in public and often provided informal translation during the sessions. By the end of the course, many women had improved their skills and learned to speak in public. As Lucinda noted, "Before we weren't confident. Now we can speak, now the fear is gone, the shame, now we can talk in the assemblies."

Under the larger framework of the identified and accepted need to improve health, this project opened a space to discuss concerns specific to women's health and sexuality, a significant advance. Male health promoters were not often knowledgeable about women's health issues, nor was it generally considered appropriate to discuss these concerns in front of men. At the Moisés Gandhi meeting, participants also voiced their concerns that women avoid going to male health promoters for many illnesses.

Women were unaccustomed to talking about their bodies, even among other women. However, when some of the older urban women began discussing their vaginal infections, other women began to join in. The *promotoras* were especially interested in the types of treatments they could offer that would not involve their patients consulting a male health promoter or going to a pharmacist. Although there were practicing midwives in the area, for most health concerns other than pregnancy women sought treatment at local hospitals and clinics. Many women preferred to suffer their ailments silently, which is not surprising given the bad treatment they often experienced. Most of the *promotoras* had experienced the disregard of their symptoms. They had been told by doctors, "No, you don't have a problem, your head just hurts because of your work," which was coupled with patronizing treatments "Here, have an aspirin [or a B vitamin shot]."

This sense of their vulnerability as poor indigenous women when dealing with medical practitioners intensified when our discussions turned to sex and family planning. Many *promotoras* spoke of cases of nonconsensual insertion of an intrauterine device (IUD) by doctors at government-run clinics after women gave birth, and even of sterilization. Although some of the stories were hearsay—from extended family members or about women from other places—one of the women in the project spoke of her own experience. She began to bleed intensely a few months after giving birth at a local government-run clinic. She went to a hospital run by a private charity for a check-up, and the doctor told her that her IUD was the problem. She was unaware of having an IUD. In spite of these accounts of violation, there was not yet a move to organize public steps to denounce this treatment. Doña Romelia told me, "*Nos da vergüenza* [We feel embarrassed]. We can't tell everyone about these things that have been done to us. We know it's wrong and that we have to complain about the *mal gobierno*, but . . . not yet." The first step was to begin discussing these kinds of concerns with other women.

Upon returning from a course, the *promotoras* would generally call an assembly to report on what they had learned and make plans for community work. In some places, these assemblies re-created the women's space of the courses and could be used to discuss sensitive issues. In others, the meetings were attended by both men and women and focused more on general health. Most people supported the *promotoras'* efforts; however, failing to report back eroded community support. In these cases, the women were criticized for not fulfilling their obligations to the community. In locations where the work advanced, other existing projects were also strengthened and, in turn, supported the health project. In Las Calabacitas,[17] the women's bread collective donated money for the *promotoras'* transportation and even gave them extra money so that they could buy themselves a treat while at the course. Where no projects existed, these health-specific assemblies helped to dispel lingering stereotypes of women as less trustworthy, committed, and responsible. The newfound respect for women's organizing often led to plans for income-producing projects, such as collective gardens, milpas, and bakeries, which had previously been deemed too risky.

While the actual project training was conducted exclusively for women, women's work within their communities was linked to the work of male health promoters, and in a number of cases, knowledge and resources were shared. Promoters in two communities merged their health centers and jointly attended to patients, choosing the best methods of treatment from all the options available. These practices reinforce ideas of equality, but with difference. In this case, women's work in health in the autonomous township of 17 de Noviembre has changed gendered relations of power in a way that could be characterized as complementary, although not in the essentialized sense that is often portrayed by casting women as the bearer of culture through motherhood (Nash 2001). Instead, it is a complementarity whereby men and women work together toward common goals, each bringing certain culturally defined qualities that the community values, which can also change over time.

POWER PLAYS: MILITARY VIOLENCE, LOOKING FOR NEW HUSBANDS, AND OTHER STORIES

This process of transformation was not without repercussions. The *promotoras* faced numerous internal and external challenges, which underscore the significance of the changes. One state response to women's organizing hinged on the control of women's bodies, instilling fear through the deployment of threats of violence and censure. Soldiers raped three young Tzeltal women at a military checkpoint in Altamirano in June 1994. Although this was the only case of rape that was publicly denounced in this region, women spoke about being constantly harassed at military checkpoints. Others discussed threats by local government collaborators who identified them as Zapatistas. Carmen told me, "They have my photo. Once in Altamirano, I had to run to Alicia's house and hide for hours and then walk [two hours] home at night." In January 1998 the Mexican Federal Army made incursions into a number of villages in this township. Women drove them off; many were beaten in the process. Although the army's day-to-day presence was less in this region than in others, the possibility of violence was always present, part of an official strategy to limit organizing.

In 1999 I traveled to San Emiliano[18] on public transportation. Clara, Rosa, and Ana were surprised and upset that I was alone and set to finding me *compañia*—someone to travel back with. When I asked why, they told me about the *cortacabezas* (headhunters) who were operating in that part of the canyon. The internationally circulated story varies from version to version, but the general narrative in the Cañadas is that a fluctuating number of headhunters (often identified as government supporters) prey on travelers or people out walking at night. After grabbing a person, they chop off his or her head, often leaving the body behind as evidence. A local related story is that the headhunters then sell the skulls to the federal army for use in bridge construction. The bridge at San Quintin, the largest military base in the jungle, was rumored to have been built with thousands of skulls. Although the *cortacabezas* stories have circulated for years and the Zapatista regional authorities reject them as a government rumor to frighten the people, many still believed them. Certainly, the ongoing low-intensity warfare provided enough instances of violence to sustain people's fear. Aside from official violence, members of opposition parties and other peasant groups had attacked and even killed Zapatistas. Women never travel alone; if their partners could not attend a course, women would find replacements or stay home.

The most common challenge for the *promotoras* was simply the community's lack of support of their work. As Aída phrased it, "No nos hicieron caso" (They didn't pay any attention to us). In many cases, the *promotoras* kept working, despite not receiving bus fare or help with their tasks, believing that the struggle was primary. And as Aída said, "One day people will see their errors."

Another type of control was the assertion of patriarchal rights. The women I interviewed consistently pointed to the right to participate and leave their homes without having to ask "permission" as one of the most significant changes since 1994. Clara, a woman in her mid-forties who moved from an *ejido* to a Nuevo Centro, said:

> Women were like chickens, locked up in the kitchen. Before I was married, I had to ask my father's permission to leave the house to visit my relatives. After I married, I had to ask my husband's permission if I wanted to go to visit my mother or to go into town, so he would know who I was with. . . . Now, women are free to go to meetings to learn, and the only thing stopping them is their own fear.

However, even if their right to leave and organize can no longer be denied, actualizing this right involves extensive negotiation among women, men, and their extended families over chores and taking care of the children.

Maria, in her mid-twenties, was the daughter of a health promoter and had completed health training in nearby Altamirano. Already an allopathic health promoter, her community named her to also become a promoter of medicinal plants. Two years earlier, she had married a former Zapatista insurgent who was initially supportive of her work. After their first child was born, Maria said that her mother-in-law began complaining that a wife should be at home with her children and taking care of her husband. Then she said, "My husband told me I couldn't leave anymore because I wasn't fulfilling my responsibilities." These responsibilities included making tortillas and food for her family, collecting firewood, and taking care of her son. Her husband threatened to leave her and find "another woman," and his mother threatened to take Maria's son away. After dropping out of courses and leaving her work for six months, she appealed to a community assembly. At the meeting, the local authorities told her husband he could not stop her from serving the community. If he continued, he would be punished. As a result of this assembly, her husband apologized and asked for her forgiveness, and she resumed her health work.

Most attempts to contain women were not this direct but took the form of rumors, gossip, and criticism. *Promotoras* noted that rumors were not new; before the uprising, there were rumors circulating of infidelity, of women going to town to buy household items but secretly meeting lovers. During the training, the most commonly circulated rumors were that women were going to courses to meet men. Although these rumors, spread by men and women, did not necessarily prevent women from attending courses and meetings, they undermined their standing in the community. The absurdity of the "looking for other husbands" rumor—women travel many hours to work for three days from 8:00 A.M. to 6:00 P.M. and sleep on wooden slats in a cold dormitory with forty other women and their children—did not diminish its force, however. Clara said, "*Da rabia* [It makes us angry]. Here we are suffering to carry out our work. They're jealous." Doña Romelia, a woman in her mid-sixties who said she has dealt with these situations for years while organizing with the Catholic Church, said that she answers, "Who would want another man? One is more than enough to take care of!" This type of accusation was the easiest to level and sustain. No proof was needed; in one case, just the suggestion was sufficient to discourage a woman enough to quit. In some cases, the positive effects of the *promotoras*' work in their communities helped to counteract the rumors.

Other conflicts involved the control of resources. Through the health work, women gained access to materials and knowledge not available to all members of their communities. A goal of the health work was to share the resulting skills with others. Men in a few communities complained that they should have their own courses rather than learn from the *promotoras*. In one community, men's jealousy over the project meant that no women were named to participate. Rumors also circulated that the women were getting paid or taking money. Elsa and Virginia, *promotoras* from the community of Primero de Mayo,[19] showed up at a course agitated. They had been accused of receiving payments and requested a letter to present at a community assembly stating that they were doing their work voluntarily.

In urban areas, health-related skills have a greater potential for income generation. One woman from an Altamirano neighborhood dropped out of the course and began taking patients for money. Although the other Zapatistas who had supported her work were upset since she kept the course materials that were supposed to be for the use of the whole neighborhood, they had little recourse. In smaller, rural communities, such as the Nuevo Centros, it was easier to hold people accountable for these types of actions. The *promotoras* in Altamirano were also unable to plant gardens—the small amounts of land available to them were unprotected. After planting in a lot given to them by the local Catholic church, the women noticed that someone cut the fencing they had put up. Some months later, they discovered marijuana planted amid their herbs.

Finally, one challenge came as a mixed blessing—positive for the individual women and the EZLN but negative in terms of community health. Because of their outstanding work in this project, a number of skilled *promotoras* were named to other *cargos*, including positions of regional authority. Although women were selected to replace them, the new *promotoras* had to start the course from the beginning, undermining the steps that had been taken to improve the general health of a particular community. However, these changes strengthened women's participation and organizing in the autonomous township and fostered the idea of knowledge as accessible and transferable.

IN SEARCH OF AUTHENTICITY

Another obstacle to *promotoras* gaining respect for their work came, ironically, in the context of efforts that relied heavily on notions of indigenous authenticity intended to protect indigenous culture, intellectual property, and resources. Although scientists have pursued ethnobotanical research for decades, the growth of plant-based medicine over the past few decades into a massive transnational business has led to bioprospecting projects for "miracle cures" and to the near extinction of many wild species. The herbal medicine project in the autonomous township of 17 de Noviembre began shortly before Chiapas became the center of an international controversy in the late 1990s, centered on the Maya International Cooperative Biodiversity Group's (Maya ICBG) bioprospecting project to research, harvest, and commercialize plants in the highlands. The Maya ICBG project, dubbed "biopiracy" by critics, touched off a firestorm that picked up momentum in 1999 and led to its indefinite postponement.

One of the groups leading the opposition to this project was the Organization of Indigenous Healers of the State of Chiapas (OMIECH) based in San Cristóbal de las Casas. The organization was formed during the shift in health care practices in the 1980s when INI and government projects were integrating groups of local healers. OMIECH, an independent group with its own facilities, opened the Museum of Mayan Medicine in 1997 with the support of foreign donors. Steffan Ayora Díaz (2000:179), a researcher who spent years in the region, criticizes the representations in the museum for fostering "the romantic nostalgia that characterizes the tourist gaze and longs for the traditional 'indigenous' community and the harmony between indigenous culture and nature."

Two groups of *promotoras* traveled to San Cristóbal to visit OMIECH to have an exchange with its members. Although the first visit in early 1999 had been set up months in advance, only members of the OMIECH's women's area received the visitors. However, the entire day was spent exchanging information, discussing concerns, and making contacts. During the second visit in 2000, the women were received by male and female board members and advisers but were treated like outsiders—as if they were visitors from any foreign locale. The *promotoras* were first given a tour of the museum, the medicinal plant garden, and the processing facilities. The tour was conducted as professionally as any tour would be: there were brief explanations in the museum, a few questions were answered about the garden, and plant remedies were offered for sale at the end. After the tour, the group met again with the members of the women's area and had useful discussions, mainly about women's reproductive health.

My point here is not that the *promotoras* were treated poorly; they were not. Rather, they were accorded a certain value status at each visit: during the first, as women and therefore not important; during the second, as "migrants."[20] Although some of the women were *curanderas,* following a religious healing tradition, and others were herbalists trained by family members, because of their social and geographic location, they were not perceived to be authentically indigenous. These experiences and the issues that emerged from the bioprospecting debates raise important questions about how to recognize the rights of indigenous peoples to their knowledges and resources without falling into the trap of predetermined identities.

As Ayora Díaz (2000) discusses, what others believe are "authentic" Mayan practices can influence groups such as OMIECH for a variety of reasons, including mobilizing support to protect their resources from transnational pharmaceutical companies. However, these strategies of "authenticity" can be risky for indigenous peoples' struggles, even though they might help with a particular demand.[21] What if indigenous peoples themselves are attempting to recuperate practices that they view as tied to a pre-Hispanic past, but their goals are to transform these for the present? Can and should this diminish a claim to an indigenous cultural identity and medical practice? Obviously, the *promotoras* also had to contend with what we outsiders brought to their project in the name of supporting their self-sufficiency. Our ideas of herbal medicine quite likely more closely resembled Western clinical models and undercut the women's own contributions to developing a local healing practice and transforming their identities.

"NO HAY PASO POR ATRÁS"

The only way to obtain what we need is to organize ourselves well, to be strong in our resistance in our autonomous townships. But to be able to do this work it is necessary that we all participate, that everyone make an effort. That we women don't stay behind. Only in this way can our struggle triumph. (Comandanta Rosalinda, Oventic, August 9, 2003)

The *promotoras*' work is part of a movement for self-determination and autonomy; their struggle to improve community health responds to demands for material resources, at the same time that it strengthens their identities and rights. Their work in their communities and neighborhoods was aimed at improving community health by using the recuperated knowledges and practices of their ancestors and blending these with new elements drawn from their encounters with one another and with people from "outside." Through the work, women also gained important skills and carved out significant spaces for women's organizing within their communities and the EZLN as a movement. The themes that emerged from the *promotoras*' performance of skits and plays at cultural events and graduation ceremonies illustrate this multiple process.

The most common dramas were about their treatment in local hospitals, their work in the communities, the criticism leveled at them, and the problem of men's drinking. They drafted me, the only *kaxlan*[22] present, to participate in a skit about the results of women seeking medical treatment at the local hospital in Altamirano. Aída told me:

> You'll be the doctor first and then the person working in the pharmacy. And you'll pretend you can't see us and make us wait a long time. Then you'll act like we don't know anything and tell us we don't have any problems, it's all in our heads and just give us a prescription. And when we go to the pharmacy, you'll ask for a lot of money and when we don't have it, tell us to go away.

In the plays, each scene has a positive ending: people break loose from their dependence on the government and its hospitals; they learn to value local medicines; the *promotoras* ignore their critics and unite their communities through their efforts; and, by using the Women's Revolutionary Law and education, they defeat alcoholism and domestic violence. These plays attest to the oppressions the women experience and their own sense of the value of their work toward strengthening autonomy.

Margara Millán (1996b) noted that the presence of women's words in the uprising altered the discourse of autonomy; women's actions alter its content and practice. The *promotoras* work with what they consider to be aspects of traditional or local medicine and challenge those who would treat them as children without the ability to respond to their own needs. Reasserting the importance of these healing practices contests the local hegemony of Western medicine, which had supplanted community traditions. The Zapatista communities participating in the project were not rejecting Western medicine as a healing practice but as a space of domination tied to assimilationist and neoliberal policies. Despite the focus on medicinal plants and the circulating desires for authenticity, indigenous identity was not reinforced by the inscription of an essence tied to nature. The majority of *promotoras* in this project saw their work not as a reformulation of what it meant to be truly "Tzeltal" or "Tojola'bal" but instead as a dynamic indigenous Zapatista identity constructed through their gender, class, and ethnic contestations.

One critique of these types of projects that resist neoliberalism through self-sufficiency is that they may ultimately run the risk of reinforcing neoliberalism. This critique certainly warrants more attention than this chapter permits. However, many of the projects that sustain Zapatista autonomy run counter to neoliberalism in significant ways. One is that through their work, the *promotoras* were seeking community solutions to health care needs, rather than individual ones, while actively creating new types of social bonds. Another is that the EZLN has never withdrawn their demand for high-quality universal health care from the state. Finally, the neoliberal multicultural project requires participation—whether this comes in the form of participating in assistance programs, citizen forums, or voting. By refusing to engage and instead continuing to pursue their autonomy through projects such as this herbal medicine training, the Zapatistas are actively resisting becoming a part of the neoliberal project and are creating new types of community.

NOTES

1. "Neoliberalism" refers here to a series of policies produced according to the logic of transnational capitalism.

2. See Wade 1997 for an in-depth discussion of the terms "race" and "ethnicity" and their uses in Latin America.

3. All translations from the Spanish are mine, unless otherwise noted.

4. See Rus 1994 for a more in-depth discussion of the relationship between the INI and Chiapas state politics.

5. For more information and publications, see www.oportunidades.gob .mx/. The institutional program for *Oportunidades* 2002–2006, part of the National Development Plan 2002–2006, can be located on this site.

6. From the *Oportunidades* web page "Who Are We?" (www.oportunidades .gob.mx/htmls/quienes_somos.html).

7. On December 22, 1997, a heavily armed group of local paramilitaries killed forty-five men, women (four of whom were pregnant), and children in the highlands village of Acteal. Another twenty-one people were severely wounded. Those who were killed were members of the pacifist religious group Las Abejas (the Bees).

8. To protect their privacy and security, I have used pseudonyms for the women I interviewed.

9. This convention concerning tribal and indigenous peoples and their culture and rights was adopted in 1989 and entered into force on September 5, 1991. Mexico was the first signatory in Latin America in 1990.

10. There is not yet a common usage translation for this phrase. I have chosen to translate *Juntas* as "councils" since it reflects the type of structure in practice, and although *Gobierno* could also be translated as "government," the term "governance" more closely captures a sense of process, which is a key element.

11. Literally, "walking equally," used to mean organizing and advancing on an equal basis with men.

12. Although not the most exact term, it is often used. "Cosmopolitan" (Ayora Díaz 2000) and "allopathic" are used less frequently. In Chiapas, I frequently heard the term "pharmacy medicine."

13. "Fourth: Women have the right to participate in the affairs of the community and hold positions of authority if they are freely and democratically elected" (*El Despertador Mexicano,* January 1, 1994).

14. Stanley Millet, affiliated with the Instituto Mexicano de Medicina Tradicional (Mexican Institute of Traditional Medicine), discusses the usage of terms for what has been called "traditional" medicine and notes, "There are many ways in which health and sickness can be understood and dealt with. Some are simple; some are complex. However, one way of understanding health and sickness and dealing with it has become hypertrophied and has monopolized the name of medicine. That is the real problem with which we deal" (1999:205).

15. Literally, "bad government," shorthand for the Mexican federal and local government. Now juxtaposed to the Good Governance Councils.

16. Literally, "walking," used to mean working for her community.

17. For the security of community members, I have replaced small village names with pseudonyms.

18. Pseudonym.

19. Pseudonym.

20. When discussing the work of this project with a medical anthropologist working in the highlands in 2003, she disparagingly referred to groups in the Cañadas as "migrants"—with the coded meaning, not the "real" thing.

21. A Global Exchange memo circulated on the Internet in September 2002 belies this danger. While the situation of the communities threatened with eviction in the Montes Azules Reserve is critical and the government's divide-and-conquer strategy has been highly effective, I believe that the problem cannot be couched in "good Indian/bad Indian" terms. This leaves the door open for questioning the authenticity of all groups of indigenous peoples. I heard the main argument of the memo being used publicly by NGOs and Zapatistas to undercut the Lacandon people's claims to the jungle because they were not *originally* from there.

> Unfortunately, the current situation in Montes Azules is plagued by a number of myths. The first is the so-called Lacandon Indians *[sic]* are the "true" inhabitants of the region. In reality, the Lacandons were eradicated roughly three hundred years ago at the hands of the Spanish conquerors. The indigenous peoples currently living in the region, in fact, originated from eastern Campeche and are actually of the Caribe Indigenous People. Evidence reveals that the Caribes migrated to the Lacandon jungle over the last two centuries. The Mexican government used the misnomer "Lacandon" to refer to them and granted them huge land concessions in one of the most fraudulent land distribution schemes in Mexican history.

22. *Kaxlan* is a Tzeltal word that has a number of related meanings; it can mean "outsider," "rich person," or "mestizo," depending on the context.

SEVEN

RIGHTS AT THE INTERSECTION
Gender and Ethnicity in Neoliberal Mexico

SHANNON SPEED

The women were gathered in the dark front room of a house in the community of Nicolás Ruiz, Chiapas.[1] They had gathered to discuss with me their experience with social movement participation, as base supporters or *milicianas* (militia members) of the Zapatista National Liberation Army (EZLN). The talk wound through various topics before finally making its way to the conflict among women in the community that had surged the previous year. I was worried about the topic. "What happened?" I asked uneasily. The talk became suddenly animated, leaving behind the reserved decorum of our earlier discussion. The women talked over each other, anxious to add details or elaborate their perspectives. Finally, one woman's voice rose above the others, who fell silent. "*Lo que pasa,*" she said with emphasis, "is that in this community, we don't want *protagonistas* [those who assert themselves forcefully in a certain situation, usually for personal gain of prestige or power]." "We women want to organize for our rights," she said, "but we want to do it *collectively.*"[2]

Her words spoke directly to the theoretical questions I had been struggling with as a feminist, an activist, and a researcher, regarding the presumed contradiction between indigenous communities' collective rights to maintain their culture and the rights of individual community members, in particular, women, that might be violated by those cultural norms and practices. Taking Nicolás Ruiz as a starting point, I examine here the tension between individual and collective human rights and the specific issues raised by gender and ethnicity in that tension. I argue that resolving this tension is not possible and that focusing our analytic efforts on establishing whether individual or collective rights should have primacy is unproductive and obscures as much as it clarifies. In fact, the conceptual dichotomy individual/collective often serves to deny many women's—especially indigenous women's—experience as lived in both realms. Further, I suggest that indigenous women's gender demands, constructed at the intersection of individual and collective rights, represent an alternative way of thinking about rights that has powerful implications for resistance to neoliberal logics and forms of rule.

THE INDIVIDUAL AND THE COLLECTIVE IN THEORY AND PRACTICE IN CHIAPAS AND MEXICO

We have to struggle more, because we are triply looked down on: because we are indigenous, because we are women, and because we are poor. (Comandanta Esther, 2001a)[3]

The Zapatista uprising began in January 1994, just as Mexico entered the neoliberal world order through the North American Free Trade Agreement. It was a key moment, in which relations between the state and civil society were shifting dramatically, as the corporatist state gave way to the neoliberal multicultural model. This shift had been set in motion two years earlier with the changes to the Mexican Constitution that ended agrarian reform and other nationalist and corporatist policies while simultaneously recognizing its population for the first time as "pluriethnic."

This process was not unique to Mexico but was under way (or soon to be under way) in a number of Latin American countries. Legal and constitutional reforms implemented to "neoliberalize" states—shrinking state functions and giving priority to ensuring stability and the free market—were regularly accompanied by legal recognition of indigenous populations and, to differing degrees, their rights. Charles R. Hale (2002) uses the term "neoliberal multiculturalism" to refer to this process, suggesting that the two—neoliberalism and multiculturalism—are integrally linked. As I argue below, multicultural recognition is a part of the new logics of governance that predominate in the neoliberal state.

It is thus not a coincidence that the constitutional reforms designed to transform Mexico into a neoliberal country simultaneously recognized its pluriethnic status. In the very same set of constitutional reforms implemented in 1992 in preparation for the North American Free Trade Agreement, Article 4 was altered to recognize Mexico's pluricultural composition. In Mexico, the implications of such a shift in forms of governance and the state-society relationship were significant. The ruling party, the PRI, had long governed through corporatist strategies, drawing different sectors of the population into the state project by mediating social inequality through a variety of means, from agrarian reform to state-sponsored labor unions and the National Indigenous Institute. The 1992 constitutional reforms signaled the shift in forms of governance that was under way: they dealt a death blow to corporatism by (among other things) ending land reform, diminishing rural subsidies, and opening communal lands to privatization, at the same time highlighting a new relationship to indigenous people—one of recognition rather than assimilation. Mexico was on the road to neoliberal multiculturalism.

However, it was not the reforms but the Zapatista uprising that put indigenous rights on the national radar screen, and in the process drew out the tensions and contradictions with which this shift was fraught. The reform of Article 4 had acknowledged Mexico's pluricultural makeup, but it did not recognize indigenous peoples as "peoples," nor did it provide indigenous groups with any specific rights. Such a move would have been a much more dramatic break with the past, as Mexico's 1917 Constitution is founded on liberal concepts of the equality of each individual Mexican before the law. But these two concepts, equality and the individual as rights bearer, were called into question by the demands of the Zapatistas and other indigenous groups throughout Mexico for real collective rights based on their cultural difference.

The question of equality and individual rights was a thorny one for the state, and also for the Zapatistas. Notably, it was not just indigenous people who stepped onto the national stage to assert their rights but also, quite prominently, indigenous women. From the start, the EZLN highlighted the presence of women in their leadership and elaborated a strong rhetoric of indigenous women's rights. Women constituted 30 percent of the Zapatista army, and the Revolutionary Women's Law represented a clear and systematic elaboration of the movement's support for "women's just demands of equality." As Karen Kampwirth (2002) notes, this is similar to the percentage of women involved in the Central American guerrilla movements of the 1980s, but the fact that the women participating in the Chiapas uprising were almost exclusively indigenous made this level of participation notable and distinct. Some feminists criticized the Zapatistas' "masculinist" approach to resistance[4] and argued that the women's laws were limited and did not constitute feminist demands (Rojas 1994).[5] Others, while noting that in many communities little had changed for women on the ground, nevertheless argued that the Zapatista movement contributed to creating a cultural climate in which gender relations could be renegotiated and opened spaces in which new forms of women's participatory citizenship could flourish (Hernández Castillo 1998a; Olivera Bustamante 1995; Garza 2002).

In the intervening decade, few would deny that Zapatista women have made a vital contribution to the advancement of the indigenous women's movement (see chapter 1, this volume). By drawing attention to the multiple oppressions suffered by indigenous women—typified by Comandanta Esther's statement, "We are triply looked down on: because we are indigenous, because we are women, and because we are poor"—the Zapatistas made it clear that while the Mexican Constitution established equality, including women's equality, in legal practice and everyday life, some people enjoyed "real" equality considerably less than others: indigenous people and women.

The tension between individual and collective rights, rendered highly visible and contentious by the Zapatista uprising, was one that Mexico, like other neoliberalizing states, would have to grapple with. Political theorists have struggled to reconcile liberal principles of individual freedom with the rights claims of collectivities through a "politics of recognition" (Kymlicka 1997; Taylor 1994). They understand collective rights as inherently antagonistic to the liberal concept of individual equality but believe that this is an antagonism that states nevertheless must resolve in the interests of doing justice to the individuals who make up those groups. But other theorists have suggested that the increasing prevalence of a state recognition model and multicultural reforms, rather than a necessity of the democratic state in pursuing democracy per se, in fact serve to reinforce the underlying goals of neoliberal economic and political strategies and limit the force of collective indigenous demands (Gustafson 2002; Hale 2002; Postero 2001). As I argue further below, the limited recognition of collective rights is an integral part of neoliberal subject formation and the construction of neoliberal rule.

The flourishing of demands for community autonomy and personal autonomy combined with the shifting terrain of governance and public policy to generate a national debate about collective and individual rights, about equality and cultural difference. The demand for autonomy in Mexico—as elsewhere in Latin America—has been built on the concept of *usos y costumbres* (traditional practices and customs). *Usos y costumbres* usually refers to consensus decision making, local administration of justice, and the election of authorities through traditional means, but it can also encompass virtually anything a community or its leaders define as "tradition." In the autonomy debate, government officials, as well as some prominent jurists and intellectuals, argued that indigenous peoples' *usos y costumbres* served to justify local power relations and that collective norms frequently violated individual rights. Some went so far as to argue that indigenous people should not be permitted by the state to any measure of autonomy based on their *usos y costumbres* because they had antidemocratic tendencies and would almost certainly violate the basic human rights of individuals in the community (Krauze 1999; Bartra 1997; Burgoa 1997). Often, women's rights served as primary examples: *usos y costumbres* such as arranged marriage, exclusion of women from political participation, and male-line inheritance were cited as examples of practices that violated women's rights to personal autonomy, civic participation, and economic sustenance.

These arguments echoed debates in the literature on gender and human rights, which has a "central concern" regarding the struggle for cultural rights "when respect for customary law or traditional customs and practices violates the individual rights of women" (Deere and León 2001:76). There is a growing literature on questions of "cultural rights" and "women's rights" (Deere and León 2001; Okin 1999; Gunning 2000; Obiora 2000; Sierra 2001; Hernández Castillo 2002a; Otzoy forthcoming). One group of analysts has argued that collective rights claims based on cultural difference tend to violate women's rights, conceived largely in universalist and individual terms. This argument is made against a position that, though rarely in fact articulated, is seen to argue for the full autonomy of groups—even to discriminate based on sex—because of a right to culture or a relativist position that denies the moral and legal validity of universal human rights. Thus the debate has been framed as one between cultural relativists who believe that culture is the principal source of validity of right and rule and feminists concerned that such a position requires accepting the subordination of women and negating indigenous women's individual human rights. In this framing, given the direct contradiction between collective claims to culture and women's individual human rights, one is forced to side with one position or the other.

Cultural rights are thus positioned against gender rights in both academic writings and public discourse. In Mexico, such arguments were made by a broad range of people, from feminists to conservative constitutionalists. Some critiques were made by people with a long-established commitment to women's rights; others were more concerned with raising the issue of women's rights to demonstrate the supposed authoritarian and undemocratic nature of indigenous communities. But while the actors making these arguments are diverse, they are nevertheless united by an underlying adherence to notions of liberal individualism inscribed in the Mexican Constitution and the popular consciousness of much of Mexico—that the rights and equality of individuals should always have primacy and that these rights are always inherently put at risk by the collective. Even more problematic is the implicit notion that indigenous culture is "the problem" and that therefore individuals in indigenous communities are in need of external protection from the civilized Mexican state to keep the cultural collective from running amok.

The multilayered paternalism and ethnocentrism in this position are perhaps readily apparent, and it is hard not to recall Gayatri Spivak's (1988) reference to the commonplace ideology of colonialism: "white men saving brown women from brown men." It is also somewhat ironic given that there is little to indicate that the state is willing or able to intervene on women's behalf. For example, the state has done very little to protect individual women from suffering violations of their rights implied by particular customs, such as those I have mentioned. Moreover, it is not at all clear that the judicial system of the Mexican state is entirely disposed to protect *any* women's rights, even those of nonindigenous women (see Azaola 1996). Comandanta Esther recognized this in a speech on International Women's Day, shortly before her address to the Mexican Congress: "Women who are not indigenous also suffer. That is why we are inviting all of them to fight, so that we will not continue suffering. It's not true that women don't know, that they're not good for anything except being in the home. That doesn't happen only in the indigenous communities, but also in the cities" ("Mexico: Words of the Rebel Women," March 8, 2001).

Perhaps more important, usually those advocating for the regulation of indigenous culture to protect individual women are not themselves indigenous women. This is in part distrust of the state and its laws, but also, importantly, because indigenous women have difficulty separating out distinct realms of individual and collective experience. Recognizing this, and in part drawing on the arguments of indigenous women themselves, some recent writings have advocated a third position, one that asserts that culture is continually changing and that indigenous groups are capable of both defending their culture and transforming it from within (toward better gender equality). This position rejects the dichotomy between relativism and women's rights and interrogates the definition of culture that underlies both the relativism and universalism stances (Engle 2005; Hernández Castillo 2002a; Merry 2003; Kapur 2002; Sierra 2001). In the following sections, in the context of one community's experience, I focus my discussion on the articulation of the individual and the collective in women's experience and the implications of their integration into a unified struggle for women's rights for indigenous men, individualist feminists, and even the neoliberal state.

NICOLÁS RUIZ:
THE MULTIPLICITY OF LOCAL EXPERIENCE

The community of Nicolás Ruiz has lived the effects of the recent social dynamics outlined above. This community and municipality in the Central Zone of the state was founded 270 years ago by Tzeltal Indians. Yet for many decades it has not been defined, internally or externally, as an indigenous community. Today in Nicolás Ruiz there is a reassertion of indigenous identity and the community's right to govern itself based on its *usos y costumbres*. Like many other communities in rural Mexico, residents of Nicolás Ruiz went from being "Indians" to being "peasants" and are now occupying the new "subject position" of globalized multicultural neoliberalism, that of indigenous peoples (Postero 2001).

These shifting subjectivities reflect the fact that community identity is a fundamentally relational concept, historically constructed in dialogue with external social actors and groups. During the period in which the state's relationship to rural peoples was formulated through agrarian reform and "campesinist" assistance policies, Nicolás Ruiz's Tzeltal identity gave way to *campesino* identity. As the Chiapas conflict brought Nicolás Ruiz into dialogue with new interlocutors, giving them increased interaction with the discourse of human and indigenous rights, and as the discourses of the state shifted from agrarian corporatism and toward the indigenous as a basis for rights claims, people in Nicolás Ruiz reinterpreted their history and their practices in ways that altered their community identity.[6]

Nicolás Ruiz does have traditional customs and practices, whether or not they have been defined in the recent past as indigenous. Since the community's formation, land has been held communally. Men become *comuneros*, meaning that they are entitled to work a parcel of land and have a voice in the community assembly when they become heads of household. Decisions about virtually every aspect of community political life are made in the community assembly by consensus, in which all *comuneros* participate. Even candidates to the municipal presidency are chosen by consensus in the assembly and then voted for in the official election. In other words, leaders are chosen through the *usos y cos-*

tumbres of the community and then ratified through the official electoral process. Those who are elected are expected to carry out—not to make—the decisions that affect the community. That is, decisions are made in the assembly, then implemented through the elected officials. This is the predominant mode of decision making in indigenous communities in Chiapas. While there is significant variation throughout the state, where many indigenous communities were once governed through civil-religious hierarchies (*cargo* systems), the assembly is today the principal space, and consensus decision making the principal form, of local governance.[7]

Consensus is crucial to the community's understanding of itself. The violent conflict that emerged there in recent years is a clear demonstration of this: for decades following the Mexican Revolution, during which the community supported the seventy-year ruling party, the PRI, consensus decision making in the assembly worked relatively smoothly. Things changed, however, with the Zapatista uprising of 1994, which challenged the PRI's hegemony and presented alternatives for political organization and struggle. In 1995 the *comuneros* of Nicolás Ruiz shifted their loyalty to the center-left PRD by consensus decision in the community assembly and in 1996 elected the first PRD municipal president. Also in 1996 Nicolás Ruiz declared itself a "comunidad en resistencia," meaning that it became a Zapatista base community. But when twenty-three families officially returned to the PRI in 1998, conflict broke out. The majority felt that this dissent was an intolerable violation of the community norm of consensus. As one resident expressed it, "We were in agreement for 264 years, and this changed everything."

The *comuneros* revoked the land rights of the dissenting community members, who were refusing to participate in the assembly. This resulted in a massive raid by the army, state and federal police, and immigration officials in defense of the ruling-party loyalists. Dozens were arrested, and several persons spent more than a year in prison. Their legal defense was similar to that of authorities in several other Zapatista autonomous municipalities that were raided in the same period. They argued that they were acting based on their *usos y costumbres,* which they had a right to do. By "usos y costumbres," they were referring to their traditional practice of decision by consensus and the concomitant responsibility to participate in the assembly, both of which had been violated by the dissenting members.

It is worth noting at this point that in Nicolás Ruiz, as in most indigenous communities in Chiapas, there is some internal differentiation—in class position (this is limited in Nicolás Ruiz and is more evident in some highland communities, where caciques have enriched themselves, creating greater social divides), political and religious stances, and, of course, along gender lines. In situations of internal discord, all sides are likely to legitimate their actions based on "customs and traditions," rendering the debate, in many cases, one over which "traditions" are the legitimate ones. In Nicolás Ruiz, the dissenters argued that the community tradition was to be Priísta, that is, in support of the PRI.

Y LAS MUJERES, ¿QUÉ? (AND WHAT ABOUT THE WOMEN?)

In Nicolás Ruiz, as in many communities, consensus means consensus of the men. Women do not hold land and therefore do not participate in the community assembly. Nevertheless, women in Nicolás Ruiz have a history of organizing that predates the Zapatista uprising. This has been especially notable in moments of conflict, when women organized to support the men, but also on occasion to wrest benefits from the state, for example, a corn mill that reduced the labor involved in producing tortillas.[8]

After the community became Zapatista, women began to have new types of interactions with people from outside the community. Some became involved directly in "the organization"[9] as *milicianas,* actively training with and responding to Zapatista leadership. Others became involved with "civil society" activists—generally pro-Zapatista but not tied directly to the organization. Several of these activists were feminists with long histories of activism in the region.

The work of women with civil society groups had a high profile, whereas that of the women with the organization was of necessity clandestine. The women formed two committees: a health committee that studied and practiced herbal medicine and a "political committee" that did political support work, such as providing a "presence" at political events in other communities. A prominent figure among these women was Doña Matilde, coordinator of the health committee. Over the course of several years, Doña Matilde became something of a spokesperson for the community and was often seen at rallies with a microphone or megaphone. An ode to Doña Matilde's strength and courage circulated on the Internet.

Not surprisingly, as women became increasingly organized and had increased interaction with outside actors with a women's rights orientation, some began to question and challenge their lack of political voice in the community. A women's assembly was formed, parallel to the men's assembly. Though they did not have the power to make decisions affecting the community as a whole, they could address the men's assembly on certain issues and try to sway opinion there. Women from both the organization and civil society groups participated in the assembly, and it seemed a big step forward in women's right to political participation. Doña Matilde was the president of the women's assembly.

Less than a year later, when I returned to the community after a period in the United States, I found that the women's assembly had been officially dissolved, the committees were no longer meeting, and Doña Matilde was all but censured in the community. Shocked by this turn of events, it took me some time to piece together a picture of what had happened from the various and distinct versions. There had been a rift among the women, along lines that could be roughly divided into those affiliated with "civil society" and those affiliated with the Zapatistas. Tensions grew into open rupture, and the issue was brought into the general assembly. After a very tense meeting in which Matilde addressed the assembly, the male authorities of the community discontinued the women's assembly.

This was clearly an unhappy episode for the women involved—one that affected women's solidarity and their advances in political participation within the community. I have not recounted the details of the conflict because it would be fruitless to attempt to establish who was right and who was wrong. I personally have respect for and owe a debt of gratitude to women in both camps, including Doña Matilde, for the time they spent answering my questions and telling of their lives and the life of the community. For the purposes of this analysis, it is more important to examine how the issues were perceived and interpreted by the different actors and why.

Both the male authorities and the women Zapatistas accused Matilde of *protagonismo*—of asserting her own agenda, wielding power over others, and flouting the community's norms and collective will. For her part, Doña Matilde and her supporters felt that the other women were jealous of her strong position, that the male authorities were threatened by her, and that the community's response was little more than an attempt to keep an assertive and capable woman "in her place."

One can clearly see the outlines of a classic collective culture versus individual gender rights debate taking shape. A fairly straightforward argument could be made—and in fact was made quiet cogently by a feminist sociologist close to Doña Matilde—about the violation of individuals' rights based on claims to the collective. The reassertion of indigenous identity and the mobilization of a discourse of *usos y costumbres* in Nicolás Ruiz, from this perspective, was functioning to maintain relations of power within the community, especially gendered relations of power.

I felt uncomfortable with the interpretation, as I often do with the *usos y costumbres* critiques, and this is why I was so worried about the subject of the conflict when it came up in the conversation with the Zapatista women. It was not that I doubted that the male authorities of Nicolás Ruiz are capable of exerting their power to maintain patriarchal relations, and in fact they do this in myriad ways on a daily basis. Yet I kept returning to the fact that the conflict erupted between women and to the intuitively illogical fact that it was the Zapatista-aligned women who requested that the male authorities cancel the women's assembly. Were the Zapatista women caught in the all-too-familiar bind of subverting their own gender demands to the greater struggle of the community (organization, movement)? I gingerly tried to broach this with the women and got little response. But the question continued to gnaw at me: had my query been too vague, or had they purposefully avoided it? I decided to be more direct. Had it ever been suggested to them—by men in the organization or in the community—that they put aside or on hold their own struggle for gender equality because it might be divisive at a time when a unified front was needed in the struggle? The three women with whom I was talking looked thoughtful. After a few moments of reflection, one of them said, "I think the opposite is true. It was through the organization that we began to organize [as women], that we began to become conscious of our rights as women." The others agreed. But, I asked, what about the male authorities of the community? They thought about that for a few more moments, then another woman spoke. "Some men are more *consciente* than others," she said, "but they also know that a community, to advance, must work as a collective, both men and women. That's why they supported us." Undoubtedly, other women would have had a different interpretation. But I found it interesting that, again, the Zapatista women framed the issue as one of individual versus collective.

Nicolás Ruiz's particular insertion into the dynamics of social conflict in Chiapas had a variety of results. One was the separation of the women of the community into distinct camps: one aligned with civil society and one aligned with the organization (and a third, for that matter, aligned with the PRI). The division between these groups is not insignificant, since it brought them into engagement with somewhat distinct discourses regarding women's rights: the civil society version, which, while diverse itself, was strongly influenced by feminist individualism; and the Zapatista version, also uneven across various terrains, but in which women's rights were tied continuously to the collective. The latter perspective, I believe, resonated more strongly with notions of collectivity and consensus that prevailed in Nicolás Ruiz prior to the events narrated here. This was notable in the fact that, at least in my discussions with community members, it was more often women than men who raised the issue of community norms of non-*protagonismo* being violated, in their view, by Matilde's increasingly public activism. In other words, it was not a straightforward matter of men mobilizing this discourse in order to subvert women's organizing. Given the community's historical privileging of the consensus model, particularly its heightened sensitivity to the issue in light of the current conflict between pro-Zapatistas and Priístas, it is perhaps not surprising that the view prevailed that individuals need to conform to community consensus and community norms. The individual women's rights perspective was more easily discredited, marked by many men and women as an "outsider" perspective.

RETHINKING BINARIES: MUTUALLY EXCLUSIVE OR EXCLUSIVELY MUTUAL?

> We resist hegemonic dominance of feminist thought by insisting that it is a theory in the making, that we must necessarily criticize, question, re-examine and explore new possibilities. . . . The formation of a liberatory feminist theory and praxis is a collective responsibility, one that must be shared. (hooks 1984:5)

U.S. Third World feminists have long warned us of the dangers of essentializing all women as a homogeneous group, pointing out that women in different cultural contexts have distinct experiences and understandings of gender (Anzaldúa 1987; Bhavnani 2000; hooks 1984; Lorde 1984; Moraga and Anzaldúa [1989] 2002). It should be clear that even in the localized context of one community, women's experience differed, and for that reason they had differences of opinion about gender rights. Rosalina's statement about wanting to struggle for women's rights collectively suggests that liberal notions of individual rights are not necessarily usefully applied to all women and are not inevitably the principal element of all struggles for women's rights. Overcoming the "feminist ethnocentrism" inherent in applying liberal individual feminist notions of rights to all women and reconceptualizing women's rights in ways that encompass other experiences, such as collective identities, is critically necessary at this juncture.[10]

However, this does not mean that one must be resigned to women's oppression in cultural contexts in which the collective is a significant aspect of women's experience (see Merry 2003). Such arguments are based on notions of culture as static and bounded: collective norms are "traditional" and therefore unchanging. Rather, I understand collectively held norms, like individually held ideas, to be in a state of continual change forged in dialogue both with external actors and among members of the community who challenge hegemonic configurations of power. Like all communities, Nicolás Ruiz's culture and identity are constantly being reshaped in relation to changing social forces, and there is no particular reason to think that gender norms and relations cannot be altered as part of that process.

It is not as counterintuitive as it seemed to me at the time that it was the Zapatista women in Nicolás Ruiz who emphasized the need to struggle for women's rights in the collective context of the community. Zapatista women have been among the leading voices expressing rejection of arguments that would make them—indigenous women—the reason their communities are denied autonomy. Comandanta Esther's words to the Mexican Congress as a representative of the EZLN spoke lucidly of the inseparability of ongoing struggles for gender rights and autonomy:

> We know which are good and which are bad *usos y costumbres*. The bad ones are hitting and beating a woman[,] . . . marrying by force against her will, not being allowed to participate in assembly, not being able to leave the house. . . . It is very important for us, the indigenous women of all of Mexico, . . . to be recognized and respected as the women and indigenous people we are.[11]

Not only Zapatistas but women in many indigenous communities are facing the challenges of renegotiating gender relations in the context of the movement that they support and in the communities they call home. These women struggle to change gendered relations of power in the cultural context of their communities while simultaneously defending the right of the community to define for themselves what that cultural context is and will be (see chapter 1, this volume).

Thus binaries such as individual/collective rights or cultural rights/ women's rights, while they exist on a conceptual and definitional level, are not always so clearly defined in women's lived experience. Focusing instead on how women in a particular social context understand their rights, variously and differentially, may be the best way to think about women's rights and how to gain them. Taking a relativist approach does not mean, necessarily, accepting all practices and traditions of a culture as valid. We can disagree with some practices without calling the entire culture into question (Merry 2003). And we can, as many indigenous women in Mexico now are doing, call on the male authorities of indigenous communities to alter their cultural understandings and community norms to include women's rights. But those of us who are elaborating a discourse of women's rights from outside the community also need to adjust our own historically and culturally specific notions of the individual nature of those rights, so that we may encompass the experience of women throughout the world who understand themselves and their rights as existing and being defined largely in a collective context.

CHALLENGES AT THE INTERSECTION: NEOLIBERALISM, ZAPATISMO, AND INDIGENOUS WOMEN

Avoiding theoretical binaries is crucial, not just because it should be our goal to fairly represent the women involved in such struggles and not entrap them in dichotomies foreign to their experience, but also because, I would like to suggest, it may be in this assertion of such multiple and overlapping experiences that a serious political challenge may be located. Gender has provided us with a key site for exploring the challenges presented by the Zapatista uprising to the neoliberal state. Some analysts have argued that indigenous women's demands, at the intersection of gender and ethnicity, are fundamental to the imagining and the mapping of a multicultural Mexico. I suggest that perhaps the opposite is true—that they in some way present a challenge to state multiculturalism. To the extent that indigenous women are imagining or positing a multicultural Mexico, we should be clear that this is a very distinct one from the "politics of recognition" model sporadically pursued by the Mexican state. I am concerned about the uncritical aspiration to a multicultural Mexico as an end in itself and the casting of indigenous women in the role of its emissary.

In Mexico, indigenous rights have been viewed by many not as a goal in and of themselves but rather as a means to an end—that end being a more just society, a multicultural democracy. Multiculturalism, then, has emerged as a principal goal of resistance. But at the same time, as we have seen, multiculturalism is a characteristic of the neoliberal state. This is neither coincidence nor contradiction: multiculturalism is consistent with neoliberal logics and practices, part of neoliberal state making.

Neoliberalism, the extension of liberal ideas that emphasizes and privileges the "free market," entails a variety of government policies and practices designed to ensure that the workings of economic markets are unfettered by state mediation. The neoliberal state must downsize its social welfare undertakings and remove all restrictions on the economy designed to protect those citizens with less resources, a process epitomized by the "structural adjustment" measures impelled by international financial institutions in many countries in Latin America. The state is no longer responsible for ensuring social well-being; all social relations will be established by the "free" market. And the state no longer mediates social conflict; this function is "privatized," passed from the state to industry and business (corporate social responsibility), communities and individuals, and especially civil society organizations such as nongovernmental organizations (NGOs) (Deleuze 1994; Guehenno 1995; Hardt 1998; Hardt and Negri 2000). Thus, as the market is prioritized and the state is divested of responsibility for social welfare, relations between social groups are defined by market forces and mediated by civil society itself (Gill 2000).

Neoliberalization entails not only the reduction of government's social functions and moves to "free" the economy but also a new set of governance practices for the state. On the one hand, the state maintains "law and order" to provide the stability necessary for the market to operate freely; on the other, it produces subjects who are autonomous and self-regulating:

> To govern better, the state must govern less; to optimize the economy, one must govern through the entrepreneurship of autonomous actors— individuals and families, firms and corporations. Once responsibilized and entrepreneurialized, they would govern themselves within a state secured framework of law and order. (Rose 1999:139)

The neoliberal state governs by creating responsibilized and entrepreneurialized subjects, on the one hand, and maintaining the structure of law, on the other.

Some analysts have provided insightful analyses of the conjunction of neoliberal governance and multiculturalism in Latin America. For example, Nancy Postero (2001) has demonstrated how the "indigenous subjects of neoliberalism" get constituted through the states' multicultural practices, which work to structure indigenous political participation in ways that imbue them with rationalities proper for adequate—and acquiescent—integration into economic markets. Postero shows how, through state policies and NGO training, concepts of individuality and self-regulation are inculcated. Neoliberal multiculturalism thus cedes rights to indigenous people but with the effect of remaking them as subjects less resistant to neoliberal economic and political policies. Hale (2001) argues that "neoliberalism's cultural project entails proactive recognition of a minimal package of cultural rights and an equally vigorous rejection of the rest. The result is a dichotomy between recognised and recalcitrant indigenous subjects, which confronts the indigenous rights movement as a 'menace' " (2002:485). Indigenous people are left policing themselves—their actions and identities—in order to remain in the recognized category, where they are defined as the subjects of rights.

Yet, in Mexico, the neoliberalizing state has *not* effectively harnessed multiculturalism to the project of rule. The initial "multicultural moves" have given way in recent years to a serious government reticence to institute multicultural policies, notably in its refusal to implement the San Andrés Accords on Indigenous Rights and Culture signed in 1996 by the EZLN and the government and in the failed Law of Indigenous Rights and Culture of 2001. This law, originally proposed as the implementing legislation of the San Andrés Accords, in the version approved by the Congress actually set indigenous rights back by limiting indigenous jurisdiction, by denying rights to territory and to natural resources, and by passing the definition of indigenous peoples and what rights pertain to them on to the individual state-level governments. It is clear, particularly in the Indigenous Law, that the Mexican government is not prepared to cede rights to indigenous peoples to the extent that some other Latin American countries have.

Some analysts have suggested that this failure to move forward on implementing multicultural policies is due to the Mexican government's incompetence or intransigence, or because it is more interested in catering to transnational capital than in creating a new relationship with its indigenous population. Yet elsewhere it is precisely in the process of neoliberalizing and making themselves viable to international capital that many countries have instituted reforms that are salutary, in principle if not in their effects.

One important reason for Mexico's reversed course is undoubtedly the Zapatista uprising. The uprising raised the stakes on indigenous rights substantially. The political fears generated by the indigenous rebellion made ceding indigenous rights and creating a multicultural state more dangerous. However, other Latin American countries have oppositional indigenous movements. What is it about the Zapatista movement that has made it so risky?

I have argued elsewhere that the fundamental challenge of Zapatista autonomy is that it is taking place essentially outside the state, developing in a unilateral process that does not seek state recognition in order to verify or make real its existence. Because they are outside the state, these discourses and practices cannot be harnessed by the state to the task of limiting the scope and impact of indigenous rights, or of constituting new neoliberal subjects (Speed and Reyes 2005). It is worth considering how autonomy itself might play into neoliberal logics by relieving the state of the need to govern and producing self-governing populations still largely beholden to state power. But Zapatista autonomy as it has been elaborated so far cannot be understood to do so. This is because it presents an alternative form and logics of governance to that proffered by the Mexican state. While the various aspects of that alternative are outside the scope of this chapter, one important piece is central to my discussion here: their interpretation of individual and collective rights.

The line between individual and collective rights is one of the most difficult faced by neoliberalizing states. After the Zapatista uprising, Mexico halted the process it had undertaken with the 1992 constitutional reforms toward a politics of recognition of collective rights and strongly reasserted the primacy of the individual. Perhaps the clearest and most evident response against the Zapatistas' autonomy project was waged, both by government officials and in public discourse, on the sanctified terrain of individual rights. While gender issues were not the only site where individual rights and collective ones were said to clash, it was undoubtedly the most prominent in public debates (with religion a close second). Indigenous women, put forward as the poster children of the primacy of individual rights, refused this position and reaffirmed their commitment to collective goals and to maintaining the conjunction of the individual and the collective as central to their struggle.

This it is not to argue that "the collective" is always inherently progressive or challenging. It is precisely at the intersection of gender and collective rights that the inaccuracy of such a claim is made clear, when "the collective" is marshaled to justify and defend practices that are harmful to specific members or groups within that collective. However, through their "double activism" (see chapter 1, this volume) that refuses to conceptualize women's rights outside of their collective context, women present a double challenge to oppressive relations of power. The first challenge is to men within their communities and organizations to recognize women's rights and change "traditional" gender norms; this challenge is strengthened because it is not a product of paternalistic external protections and because it cannot be discounted as the discourse of outsiders. The second challenge, which arises by their refusal to disarticulate their struggle for women's equality within their communities from their struggle for rights based on cultural difference, is to the multiculturalism of the neoliberal state in Mexico, drawing the contradictions to the fore and offering an alternative logic.

Mexico has not "multiculturalized" in the manner that some other Latin American countries have for a variety of reasons. One of them, I have suggested, is that indigenous challenges from within made the internal contradictions of such an undertaking too difficult to overcome. Zapatismo and the indigenous women's movement that has gained force since the Zapatista uprising are a part of that internal challenge. Given the potentially negative effects of the multiculturalism that is an essential part of the neoliberal project, it seems prudent not to uncritically embrace it. Indigenous women, due to their location at the juncture of multiple identities of race, class, and gender, may well be at the forefront of contributing to a new multicultural Mexico. However, the one they advocate is not only different from but also challenging to that of the neoliberal state.

This process is not without contradictions and complexities. In Nicolás Ruiz, as in many other communities, these positions are still being struggled over, among women and between women and men. But even on this uneven and shifting topography, there is more, I want to suggest, at the intersection of gender and ethnicity than the collision of individual and collective rights. By overcoming feminist ethnocentrism and thinking beyond these binaries to the meanings of their conjunctions, we may see many indigenous women fostering potentially powerful new ways of conceptualizing rights and resisting oppressive power relations and forms of rule.

NOTES

1. To protect the privacy and security of the community and its members, all names in this chapter except those of public figures are pseudonyms.

2. This and all translations of verbal exchanges were recorded, transcribed, and translated into English by the author. I have used italics both for words left in Spanish (when no adequate English equivalent exists) and to indicate verbal emphasis placed on certain words by the speaker.

3. Comandanta Esther's complete speech of March 8, 2001, is available at www.infoshop.org/news_archive/mex_woman.html.

4. For example, in the volume *Chiapas: Y las mujeres que?* published in 1995 (another volume with the same title was published in 1996), the editor, Rosa Rojas, and other contributors questioned, from their own feminist perspectives, Zapatismo's liberatory effects for women. In particular, Bedregal argues that women are inherently more peaceful than men and that by taking up arms and inserting themselves into male hierarchical structures (such as that of an army) women concede too much from the start.

5. The Women's Laws did not constitute feminist demands because they did not contain a critique of patriarchal social relations. In the terms of the feminist debates of the day, they were seen as "practical" demands for bettering women's lives rather than "strategic" ones for challenging and altering unequal relations of power between men and women (Molyneux 1985; and see Stephen 1997 for a discussion of this debate).

6. See Speed 2002 for a more thorough examination of this process.

7. Hernández Castillo (2002a) discusses the different meanings concepts such as "customary law" and "traditional authorities" have in different regions of the state, depending on the local history.

8. Interview, Doña Matilde, June 1999.

9. "The organization" is shorthand for the EZLN.

10. Hernández Castillo (chapter 1, this volume) notes that this perspective has been accepted by some Mexican academic feminists (as it has by many academic feminists in other parts of Latin America and in the United States). However, in both the United States and Latin America, academic or "hegemonic" feminism has remained focused largely on the specific goals of reproductive rights and domestic violence. While these issues are relevant to indigenous women, their dominance continues to marginalize and exclude indigenous women's specific demands from the feminist agenda.

11. See Comandanta Esther's speech in Section 1 of this volume.

EIGHT

"WE CAN NO LONGER BE LIKE HENS WITH OUR HEADS BOWED, WE MUST RAISE OUR HEADS AND LOOK AHEAD"

A Consideration of the Daily Life of Zapatista Women

VIOLETA ZYLBERBERG PANEBIANCO,
TRANSLATED BY MARÍA VINÓS

More than ten years have passed since the Zapatista National Liberation Army (EZLN) came into public view. One of the aspects that has most captured public attention since the beginning is the presence of women in the movement. Also notable is the Women's Revolutionary Law (see Section 1, this volume), which sought to contribute to the elimination of gender inequality within the framework of a larger struggle against inequality and injustice.

The Zapatista movement's political relevance in the transformation of gender relations among indigenous peoples has been widely recognized. The Women's Revolutionary Law and the statements of Zapatista rebels published in the press awakened enthusiasm for the new horizons of visibility that were opened for indigenous women in Mexico (see chapter 2, this volume), as did the emergence of a new political discourse combining gender, class, and ethnic demands for this sector of the population (Hernández Castillo 1994b, 1998a; Marcos and Ponce de León 1997; Lagarde 1997).

Women participate within the EZLN at all levels. At the top is the Clandestine Indigenous Revolutionary Committee (CCRI), which, although not part of the military structure, is in charge of organizing communities and regions. Both male and female comandantes—Esther and Ramona among them—are members of the CCRI. Below the CCRI is the military and regular structure of the EZLN, composed of men and women who live in the military camps in the region's mountains. At the third level are the women's militias, composed of women who live in their communities but who have had military training; they form irregular troops that are called into action at specific times. Finally, there are the women who are part of the support bases. They take part in all EZLN initiatives, such as marches and opinion polls, land occupations, demonstrations, and other resistance actions at specific times. The support bases also support the Zapatista movement by, for example, providing food to the insurgents or others who visit the communities in solidarity with the movement.

The women I am writing about here are part of the support bases and generally are not thoroughly steeped in politics. They are not skilled public speakers, nor are they very visible in the media. These are women who live in the communities and engage in a daily struggle to have their rights respected, sometimes at great personal cost. These are women without whom the Zapatista movement would be not only impossible but meaningless as well.

The discourse against women's oppression expressed by the leadership of the EZLN is appropriated, resignified, and reelaborated in different ways when used within the communities. The processes each community and its residents experience are not homogeneous; achievements and challenges vary from one community to another and from one individual to another. The political and organizational history of each region, community, and individual determines the various ways in which the Zapatista discourse is appropriated and the impact it has on everyday life.

Little is known about the women who form the Zapatista support bases, about their daily struggle to survive under the low-intensity warfare that besieges their communities, to transform the "traditions" that regulate their lives.[1] Looking closely at the daily lives of women in "communities in resistance" (Zapatista base communities) allows me to trace the process of debate and change that they are experiencing, a complex process that includes struggling to maintain certain traditions while at the same time transforming community norms. This examination entails recognition of their achievements and of the spaces they have won but also of the limitations, obstacles, and challenges they have faced.

SITUATING MY KNOWLEDGE

The excitement generated by the Zapatista uprising throughout the country was reflected, in my case, in my choice of career. When I first visited the community of San Francisco,[2] I had just finished high school, and it was my experience in the community that motivated me to study anthropology and generated my interest in the questions discussed in this chapter.[3] How has Zapatismo affected women's lives? This was the question that gave rise to my research, though this was not the original motivation for my arrival in San Francisco. This question emerged from my interactions with people in the community. Perhaps it was my personal history—growing up in an urban middle-class environment, the daughter of Argentine exiles, and educated in activist schools—that led me to become interested, from the start, in the marked differences between men and women in the community. The community was a place unlike any I had known, and I sought to understand the extent to which the Zapatista rebellion had had an impact on it and in particular on the lives of the women.

In recent years I have had the opportunity to visit San Francisco on numerous occasions, and during this time, I have observed some of the problems faced in daily practice by the communities of the EZLN support bases in their attempt to eliminate gender inequality. This chapter attempts to reconstruct some of what I observed, starting from the impact the EZLN has had and its influence on the daily dynamics of the support base communities, illustrated though the specific experience of a Tzeltal community in the Lacandon jungle.

This analysis does not intend to hold up the experience of San Francisco as an ideal for Zapatista support bases. I know that there are some communities in which women have gained important spaces of participation and power and others in which women still do not even have access to the community assembly (see chapter 5, this volume). Previous organizational experiences, the level of consolidation of internal structures, the manner in which they have experienced low-intensity warfare, and the presence or absence of links to other organized women are some of the factors that influence how gender relations are restructured (or not). The present experience is only a window upon one of the various facets of daily life for Zapatista women.[4]

It is of critical importance to recognize indigenous women as diverse subjects of concrete histories who are elaborating their own horizons of change. In this chapter, I do not attempt to speak for indigenous Zapatista women (they speak for themselves) but rather to speak about them, with them, and with other social actors who speak about and with them. I recognize that my perspective, the interpretation in this analysis, is a partial one and that there can be many others. If our location, geographic, cultural, social, and political, that is, the place from which we speak, conditions our perspective, I would like to reiterate the position from which I speak: as a middle-class, mestiza, activist, child-of-exiled-Argentines anthropologist. These are some of the places from which I saw and engaged in dialogue in this research. By recognizing the places from which we speak, we can build bridges and listen to others in their own context, accepting the differences that exist without having them imply inequalities in daily life, in politics, and in academia.

DAILY LIFE

I first visited San Francisco in June 1995. A month before, the people of San Francisco had finally returned to their homes after being forced to flee by the Mexican Army. María Angélica reconstructs her experience as a displaced person: "We had to go to the mountains when the army came. We stayed away for about three months in fear of the army. We weren't able to take our things along, we left in such a hurry." What the people of this community found when they returned is something they have in common with all the other EZLN support bases who chose to abandon their homes on February 9, 1995, to escape from the federal troops: all their belongings had been destroyed, their animals had been stolen or killed to feed the soldiers, and the corn and beans from the year's harvest were scattered on the ground, mixed with the soldiers' feces and urine.

Since the 1995 military mobilization, an army camp was set up on farmland belonging to the community. San Francisco, like other resisting communities, has experienced what has been called low-intensity warfare.[5] Everyday life is marked by military occupation, by forced displacement, by constant surveillance, by a latent threat. Everyday life is lived under violence. The presence of federal troops has altered how the people go about their daily activities.

The way in which women carry out the task of supplying their homes with basic resources, such as firewood and water, has been impeded. The army set up quarters where women used to gather firewood, so that now every day they are forced to walk farther to fetch it and must always pass in front of the army camp. Thanks to the recent installation of water systems by civil authorities, the women need no longer walk to the river for water; however, the hoses that carry the water are often cut by unknown individuals. When this happens the women must walk to distant springs because the river that runs nearby has been polluted by wastewater from the army camp.

THE COMMUNITY

The Mexican Federal Army settled in San Francisco in 1995 because it had pronounced itself a community in resistance after the EZLN uprising. This implies, among other things, the rejection of government institutions and of the official municipal authorities, which were considered illegitimate and replaced with autonomous authorities.

There are many reasons why the communities organized to form what today is the EZLN, and much has been written on the subject (see, e.g., Benjamin 1995; Gonzáles Casanova 1995; Gonzáles Esponda and Pólito Barrios 1995; Gilly 1997; Harvey 2000; De Vos 2002). The causes of the struggle are not the subject of this chapter; obviously there are many, and they operate at various levels of the social structure. Some are the result of historical processes; others are the product of junctures. In the history of San Francisco we can highlight, among others, migration, participation in political and productive organizations, and the inspiration of liberation theology (see Ascencio and Leyva 1996; Harvey 2000; De Vos 2002).

My concern here is to identify transformations in the lives of women in a community that forms part of the network of EZLN support bases. However, I want to emphasize that beginning with the town's participation in the Zapatista movement there have been changes in various aspects of community life that have had direct or indirect influence over women's daily lives.

First, in the initial days of the EZLN uprising the community occupied large areas of land belonging to plantations and big landowners in the area. The land was assigned to Zapatista farmers, which, in the case of San Francisco, has meant an increase in crops (mostly maize and beans). As a result, today San Francisco is able to produce enough food for the entire community; the occasional excess is sold or traded for other goods, such as salt, sugar, coffee, and clothing.

This increase in production, complemented by the Zapatista prohibition of alcohol consumption, means a better standard of living. Men spend the little money left over on necessities instead of alcohol.

Second, since San Francisco became a community in resistance, civic organizations and individuals, both national and international, have been present in the community. This presence has given rise to various projects that have brought improvements to the community. A new water system, for example, benefited women directly, since they were the ones who used to fetch it from the river. An autonomous health clinic was built, which provides free medical care. This clinic, staffed originally by members of civil organizations—doctors and medical and dentistry students—was over time increasingly staffed by health promoters from the communities themselves and is now entirely staffed by them. This has been a significant improvement: people no longer need to travel miles to the city of Ocosingo to see a doctor or worry about money to buy medicines. The recent influx of visitors to the community has also made possible the establishment of community and regional co-ops to supply them with basic goods. The money made in these co-ops goes into an emergency fund or is used for special projects.

A careful study of what this outside presence has meant for Zapatista communities—how cross-cultural dialogues have changed their political and ethnic identities—remains to be done. It is evident that the women of San Francisco have widened their vision of the community, the nation, and the world through their dialogues with visiting women.

CHANGES AND CHALLENGES
THROUGH WOMEN'S EYES

María Angélica is a thirty-three-year-old Tzeltal woman. She is also a Zapatista, and holds a religious post in the community. She is a member of the sewing workshop that the Catholic missionaries helped to organize, as well as a health promoter, an activity also initiated by the Catholic church and then continued by other organizations, including the EZLN. In addition to her housework, María Angélica sometimes bakes bread to sell in the community and does embroidery that she sells to visitors. In contrast to other women in the community, María Angélica leaves her home to sell bread door-to-door, speaks with visitors, and sometimes travels as far as Ocosingo to get supplies.

After several days of establishing a "formal" relationship with the device, María Angélica speaks haltingly in front of the tape recorder. She finally accepts that her thoughts and words will be recorded, and she speaks.

She is a Zapatista, and she says it with pride and not a trace of doubt. She can see the changes wrought in the women of her community since the EZLN uprising.

> Before we became Zapatistas, there was nothing that would move us. We just sat there, as always. We didn't know if we had it in us to take part, if we had the courage, if we could carry out work or form some kind of collective. But when the struggle began, that was when women started

to know how to do things, how we could have freedom, how we could relate to men.[6]

As Zapatista base supporters, the people of San Francisco have participated in demonstrations, actions, and events called by the EZLN. In 1997 one of the oldest and most respected women in the community represented them in the March of the 1,111 Zapatistas to Mexico City. In 1999 when the poll for the Recognition of Indigenous Peoples took place, 2,500 men and 2,500 women from the support bases traveled to cover each state in the nation. Two men and two women from San Francisco traveled as representatives of their community to the northern states. In March 2000 María Angélica was one of the people chosen to represent her community in the march to celebrate International Women's Day. She tells with pride of her participation in the seizing of a radio station in San Cristóbal de las Casas on March 8. It was she who spoke about women rights, about the situation of women in their communities, and about the impact of the military presence in their lives.

For María Angélica, as for most women in San Francisco, the Women's Revolutionary Law issued by the EZLN on January 1, 2004, is a symbolic referent of the "women's dignity" that the Zapatista fighters have demanded, although neither she nor the other women knew its specific content. Most of the men and women we interviewed said that they were aware of the law but not of its exact content. Some said they had not known it existed. However, there is no doubt that Zapatismo ignited new ideas in the community that are reflected in the changes in the community's norms in recent years. Many of these changes have been in reference to women. Thus the current community norms that govern day-to-day life in San Francisco include some of the aspects called for by the Women's Revolutionary Law.

For example, women were given the right to choose their spouses and to not be forced or sold into marriage by their parents, the right to take part in community politics and hold leadership posts, and the right to be informed about family planning methods and to use them if they choose. Physical violence against women is also prohibited. The prohibition against alcohol consumption is considered also a preventive measure against domestic violence:

> Men used to drink a lot before, and then they would hit their wives. When this struggle was taking shape, it was decided that drink was not a good thing, that there should be no more drinking, because from drink

comes the mistreatment of the *compañera*, the partner, and the mistreatment of the children.[7]

Some men appear to understand now, some have stopped mistreating women, but some seem to keep going. But women know what their rights are, and what they can do if they are mistreated. Some might not know, and may still be beaten by their husbands. Who knows? But today we know how to defend ourselves, and if women fail to report mistreatment to the authorities, they have only themselves to blame.[8]

Indeed, violence against women has decreased in the community, although the problem has not gone away completely. And though the changes in community rules stipulate that a mistreated woman may request that the man who is responsible be punished, some still hold out for fear of retaliation.

In other spheres the winds of change have affected the behavior of Tzeltal men and women more profoundly. It has become normal to find young women of twenty-one or twenty-two who are still single (until ten years ago, Tzeltal women married between the ages of fourteen and sixteen) and who consider marriage a limitation on their participation. The norm now is that young men and women choose their spouses rather than their parents choosing for them. Lorena, twenty-one and still single, is an example of the new generation of Tzeltal youth who have confronted marriage traditions: "I was asked once before, but I did not want to marry, I was too young. I want to enjoy life and get married when I am twenty-five or twenty-six, and I do not know if I want children. Children are a lot of work. Maybe I will have only one or two."[9]

Francisca, Lorena's mother, lived through a different time, and she did not have a chance to decide for herself. She said that when she was about fifteen, a man asked for her. She did not want to go with him, but her mother gave her in marriage anyway. She says the man had also been under pressure from his own parents to get married. After a few years, he abandoned her for another woman. Her rejection of forced marriage comes from her own experience: "It is not a good thing to force young people to marry someone they don't want. It brings problems and mistreatment."

The use of birth control pills has become commonplace among married women in the community. Some of the women we interviewed asserted that using birth control did not mean they were rejecting motherhood but that they wanted their pregnancies to be spaced further apart, so they could have time to recover. "Children," one woman said, "are no longer born so small." But the right to "decide the number of children they want to bear and raise," included in Article 3 of the Women's Revolutionary Law, has been recast in this community as the couple's right to decide. "The couple should talk about it, it is not for the woman to decide on her own," a man from the community commented.[10] There are also those who choose not to use any birth control, in obedience of Catholic precepts, which state that a woman should have the number of children God sends her.

Also as a result of the Zapatista uprising, men are increasingly helping women with tasks that were previously considered exclusively women's domain, such as shucking the corn from the cob or feeding the chicken and swine. It is interesting to hear what men have to say on the subject: "If I finish early with my work, I can help. Women have a lot of work, and there are things we can help with."[11] However, that men help with some domestic tasks does not mean that the view that only women are "fit" for certain jobs—such as housekeeping, cooking, and child care—has changed. A man from the community said about the possibility of changing roles with women: "No I don't think it can be done. Well, I could grind corn, but I could not make tortillas. I could not stand the smoke."[12]

Participation spaces for women have also widened. Community assemblies, in the past considered exclusively the men's domain, are now open to women. Women use their new right by attending assemblies, but in most cases their participation is limited to listening and commenting among themselves. Seldom do they speak openly at the assembly. Even so, this limited participation is an improvement on waiting at home for husbands, fathers, or brothers to return from the meeting to tell them (if they are so inclined) what was discussed, what the issues were, and what was decided.

Women's scant participation responds to a certain logic. Women have heard all their lives that they are not supposed to participate, so they can hardly believe now that they can. This fear of speaking in public and participating is illustrated in the testimony of a woman at an Indigenous Women's Meeting: "We have been taught since we were little girls to do as we were told, to be quiet, not to talk back, to put up and shut up, to stay away from participation."[13]

Although San Francisco's community rules permit it, there are still no women in leadership posts. Some argue that it is difficult for a woman to get chosen since married women already have many responsibilities and most do not wish to add to their already heavy schedules or think that they might not do a good job. In other instances, the husband may not be willing, since it would mean that his wife might "neglect her housework." On the other hand, unmarried women, who have more free time and fewer duties, are perceived by the community as "too young, unknowledgeable, shy, afraid of gossip, and irresponsible," or as "only looking for a boyfriend; once they catch a man, they get married and forget about work."

Lack of time, fear, and concern about what others will say are some of the reasons women put forward to explain their reluctance to use the newly opened spaces of participation. Rumors and gossip, as manifestations of power relations, have had a hand in keeping women from participation beyond their housekeeping tasks. However, even with all the obstacles and limitations they face, some women have chosen to participate in various community projects. An example of this is the women's co-op shop, where women sell their goods, manage tasks, and make all the decisions. Women also participate in various health, education, and sewing workshops.

Valentina, twenty-six, was eighteen when she married, just after the Zapatista uprising. She says if she had known that such spaces would be opened to women, she would have delayed marriage. Now it would be difficult for her to take part. She has four small children, and even if her husband agreed to let her work, she does not have the time. Doña Juana is fifty-two and has twelve children; she is the only married woman who participates in the co-op. "My husband tells me to leave the shop, he thinks since I am married people are going to think that he is too meek, that he has no authority," she explains. This reflects an undeniable reality: it is not just women who are the victims of rumor and gossip; in many instances, men are also affected. If a woman spends too much time away from her home, if she participates in several activities, the general feeling in the community is that her husband or father has not got a handle on her, that he is "not man enough." In this sense, it is helpful to recall that this is a complex process since it is not only women who have to break away from the preconceptions of what a "good woman" should be like or how she should behave. The local representation of femininity is tightly linked to the representation of masculinity, to the parameters and stereotypes of what it is to be a "good man." The challenge of a real transformation in gender inequality is that the community as a whole must recast gender relations.

Regarding women's participation in various projects, María Angélica states:

It is a good thing that women participate, get training, work, and feel encouraged. Not everyone feels able to do it, some can, some can't. . . .

But we are not all the same, and not everyone understands. Some women do understand their importance, but others think differently, they don't believe they have rights, they feel there is nothing they can do. I was afraid to participate too. My voice would tremble when I spoke, and I stuttered. Thank God, they put me in charge of the Word of God, and overcame my shyness there. Now I am not afraid to speak, I am not afraid to participate.[14]

María Angélica has taken the risk inherent in breaking away from traditional gender roles and crossing the boundaries of domestic unity. She takes part in political and community activities and promotes this work with other women: "We can no longer sit there with our heads down like hens, we have to raise our heads."[15]

The fact that María Angélica leaves her home often to sell bread, embroidery, to give interviews to visitors, or to participate in the sewing workshop has made things difficult with her husband and his family. Recently, the situation between them had grown complicated. Someone in the community accused her of having a lover, and this made things unbearable between them. She decided to leave her husband and return to her parents' home.

The story of how María Angélica's problem was resolved is long and far from simple. The community had to use all the mechanisms available to resolve internal conflicts. Initially, the community leadership (twenty-two men, those with land responsibilities and those with religious posts) tried to mediate. When they failed to find a suitable solution, they passed the case to the community assembly. I had the opportunity to attend that gathering, which turned out very interestingly, not only because this was the first time a woman was leaving her husband, which had all the community paying attention, but because in the discussion that ensued both the new rights and norms and the old norms of good behavior accepted traditionally by the community were debated.

María Angélica's husband's argument was that she had lost respect for him: she no longer asked permission to go out or told him where she was going. That is, she no longer complied with the implicit rule of being a "good woman," and this affected them directly, since the community considered he was unable to command his wife or to support her, which is why she had to go out to sell things. In short, he was not "a good man."

María Angélica also spoke before the assembly. Women seldom address the assembly, and no one before her had done it in the tone she used. She spoke strongly, and she was visibly angry. She denied the accusations of infidelity, defended her rights, and justified having left her husband because of the way he and his family were treating her; she repeated that she was not going to go back to him and asked the assembly to separate them. Here another issue was put forth: because they were married by the church, it was beyond the assembly's powers to grant them a divorce; in addition, people were afraid that if the assembly accepted the separation of the couple, it would set a precedent and such cases might increase. The assembly refused to recognize the separation and after insisting they should forgive each other, granted a period of time to think things over.

In contrast to other women who have had problems in the community, María Angélica, certain that she was not to blame, continued to attend church services, assemblies, and festivities; she danced and sold bread and embroidery. Finally, after two months of separation, she and her husband reached a compromise, and she returned home. This solution left many unsatisfied. Those who were of the opinion that he should not have forgiven her leaving and taken her back thought he should have taken another wife.[16]

Although the community has modified its discourse and norms to a certain extent regarding, among other issues, women's rights, daily interactions still reproduce gender inequality. There are implicit norms that only recently have come into question, but they are still reproduced. These are norms that no one agreed to but which are known and complied with by all. An example of this is the unspoken rule that women should not be walking about town or speak to any man who is not a relative since doing so would give way to gossip, would give people "something to talk about," would look as if she was looking for a boyfriend (if she is single) or a lover (if she is married). These assumptions are reproduced both by men and by women. Gossip is one of the important ways in which power relations become manifest; it carries implicitly the boundaries of acceptable behavior, which, if trespassed, are accompanied by problems with the husband, the family, and the community.

Although Zapatista women participate in the movement and fight for their rights and a change in their situation, it is evident that they face obstacles and resistance inside the EZLN as well as in the support base communities. Many men say that they understand and support women's demands, but this understanding seems to evaporate the instant they find it is their own wives, sisters, or daughters who have an opinion, who participate in meetings and assemblies, who are part of a project. María Angélica points out the double standard of many of her Zapatista *compañeros* who seem to support women's demands in their discourse but in practice limit their wives' participation: "It appears that men are good, but appearances don't tell all. You see a face, but you don't see a heart. Men seem to have two hearts, good heart and bad heart, which is why we can't tell in any given moment if they are good, if they are bad."[17] However, María Angélica recognizes that this is not a struggle against men, that both men and women are working together to change things.

An EZLN communiqué recognizes the obstacles women face:

Zapatista women, both combatant and noncombatant, are fighting for their own rights as women. In addition, they face the macho culture of Zapatista men, which is expressed in different ways. Zapatista women are not free because they are Zapatistas; they still have a long way to go and a lot to gain. We understand this is not a struggle against men, but a struggle for women's rights.[18]

Concerned about the situation of women in the community and focusing on how to continue to change this situation, María Angélica commented:

I don't know what can be done, I don't know what they think Esther, because it's not just in this community, but in the majority of communities. One or two that understand what it means [women's rights] and many others that don't understand and even though you want to tell them, this is what you're going to do, what you can do, if they don't want to, then how? I don't know, even if you want to put your heart into it, but they don't want to . . . I've told them so many times: look, *compañeras*, . . . what is being said about our struggle, that we are going to have rights, that we women also have a right to participate, but if we don't want that, don't accept that, how is anything going to change, nobody is going to come and change it if we ourselves don't.[19]

And, regarding the possibility of women changing, María Angélica said:

I believe that they can change if they themselves want to, that can be done, even if they are not accustomed to participating or talking to just anyone, if they want to little by little that fear fades, but I don't think they want—or they can't decide—to change their way of thinking. The idea they hold is that they cannot change, but they can. If we want to we can change everything.[20]

What I have briefly presented in this chapter and what María Angélica has said would seem to coincide with what other Zapatista communities have expressed:

We are men and women, like any, with our lows and our selfishnesses, with our weaknesses and errors. We are not "the new men" and "the new women." Zapatismo is not the new world. Zapatismo is an effort, an institution, a desire to struggle for change, to change everything, including ourselves. We are men and women who want to change and change ourselves and we are men and women willing to do anything to achieve it.[21]

FINAL REFLECTIONS

Everything that Zapatismo has engendered and signified for society in general, as well as the transformations of unequal relations of power that indigenous women live daily, is of vital importance. The Zapatista movement marked a change in the image that many held of the indigenous woman; with their actions and their words, these women are questioning stereotypes of indigenous women as submissive victims, as inactive and passive.

Indigenous women's demands make manifest the break with the common frame of reference prevailing in indigenous communities (and in much of society), in which gendered inequalities are seen as "normal" or natural. With their discourse and practice, indigenous women have begun to denaturalize inequality. What was previously assumed to be natural has ceased to be so and is now within the realm of what can be questioned and debated.

Nevertheless, this is just the first stage in a long process in which indigenous Zapatista women are struggling daily to make the new discourses bring about changes in their lives. Throughout this chapter, I have tried to present some of the difficulties they confront in daily practice in the EZLN base support communities when trying to eliminate gender inequalities. The dimensions of the challenge and the complexity that a process of this type represents are great.

Social movements are constructed, and this implies breaking with ideas and social practices previously experienced as natural. This construction occurs in a process of critique and permanent confrontation, of rupture and the creation of new values, of other forms of perceiving life experiences, about what is possible and legitimate (Bourdieu and Wacquant 1995, cited in Garza Caligaris and Toledo 1998). While San Francisco is living a process of change and some results are visible, it is true that daily practices and beliefs that have historically justified oppression and exclusion cannot be changed by decree. No one can change in the course of a few short years practices that have been maintained through centuries. As Iris Marion Young (2000:75) has asserted, oppression is structural and cannot be eliminated simply by the fact that certain norms, habits, and symbols—that is, assumptions, "seemingly absurd, often unconscious reactions from people who in normal social intercourse have good intentions"—go unquestioned. Oppression in this sense is structural and cannot be eliminated by "getting rid of governments or making a few new laws, because oppression is reproduced systematically in the most important economic, political and cultural institutions" (Young 2000:75).

In Zapatista communities, as in society in general, the elimination of gender inequality continues to be an ideal to achieve more than a lived reality (Hernández Castillo and Zilberberg 2002). The women as well as the men of San Francisco and other communities are conscious of this and do not believe that they have achieved the elimination of oppression, or that women are enjoying the full range of their rights. They know it is a long road, a road they have just begun to travel. Many women, among them indigenous women like María Angélica, are working in national and in community spaces to turn discourses of women's rights into daily practices.

NOTES

Portions of this chapter appeared in the article, coauthored with Aída Hernández Castillo, "Impactos locales y nacionales del zapatismo en la vida de las mujeres indígenas," in *Tejiendo historias: Chiapas en la mirada de las mujeres*, ed. Maya Lorena Pérez (Mexico City: INAH, 2004). This chapter is a product of the collective research "New and Old Spaces of Power: Indigenous Women, Collective Organization, and Resistance," sponsored by CONACYT (38784-S).

1. Among the few studies about women in the support bases are Eber 1998, 2002.

2. "San Francisco" is a pseudonym. I have used a pseudonym to protect the safety of the community's inhabitants and at their express request. San Francisco

is an *ejido*, but I have used the term "community" because that is how the inhabitants themselves refer to it.

3. The information presented in this chapter forms part of a larger study for my undergraduate thesis in ethnology at the Escuela Nacional de Antropología e Historia (ENAH), titled "Género, etnicidad y resistencia: Movimiento zapatista y mujeres en Chiapas" and presented in August 2004.

4. It is important to realize that we cannot make generalizations about Zapatismo from the experience of one Zapatista community.

5. Low-intensity warfare (LIW) was first developed as a concept during the Vietnam War. It describes an irregular armed conflict in which the people directly affected live under immediate danger of their lives but in which for the armed forces it is a subtle, indirect, and long-term war. The main difference from conventional war is its low intensity; its military strategy is based on psychological effect. Gaining knowledge about the private life of the enemy's armies and communities is one of the main objectives in this type of conflict; see Rangel 1997:87. For more on this, see Pineda 1996.

6. Interview, San Francisco, February 2001.

7. Interview, San Francisco, February 2001.

8. Interview, San Francisco, February 2001.

9. Interview, San Francisco, February 2001.

10. Interview, San Francisco, February 2001.

11. Interview, San Francisco, April 1999.

12. Interview, San Francisco, April 1999.

13. "El grito de la luna. Mujeres: derecho y tradición," *Ojarasca*, nos. 35 and 36, August–September 1994, 27. The text is contained in "Women Speak Their Word" in Section 1 of this volume.

14. Interview, San Francisco, February 2001.

15. Interview, San Francisco, February 2001.

16. While some of us who visited the community at that time might have felt that María Angélica's having gone back to her husband might indicate a step backward, it is important not to lose sight of the fact that the other options available were not very encouraging. One of these was to remain in the household of her elderly parents and take on all the work that that implies but without the liberty of making her own decisions; in other words, she would lose whatever personal autonomy she had achieved. Another option was going to Altamirano where she had a relative, but this meant breaking her ties to the community and going to work in the city, with all the conditions of racism and exploitation that exist there. María Angélica took into account the costs and benefits of all the possible options and decided that the best one for her was to return to her house, with her husband and child, and from there continue to fight against the things she did not agree with.

17. Interview, San Francisco, February 2001.

18. *La Jornada*, March 9, 1996.

19. Interview, San Francisco, 2001.

20. Interview, San Francisco, 2001.

21. EZLN communiqué, April 7, 1996, available at www.ezln.org.

REFERENCES

Alarcón, Norma
1990   "The Theoretical Subjects of This Bridge Called My Back and Anglo-American Feminism." In *Making Faces/Making Soul: Haciendo caras,* ed. Gloria Anzaldúa. San Francisco: Aunt Lute.
Alberti Manzanares, Pilar
1994   "Dos mitos: Las mujeres indígenas cosificadas y la etnia anquilosada." *Antropológicas* 10:7–8.
1997   "La identidad de género y etnia como base de las estrategias de adaptación de las mujeres indígenas ante la crisis." In *Estrategias de sobrevivencia de las mujeres campesinas e indígenas ante la crisis,* ed. Pilar Alberti Manzanares and Emma Zapata Martelo. Mexico City: Colegio de Postgraduados en Ciencias Agrícolas/Programa de Estudios del Desarrollo Rural.
Alexander, M. Jacqui, and Chandra Talpade Mohanty
1997   *Feminist Genealogies, Colonial Legacies, Democratic Futures.* New York: Routledge.
Álvarez, Sonia E.
1990   *Engendering Democracy in Brazil: Women's Movements in Transition Politics.* Princeton: Princeton University Press.
2000   "Translating the Global: Effects of Transnational Organizing on Local Feminist Discourses and Practices in Latin America." *Meridians: Feminism, Race, Transnationalism* 1(1):29–67.
Álvarez, Sonia E., Evelina Dagnino, and Arturo Escobar
1998   *Cultures of Politics/Politics of Cultures: Re-visioning Latin American Social Movements.* Boulder: Westview Press.
Anzaldúa, Gloria
[1987] 1991   *Borderlands/La Frontera: The New Mestiza.* San Francisco: Aunt Lute.
Arizpe, Lourdes
1980   *Indígenas en la Ciudad de México: El caso de las Marías.* Mexico City: Secretaría de Educación Pública.

Artía Rodríguez, Patricia
2001   "Desatar las voces, construir las utopías: La Coordinadora Nacional de Mujeres Indígenas en Oaxaca." M.A. thesis, CIESAS, Mexico City.
Ayora Díaz, Steffan Igor
1998   "Globalization, Rationality and Medicine: Local Medicine's Struggle for Recognition in Highland Chiapas." *Urban Anthropology* 27: 165–196.
2000   "Imagining Authenticity in the Local Medicines of Chiapas, Mexico." *Critique of Anthropology* 20:173–190.
Azaola, Elena
1996   *El delito de ser mujer.* Mexico City: CIESAS/Plaza y Valdés.
Bartra, Eli
2002   "Tres décadas de neofeminismo en México." In *Feminismo en México ayer y hoy,* ed. Eli Bartra. Mexico City: Universidad Autónoma– Metropolitana.
Bartra, Roger
1997   "Violencias indígenas." *Jornada Semanal* 130:8–9.
Becerril Albarrán, Nahela, Marcela Laguna Morales, Diana I. García, Claudia Jiménez, and Laura R. Ruiz M.
2000   "Las políticas públicas para las mujeres rurales en Chiapas." In *II encuentro indígena de las Américas: Memoria 1999, 19–21 abril, Chiapas, México.* San Cristóbal de las Casas: Sna Jtz'ibajom.
Berry, Charles R.
1981   *The Reform in Oaxaca, 1856–76.* Lincoln: University of Nebraska Press.
Benhabib, Seyla
2002   *The Claims of Culture: Equality and Diversity in the Global Era.* Princeton: Princeton University Press.
Benjamin, Thomas
1995   *Chiapas: Tierra rica, pueblo pobre.* Mexico City: Grijalbo.
2000   "A Time of Reconquest: History, the Maya Revival, and the Zapatista Rebellion in Chiapas." *American Historical Review* 105(2):417–450.
Bhavnani, Kum Kum
2000   *Feminism and "Race".* Oxford: Oxford University Press.
Blackwell, Maylei
2000   "Geographies of Difference: Mapping Multiple Feminist Insurgencies and Transnational Public Cultures in the Americas." Ph.D. diss., University of California, Santa Cruz.
2004   "(Re) Ordenando el discurso de la nación: El movimiento de mujeres indígenas en México y la práctica de la autonomía." In *Mujeres y nacionalismo: De la independencia a la nación del nuevo milenio,* ed. Natividad Gutiérrez Chong, 193–234. Mexico City: Universidad Nacional Autónoma de México (UNAM).
Bonfil, Paloma
1997   "La presencia de las mujeres en las movilizaciones indígenas contemporáneas de México." In *Estrategias de sobrevivencia de las mujeres*

campesinas e indígenas ante la crisis, ed. Pilar Alberti Manzanares and Emma Zapata Martelo. Mexico City: GIMTRAP.

Bonfil Batalla, Guillermo

1972   "El concepto de indio en América: Una categoría de la situación colonial." *Anales de Antropología* 9(3):105–124.

[1986] 1990   *México profundo: Una civilización negada.* Mexico City: Grijalbo/CONACULTA.

Bonfil Sánchez, Paloma, and Raúl Marcó del Pont Lalli

1999   *Las mujeres indígenas al final del milenio.* Mexico City: Secretaría de Gobernación and Comisión Nacional de la Mujer.

Bossen, Laurel

1983   *The Redivision of Labor: Women and Economic Choice in Four Guatemala Communities.* Albany: State University of New York Press.

Boserup, Esther

1970   *Women's Role in Economic Development.* London: George and Allen & Unwin.

Bourdieu, Pierre

1980   *Le sens pratique.* Paris: Editions de Minuit.

Brading, D. A.

1973   *Los orígenes del nacionalismo mexicano.* Mexico City: Secretaría de Educación Audiovisual y Divulgación.

Braman, Sandra

1996   "Interpenetrated Globalization: Scaling, Power and the Public Sphere." In *Globalization, Communication, and Transnational Civil Society,* ed. Sandra Braman and Annabelle Sreberny-Mohammadi, 21–35. Cresskill, NJ: Hampton Press.

Brysk, Alison

1994   "Acting Globally: Indian Rights and International Politics in Latin America." In *Indigenous Peoples and Democracy in Latin America,* ed. Donna Lee Van Cott, 29–51. New York: St. Martin's Press.

2000   *From Tribal Village to Global Village: Indian Rights and International Relations in Latin America.* Stanford, CA: Stanford University Press.

Burgoa, Ignacio

1997   "Critica jurista la iniciativa de ley de la COCOPA." *La Jornada,* March 4.

Burguete Cal y Mayor, Aracely

2003   "The De Facto Autonomous Process: New Jurisdictions and Parallel Governments in Rebellion." In *Mayan Lives, Mayan Utopias: The Indigenous Peoples of Chiapas and the Zapatista Rebellion,* ed. Jan Rus, Shannan L. Mattiace and Rosalva Aída Hernández Castillo, 191–218. Lanham, MD: Rowan & Littlefield.

Butler, Judith

2001   *El género en disputa: El feminismo y la subversión de la identidad.* Mexico City: Paidós/PUEG-UNAM.

Cadena, Marisol de la

2000   *Indigenous Mestizos: The Politics of Race and Culture in Cuzco, 1919–1991.* Durham, NC: Duke University Press.

Cancian, Frank

1990 "The Zinacantán Waiting Lists as a Reflection of Social, Political, and Economic Changes, 1952–1987." In *Class, Politics, and Popular Religion: Religious Change in Mexico and Central America*, ed. Lynn Stephen and James Dow. Washington, DC: American Anthropological Association.

1992 *The Decline of Community in Zinacantán: Economy, Public Life, and Social Stratification, 1960–1987*. Stanford, CA: Stanford University Press.

Castellanos, Absalón

1983–1986 *Informes de Gobierno*. Tuxtla Gutiérrez: Gobierno del Estado de Chiapas. Center for Human Rights (Centro de Derechos Humanos) "Fray Bartolomé de las Casas"

1998 *Camino a la masacre*. San Cristóbal de las Casas, Chiapas: Centro de Derechos Humanos "Fray Bartolomé de las Casas."

Chance, John

1990 "Changes in Twentieth-Century Mesoamerican Cargo Systems." In *Class, Politics, and Popular Religion: Religious Change in Mexico and Central America*, ed. Lynn Stephen and James Dow. Washington, DC: American Anthropological Association.

Chance, John K., and William B. Taylor

1985 "Cofradías and Cargos: An Historical Perspective on the Mesoamerican Civil-Religious Hierarchy." *American Ethnologist* 12(1):1–26.

Chatterjee, Partha

1998 "Community in the East." *Economic and Political Weekly*, February 7, 277–282.

Chiñas, Beverly

1975 *Mujeres de San Juan: La mujer zapoteca del Istmo en la economía*. Mexico City: SepSetentas.

Collier, George

1994 *Basta! Land and the Zapatista Rebellion in Chiapas*. Oakland, CA: Food First Books.

Collier, Jane

1968 *Courtship and Marriage in Zinacantán, Chiapas, Mexico*. New Orleans: Middle American Research Institute, Tulane University.

Comaroff, John, and Jean Comaroff

1992 *Ethnography and the Historical Imagination*. Boulder, CO: Westview Press.

CONAPO

1994 *Mujer rural, medio ambiente y salud en la selva*. Tuxtla Gutiérrez: Consejo Nacional de Población/Secretaría de Gobernación.

Cooper, F., and A. L. Stoler

1989 "Tensions of Empire: Colonial Control and Visions of Rule." *American Ethnologist* 16(4):609–621.

Dalton, Margarita, and Guadalupe Musalem

1992 *Mitos y realidades de las mujeres huaves*. Benito Juárez, Oaxaca: Instituto de Investigaciones Sociológicas.

Declaración del Sol
1995   Document of the first Encuentro de Mujeres Indígenas de las Primeras Naciones de Abya Yala. Organized by Confederación de Nacionalidades Indígenas del Ecuador (CONAIE) and the Coordinadora Nacional de Mujeres Indígenas del Ecuador (CONAMIE). July 31–August 4, Quito, Ecuador.

Deere, Carmen Diana, and Magdalena León
2001   *Empowering Women: Land and Property Rights in Latin America.* Pitt Latin American Series. Pittsburgh: University of Pittsburgh Press.

2002   "Individual versus Collective Land Rights: Tensions between Women's and Indigenous Rights under Neoliberalism." In *The Spaces of Neoliberalism: Land, Place and Family in Latin America,* ed. J. Chase, 53–86. Bloomfield, CT: Kumarian Press.

de la Peña, Guillermo
1999   "Territorio y ciudadanía étnica en la nación globalizada." *Desacatos* 1(1): 13–27.

Deleuze, Gilles
1994   "Postscript on Societies of Control." In *Negotiations.* New York: Columbia University Press.

De Vos, Jan
2002   *Una tierra para sembrar sueños: Historia reciente de la Selva Lacandona, 1950–2000.* Mexico City: CIESAS/Fondo de Cultura Económica.

Díaz Polanco, Héctor
1991   *Autonomía regional: La autodeterminación de los pueblos indios.* Mexico City: Siglo XXI.

1997   *La rebelión Zapatista y la autonomía.* Mexico City: Siglo XXI Editores.

Duarte Bastían, Ixkic
2002   "Conversación con Alma López, autoridad guatemalteca: La doble mirada del género y la etnicidad." *Estudios Latinoamericanos,* n.s. 18 (July–December): 15–27.

Dunbar Ortiz, Roxanne
1984   *Indians of the Americas: Human Rights and Self-Determination.* New York: Praeger.

Durán de Huerta, Martha
1994   *Yo, Marcos: Entrevistas y pláticas del Subcomandante.* Mexico City: Ediciones del Milenio.

Eber, Christine
1998   "Las mujeres y el movimiento por la democracia en San Pedro Chenalhó." In *La otra palabra: Mujeres y violencia en Chiapas, antes y después de Acteal,* ed. R. Aída Hernández. Mexico City: CIESAS/COLEM/CIAM.

1999   " 'Seeking Our Own Food': Indigenous Women's Power and Autonomy in San Pedro Chenalhó, Chiapas (1980–1998)." *Latin American Perspectives* 26(3): 6–36.

[1995] 2000   *Women and Alcohol in a Highland Maya Town: Water of Hope, Water of Sorrow.* 2d ed. Austin: University of Texas Press.

2001   "Buscando una nueva vida: Liberation through Autonomy in San Pedro Chenalhó, 1970–1998." *Latin American Perspectives* 28(2): 45–71.

2002   "Buscando una nueva vida: Liberación a través de la autonomía en San Pedro Chenalhó, 1970–1998." In *Tierra, libertad y autonomía: Impactos regionales del Zapatismo in Chiapas,* ed. Shannan Mattiace, R. Aída Hernández and Jan Rus. Mexico City: CIESAS-IWGIA.

Eber, Christine, and Christine Kovic, eds.

2003   *Women of Chiapas: Making History in Times of Struggle and Hope.* New York: Routledge.

Eckstein, Susan Eva, and Timothy P. Wickham-Crowley

2003   "Struggles for Social Rights in Latin America: Claims in the Arenas of Subsistence, Labor, Gender, and Ethnicity." In *Struggles for Social Rights in Latin America,* ed. Susan Eva Eckstein and Timothy P. Wickham Crowley, 1–56. New York: Routledge.

Ehler, Tracy

1990   *Silent Looms: Women and Production in a Guatemalan Town.* Boulder: Westview Press.

Engle, Karen

2005   "International Human Rights and Feminisms: When Discourses Keep Meeting." In *Feminist Perspectives on International Law,* ed. D. Buss and A. Manji, 46–67. Oxford: Hart Publishing.

Escobar, Arturo, and Sonia Álvarez

1992   *The Making of Social Movements in Latin America: Identity, Strategy, and Democracy.* Boulder: Westview Press.

Espinosa Damián, Gisela

1993   "Feminismo y movimientos de mujeres: Encuentros y desencuentros." *El Cotidiano* 3(53):20–25.

2005   "Entre el cuerpo y la política: Cuatro vertientes del feminismo mexicano." Ph.D. diss., National School of Anthropology and History (ENAH), Mexico City.

Espinosa, Gisela, and Lorena Paz Paredes

1988   "Pioneros del feminismo en los sectores populares: La experiencia de CIDHAL 1977–1985." Manuscript.

EZLN

1994, 1995, 1997   *Documentos y comunicados.* Vols. 1–3. Mexico City: Era.

1999   "The Agrarian Revolutionary Law." In *Rebellion in Chiapas: An Historical Reader,* ed. John Womack, 253–254. New York: New Press.

2000   *Discursos de la Delegación Zapatista a la ciudad de México.* www.Ezlnaldf.org/static/delegacion.htm.

Fitzpatrick, Peter

1980   *Law and State in Papua New Guinea.* New York: Academic Press.

Flood, Merielle

1994   "Changing Gender Relations in Zinacantán, México." *Research in Economic Anthropology* 15.

Flores, William V., and Rina Benmayor

1997   "Introduction: Constructing Cultural Citizenship." In *Latino Cultural Citizenship: Claiming Identity, Space, and Rights,* ed. William V. Flores and Rina Benmayor, 1–23. Boston: Beacon Press.

Fraser, Nancy

1996   "Redistribución y reconocimiento: Hacia una visión integrada de justica de género." *Revista Internacional de Filosofía Política* 8:30–53.

Freyermuth Enciso, Graciela

1993   *Médicos tradicionales y médicos alópatas: Un encuentro difícil en los Altos de Chiapas.* Tuxtla Gutiérrez: CIESAS-Sureste/Gobierno del Estado de Chiapas.

Freyermuth, Graciela, and Mariana Fernández

1995   "Migration, Organization and Identity: The Case of a Women's Group from San Cristóbal las Casas." *Signs* 20(4):970–995.

Friedman, Elizabeth

1999   "The Effects of 'Transnationalism Reversed' in Venezuela: Assessing the Impact of UN Global Conferences on the Women's Movement." *International Feminist Journal of Politics* 1(3):357–381.

Gamio, Manuel

1916   *Forjando patria (pro nacionalismo).* Mexico City: Porrúa Hermanos.

Gall, Olivia, and Rosalva Aída Hernández Castillo

2004   "La historia silenciada: El papel de las campesinas indígenas en las rebeliones coloniales y poscoloniales en Chiapas." In *Voces disidentes: Debates contemporáneos en los estudios de género en México,* ed. Patricia Ravelo, 151–178. Mexico City: CIESAS-Porrúa.

García, María del Carmen, et al.

1998   "Las organizaciones campesinas e indígenas de Chiapas frente a la reforma del Estado: una radiografía." *Cuadernos Agrarios* 16 (Nueva Epoca):75–94.

Garza Caligaris, Ann María

1999   "El género entre normas en disputa: San Pedro Chenalhó." M.A. thesis, Instituto de Estudios Indígenas, UNACH.

2002   *Género, interlegalidad y conflicto in San Pedro Chenalhó.* Mexico City: PROIMMSE, UNAM-IEI, UNACH.

Garza Caligaris, Anna María, and Sonia Toledo

2000   "El movimiento de mujeres en Chiapas: Haciendo historia." In *Anuario de Estudios Indígenas* 8:109–135. Tuxtla Gutiérrez: Instituto de Estudios Indígenas, UNACH.

2004   "Mujeres, agrarismo y militancia: Chiapas en la década de los ochentas." In *Tejiendo historias: Tierra, género y poder en Chiapas,* ed. Maya Lorena Pérez Ruiz, 15–19. Mexico City: CONACULTA/INAH.

Garza Caligaris, Anna María, María Fernanda Paz Salinas,
Juana María Ruiz Ortiz, and Angelina Calvo Sánchez

1993   *Sk'op Antzetik: Una historia de mujeres en la selva de Chiapas.* Tuxtla Gutiérrez: UNACH.

Gil Tébar, Pilar R.
1999   *Caminando en un solo corazón: Las mujeres indígenas de Chiapas.*
Málaga: Atenea/Universidad de Málaga, España.
Gill, Lesley
2000   *Teetering on the Rim: Global Restructuring, Daily Life, and the Armed
Retreat of the Bolivian State.* New York: Columbia University Press.
Gilly, Adolfo
1997   *Chiapas: La razón ardiente. Ensayo sobre la rebelión del mundo en-
cantado.* Mexico City: Era.
1998   "Mujeres." *La Jornada,* January 4, 8–9.
Gómez Hernández, Antonio, and Mario Humberto Ruz, eds.
1992   *Memoria baldía: Los Tojolabales y las fincas. Testimonios.* Mexico
City: Universidad Nacional Autónoma de México; Tuxtla Gutiérrez:
Universidad Autónoma de Chiapas.
Gómez Nuñez, Marcelino
2000   "Autonomous Pluriethnic Regions (RAP): The Many Paths to De Facto
Autonomy." In *Indigenous Autonomy in Mexico,* ed. Aracely Bur-
guete Cal y Mayor, 178–193. Copenhagen: International Working
Group on Indigenous Affairs.
González, Cristina
2001   *Autonomía y Alianzas: El movimiento feminista en la Ciudad de
México, 1976–1986.* Mexico City: PUEG-UNAM.
González Casanova, Pablo
1995   "Causas de la rebelión zapatista." *La Jornada,* September 5.
González Esponda, Juan, and Elizabeth Pólito Barrios
1995   "Notas para comprender el origen de la rebelión zapatista." In *Chiapas,*
no. 1. Mexico City: Era/Instituto de Investigaciones Económicas/
UNAM.
González Montes, Soledad
1991   "Los ingresos no agropecuarios, el trabajo remunerado femenino y las
transformaciones de las relaciones intergenéricas e intergeneraciona-
les de las familias campesinas." In *Textos y pre-textos: Once estudios
sobre la mujer,* ed. Vania Salles and Elsie McPhail. Mexico City: El
Colegio de México/PIEM.
Goody, Jack
1976   *Production and Reproduction.* Cambridge: Cambridge University
Press.
Grewal, Indepal, and Caren Kaplan, eds.
1994   *Scattered Hegemonies: Postmodernity and Transnational Feminist
Practices.* Minneapolis: University of Minnesota Press.
Guehenno, Jean Marie
1995   *The End of the Nation-State.* Minneapolis: University of Minnesota
Press.
Gunning, Isabelle R.
2000   "Uneasy Alliances and Solid Sisterhood: A Response to Professor
Obiora's 'Bridges and Barricades.'" In *Global Critical Race Feminism:
A Reader,* ed. A. K. Wing. New York: New York University Press.

Gupta, Akhil, and James Ferguson
1997   *Culture, Power, Place: Explorations in Critical Anthropology.* Durham, NC: Duke University Press.

Gustafson, Bret
2002   "Paradoxes of Liberal Indigenism: Indigenous Movements, State Processes, and Intercultural Reform in Bolivia." In *The Politics of Ethnicity: Indigenous Peoples in Latin American States,* ed. David Maybury-Lewis. Cambridge, MA: Harvard University Press.

Gutiérrez, Margarita
2001   Interview by Maylei Blackwell, September 1. Tape recording. Conducted at the NGO Forum of the UN World Conference Against Racism, Racial Discrimination, Xenophobia, and Related Intolerance (WCAR). Durban, South Africa. [Spanish]

Gutiérrez, Margarita, and Nellys Palomo
1999   "Autonomía con mirada de mujer." In *México: Experiencias de autonomía indígena,* ed. Aracely Burguete Cal y Mayor, 54–86. Copenhagen: International Working Group on Indigenous Affairs.
2000   "A Woman's Eye View of Autonomy." In *Indigenous Autonomy in Mexico,* ed. Aracely Burguete Cal y Mayor, 53–82. Copenhagen: International Working Group on Indigenous Affairs.

Hale, Charles R.
2001   "What Is Activist Research?" *SSRC Newsletter* 2(1–2).
2002   "Does Multiculturalism Menace? Governance, Cultural Rights and the Politics of Identity in Guatemala." *Journal of Latin American Studies* 34(3):485–524.
2004   "Neoliberal Multiculturalism: The Remaking of Cultural Rights and Racial Dominance in Central America." *POLAR* 28(1):10–19.

Handler, Richard, and Jocelyn Linnekin
1984   "Tradition, Genuine or Spurious." *Journal of American Folklore* 97(385): 273–290.

Hardt, Michael
1998   "The Withering of Civil Society." In *Deleuze and Guattari: New Mapping in Politics and Philosophy,* ed. Eleanor Kaufman and Kevin Jon Heller. Minneapolis: University of Minnesota Press.

Hardt, Michael, and Antonio Negri
2000   *Empire.* Cambridge, MA: Harvard University Press.

Harvey, Neil
1998   *The Chiapas Rebellion: The Struggle for Land and Democracy.* Durham, NC: Duke University Press.
[1998] 2000   *La rebelión de Chiapas: La lucha por la tierra y la democracia.* Mexico City: Ediciones ERA.

Hernández Castillo, Rosalva Aída
1994a   "Las voces de las mujeres en el conflicto chiapaneco: Nuevos espacios organizativos y nuevas demandas de género." Manuscript.
1994b   "Reinventing Tradition: The Women's Law." *Akwe:Kon: A Journal of Indigenous Issues* 11(2):67–70.

1996   "From the Community to the Women's State Convention." In *The Explosion of Communities in Chiapas*, ed. June Nash, 53–65. Copenhagen: International Working Group on Indigenous Affairs (IWGIA).

1997   "Between Hope and Adversity: The Struggle of Organized Women in Chiapas since the Zapatista Rebellion." *Journal of Latin American Anthropology* 3(1):102–120.

1998a   "Construyendo la utopía: Esperanzas y desafíos de las mujeres chiapanecas de frente al siglo XXI." In *La otra palabra: Mujeres y violencia en Chiapas, antes y después de Acteal*, comp. R. Aída Hernández. Mexico City: CIESAS/COLEM/CIAM.

1998b   "Indígenas y religiosas en Chiapas: ¿Una nueva teología india desde las mujeres?" *Cristianismo y Sociedad* 35(137):32–55.

1998c   *La otra palabra*. Mexico City: CIESAS/COLEM/CIAM.

2001a   "Entre el etnocentrismo feminista y el esencialismo étnico: Las mujeres indígenas y sus demandas de género." *Debate Feminista* 24:206–229.

2001b   *Histories and Stories from Chiapas: Border Identities in Southern Mexico*. Austin: University of Texas Press.

2001c   *La otra frontera: Identidades múltiples en el Chiapas poscolonial.* Mexico City: CIESAS.

2002a   "Indigenous Law and Identity Politics in Mexico: Indigenous Men's and Women's Struggles for a Multicultural Nation." *POLAR* 24(2): 90–109.

2002b   "National Law and Indigenous Customary Law: The Struggle for Justice of Indigenous Women in Chiapas, Mexico." In *Gender, Justice Development and Rights*, ed. Maxine Molyneux and Shahra Razavi, 384–413. Oxford: Oxford University Press.

2004   "Indígenas y teología india: Límites y aportaciones a las luchas de las mujeres indígenas." In *Religión y género: Enciclopedia iberoamericana de religiones*, ed. Sylvia Marcos. Madrid: Editorial Trotta.

Forthcoming   "De feminismos y poscolonialismos: Reflexiones desde el Sur del Río Bravo." In *Decolonizar el feminismo: Teorías y prácticas desde los márgenes*, ed. Rosalva Aída Hernández Castillo and Liliana Suárez Navaz. Mexico City: CIESAS/PUEG.

Forthcoming   "Descentrando el feminismo: Lecciones aprendidas de las luchas de las mujeres indígenas de América Latina." In *Viejos y nuevos espacios de poder: Mujeres indígenas, resistencia cotidiana y organización colectiva*, ed. Rosalva Aída Hernández Castillo. Mexico City: CIESAS.

Hernández Castillo, Rosalva Aída, Sarela Paz, and María Teresa Sierra, eds.

2004   *El estado y los indígenas en tiempos del PAN: Neoindigenismo, legalidad e identidad*. Mexico City: CIESAS/Porrúa.

Hernández Castillo, Rosalva Aída, and Héctor Ortiz Elizondo

1996   "Las demandas de la mujer indígena en Chiapas." *Nueva Antropología* 15(49):31–39.

Hernández Castillo, Rosalva Aída, and Violeta Zylberberg

2004   "Alzando la vista: Los impactos del zapatismo en la organización y vida cotidiana de las mujeres indígenas." In *Tejiendo historias: Tierra, género y poder en Chiapas*, ed. Maya Lorena Pérez. Mexico City: INAH.

Hernández Navarro, Luis
1999   "The San Andrés Accords: Indians and the Soul." *Cultural Survival Quarterly* 23(1):30–32.

Hernández Navarro, Luis, and Ramón Vera Herrera, comps.
1998   *Acuerdos de San Andrés*. Mexico City: Era.

Hewitt de Alcántara, Cynthia
1984   *Anthropological Perspectives on Rural Mexico*. London: Routledge & Kegan Paul.

Hobsbawm, Eric
1996   "La política de la identidad y la izquierda." *Debate Feminista* 7(14): 86–101.

Hobsbawm, Eric, and Terence Ranger
1983   *The Invention of Tradition*. Cambridge: Cambridge University Press.

Holland, William R.
1963   *Medicina maya en los altos de Chiapas*. Mexico City: Instituto Nacional Indigenista.

hooks, bell
1984   "Black Women: Shaping Feminist Theory." In *Feminist Theory from Margin to Centre*. Boston: South End Press.

Hvostoff, Sophie
2000   "¿Del indio-indito al indígena sujeto? La evolución de la agenda indígena de 1970 a 1994." In *Anuario de Estudios Indígenas* 8:57–82. Tuxtla Gutiérrez: Instituto de Estudios Indígenas, UNACH.

Instituto Nacional Indigenista (INI)
1997   *Seminario latinoamericano: La mujer y los derechos fundamentales de los pueblos indígenas*. Mexico City: INI/SEDESOL.

Jaidopulu Vrijea, María
2000   "Las mujeres indígenas como sujetos políticos." *Chiapas*, no. 9. Mexico City: Era/Instituto de Investigaciones Económicas, UNAM.

Järviluoma Helmi, Pirkko Moisala, and Anni Vilkko
2003   *Gender and Qualitative Methods*. London: Sage.

Jelin, Elizabeth
1987   *Ciudadanía e identidad: Las mujeres en los movimientos sociales latinoamericanos*. Ginebra: Instituto de Investigaciones de las Naciones Unidas para el Desarrollo Social.

Jímenez, Cándida
1999   Interview conducted by Maylei Blackwell, August 23. Tape recording. Oral History Interview I (Sides A & B). Conducted at the Offices of the Coordinadora Nacional de Mujeres Indígenas, Mexico City.

Kabeer, Naila
1992   *Realidades trastocadas: Las jerarquías de género en el pensamiento de desarrollo*. Mexico City: Paidos/PUEG/UNAM.

Kampwirth, Karen
2002   *Women and Guerrilla Movements: Nicaragua, El Salvador, Chiapas, Cuba*. University Park: Pennsylvania State University Press.

Kapur, Ratna
2002   "The Tragedy of Victimization Rhetoric: Resurrecting the 'Native' Subject in International/Post-Colonial Feminist Legal Politics." *Harvard Human Rights Journal* 15(1):1–28.
Keck, Margaret E., and Kathryn Sikkink
1998   *Activists Beyond Borders: Advocacy Networks in International Politics*. Ithaca: Cornell University Press.
Krauze, Enrique
1999   "Chiapas: The Indians' Prophet." *New York Review of Books*, December 16, 65–73.
Kymlicka, Will
1997   *Multicultural Citizenship: A Liberal Theory of Minority Rights*. Oxford: Oxford University Press.
Laclau, Ernesto, and Chantal Mouffe
1985   *Hegemony and Socialist Strategy: Towards a Radical Democratic Politics*. London: Verso.
Lagarde, Marcela
1997   "Etnicidad y género: La autonomía, un nuevo pacto con las mujeres." In *Las Alzadas*, ed. Sara Lovera and Nellys Palomo, 329–338. Mexico City: CIM/CSAPN.
Lamas, Marta
1986   "La antropología feminista y la categoría de género." *Nueva Antropología* 8(30):173–222.
1992   "El movimiento feminista en la década de los ochenta." In *Crisis y sujetos sociales en México*, ed. Enrique de la Garza Toledo. Mexico City: CIIH-UNAM/Porrúa.
1994   "Algunas características del movimiento feminista en la ciudad de México." In *Mujeres y participación política: Avances y desafíos en América Latina*, ed. Magdalena León. Bogotá: TM Editores.
Lamas, Marta, Alicia Martínez, María Luisa Tarrés, and Esperanza Tuñon
1995   "Building Bridges: The Growth of Popular Feminism in Mexico." In *The Challenge of Local Feminisms: Women's Movements in Global Perspective*, ed. Amrita Basu, 324–350. Boulder: Westview Press.
Lau Jaivén, Ana
1987   *La nueva ola del feminismo en México*. Mexico City: Editorial Planeta.
2002   "El nuevo movimiento feminista mexicano a fines del milenio." In *Feminismo en México, ayer y hoy*, ed. Eli Bartra, 120–152. Mexico City: UNAM.
Leyva Solano, Xóchitl
1994a   "De identidades y militancias en la región de conflicto." *La Jornada*, February 1.
1994b   "Sociedad y cultura en la selva lacandona." In *Chiapas, los problemas de fondo*, ed. Moctezuma Navarro, 91–98. Mexico City: CRIM/UNAM.

1999   "De las cañadas a Europa: Niveles, actores y discursos del Nuevo Movimiento Zapatista, NMZ, 1994–1997." *Revista Desacatos* (Spring): 56–87.

2001   "Regional, Communal, and Organizational Transformations in Las Cañadas." *Latin American Perspectives* 28(2):20–44.

2003   "Regional, Communal, and Organizational Transformations in Las Cañadas." In *Mayan Lives, Mayan Utopias: The Indigenous Peoples of Chiapas and the Zapatista Rebellion,* ed. Jan Rus, Rosalva Aída Hernández Castillo and Shannan Mattiace, 161–184. Lanham, MD: Rowan & Littlefield.

Leyva Solano, Xóchitl, and Gabriel Ascencio Franco

1996   *Lacandonia al filo del agua.* Mexico City: Centro de Investigaciones y Estudios Superiores en Antropología Social; San Cristóbal de Las Casa: Centro de Investigaciones Humanísticas de Mesoamérica y el Estado de Chiapas; Tuxtla Gutiérrez: Universidad de Ciencias y Artes del Estado de Chiapas; Mexico City: Fondo de Cultura Económica.

Linnekin, Jocelyn

1982   "Defining Tradition: Variation on Hawaiian Identity." *American Ethnologist* 10:241–252.

Lomelí González, Arturo

2000   "Indian Peoples and Zapatista Autonomies." In *Indigenous Autonomy in Mexico,* ed. Aracely Burguete Cal y Mayor, 216–239. Copenhagen: International Working Group on Indigenous Affairs.

López Arellano, Olivia, and José Blanco Gil

1993   *La modernización neoliberal en salud: México en los ochenta.* Mexico City: UAM.

Lorde, Audre

1984   *Sister/Outsider.* Berkeley, CA: Crossing Press.

Lorena [pseudonym]

2000   Interview by Maylei Blackwell, April 1. Tape recording. Conducted at the Segundo Encuentro Nacional de Mujeres Indígenas, Chilpancingo, Guerrero.

Lovera, Sara, and Nellys Palomo, eds.

1997   *Las Alzadas.* Mexico City: Centro de Información de la Mujer/ Convergencia Socialista, Agrupación Política Nacional.

Lowe, Lisa

1996   *Immigrant Acts: Asian American Cultural Politics.* Durham, NC: Duke University Press.

Lowe, Lisa, and David Lloyd

1997   *The Politics of Culture in the Shadow of Capital.* Durham, NC: Duke University Press.

Magallón, Carmen

1988   "La participación de las mujeres en las organizaciones campesinas: Algunas limitaciones." In *Las mujeres en el campo,* ed. Josefina Aranda. Oaxaca: Instituto de Investigaciones Sociológicas.

Mani, Lata
1998   *Contentious Traditions: The Debate on Sati in Colonial India*. Berkeley: University of California Press.
Maier, Elizabeth
1994   "Sex and Class as a Single Entity." In *Compañeras: Voices from the Latin American Women's Movement*, ed. Gaby Kluppers, 40–45. London: Latin American Bureau; Boulder: Westview Press.
Marcos, Subcomandante Insurgente, and Juana Ponce de León
2001   *Our Word Is Our Weapon: Selected Writings*. New York: Seven Stories Press.
Marcos, Sylvia
1997   "Mujeres indígenas: Notas sobre un feminismo naciente." *Cuadernos Feministas* 1(2):10–16.
1999a   "La otra mujer: Una propuesta de reflexión para el VIII Congreso Feminista Latinoamericano y del Caribe." *Cuadernos Feministas* 2(9):7–9.
1999b   "Twenty-five Years of Mexican Feminisms." *Women's Studies International Forum* 22(4):431–433.
Marshall, T. H.
1950   *Citizenship and Social Class and Other Essays*. Cambridge, MA: Cambridge University Press.
Marston, Sallie A.
2000   "The Social Construction of Scale." *Progress in Human Geography* 24(2):219–242.
Massey, Doreen B.
1994   *Space, Place, and Gender*. Minneapolis: University of Minnesota Press.
Massolo, Alejandra
1992   *Por amor y coraje: Mujeres en movimientos urbanos de la ciudad de México*. Mexico City: El Colegio de México.
Matias Alonso, Marcos
1997   *La autonomía y el movimiento indígena en Guerrero (Homaje a Sabino Estrada Guadalupe)*. Mexico City: Convergencia Socialista.
Mattiace, Shannan L.
1997   "Zapata Vive! The EZLN, Indian Politics, and the Autonomy Movement in Mexico." *Journal of Latin American Anthropology* 3(1): 32–71.
1998   "Peasant and Indian: Political Identity and Indian Autonomy in Chiapas, Mexico, 1970–1990." Ph.D. diss., University of Texas, Austin.
2001   "Regional Renegotiations of Spaces: Tojolabal Ethnic Identity in Las Margaritas, Chiapas." *Latin American Perspectives* 28(2):73–97.
2003a   "Regional Renegotiations of Spaces: Tojolabal Ethnic Identity in Las Margaritas, Chiapas." In *Mayan Lives, Mayan Utopias: The Indigenous Peoples of Chiapas and the Zapatista Rebellion*, ed. Jan Rus, Rosalva Aída Hernández Castillo and Shannan L. Mattiace, 109–134. Lanham, MD: Rowan & Littlefield.
2003b   *To See with Two Eyes: Peasant Activism and Indian Autonomy in Chiapas, Mexico*. Albuquerque: University of New Mexico Press.

McClaurin, Irma
2001   *Black Feminist Anthropology: Theory, Politics, Praxis, and Poetics.*
New Brunswick, NJ: Rutgers University Press.
Mejía, María, and Sergio Sarmiento
1987   *La lucha indígena: Un reto a la ortodoxia.* Mexico City: Siglo XXI.
Mejia, Susana
2005   "Movimientos de mujeres indígenas en la Sierra Norte de Puebla."
Ph.D. diss., Universidad Autónoma Metropolitana (UAM/Xochimilco).
Merry, Sally Engle
2003   "Human Rights Law and the Demonization of Culture (and Anthropology Along the Way)." POLAR 26(1):55–77.
Millán, Márgara
1996a   "Mujeres indígenas y zapatismo: Nuevos horizontes de visibilidad."
Cuadernos Agrarios 13:156–167.
1996b   "Las zapatistas de fin del milenio: Hacia políticas de autorrepresent-
ación de las mujeres indígenas." *Revista Chiapas* 3:19–32.
1997   "Chiapas y sus mujeres indígenas: De su diversidad y resistencia."
Revista Chiapas 4:209–216.
1999   "Mujeres indígenas y zapatismo: Nuevos horizontes de visibilidad."
In *Las Alzadas*, 2d ed., ed. Nellys Palomo and Sara Lovera, 92–109.
Mexico City: CIMAC/Convergencia Socialista.
Millet, Stanley
1999   "Reflections on Traditional Medicine." *Journal of Alternative and
Complementary Medicine* 5(2):203–205.
Mohanty, Chandra Talpade
1991   "Under Western Eyes: Feminist Scolarship and Colonial Disccourses."
In *Third World Women and the Politics of Feminism,* ed. Chandra
Mohanty, Ann Russo and Lourdes Torres, 57–79. Bloomington: Indiana University Press.
2003   *Feminism without Borders: Decolonizing Theory, Practicing Solidarity.* Durham, NC: Duke University Press.
Mohanty, Chandra Talpade, Ann Russo, and Lourdes Torres, eds.
1991   *Third World Women and the Politics of Feminism.* Bloomington: Indiana University Press.
Moisés Gandhi Relator@s
1997   *Salud en manos del pueblo: Memoria del primer foro encuentro de
promotores de salud.* San Cristóbal de las Casas: Moises Gandhi.
Molyneux, Maxine
1985   "Mobilization without Emancipation? Women's Interests, State and
Revolution in Nicaragua." *Feminist Studies* 2(2):227–254.
2003   *Movimientos de mujeres en América Latina: Estudio teórico com-
parado.* Madrid: Colección Feminismos Ediciones Cátedra.
Montoya, Rosario, Leslie Jo Frazier, and Janise Hurtig
2002   *Gender's Place: Feminist Anthropologies of Latin America.* New York:
Palgrave-Macmillan.

Moore, Henrietta
1999   *Antropología y feminismo.* Valencia: Ediciones Cátedra.
Moraga, Cherríe, and Gloria Anzaldúa
[1981] 2002   *This Bridge Called My Back: Writings by Radical Women of Color.* Berkeley, CA: Third Woman Press.
Morales Bermúdez, Jesús
1992   "El Congreso Indígena de Chiapas: Un testimonio." In *Anuario 1991,* 241–371. Tuxtla Gutiérrez: Instituto Chiapaneco de Cultura.
Muñoz Ramírez, Gloria
2003   *EZLN: 20 y 10, el fuego y la palabra.* Mexico City: Demos, Desarrollo de Medio, La Jornada Ediciones.
Nash, June
1970   *In the Eyes of the Ancestors: Belief and Behavior in a Mayan Community.* New Haven, CT: Yale University Press.
1993   "Maya Household Production in the Modern World." In *The Impact of Global Exchange on Middle American Artisans,* ed. June Nash. Albany: State University of New York Press.
2001   *Mayan Visions: The Quest for Autonomy in an Age of Globalization.* New York: Routledge.
Nash, June, and Alejandro Parellada
1995   "La explosión de comunidades en Chiapas." Document no. 6, International Working Group on Indigenous Affairs (IWGIA). Copenhagen.
Obiora, L. Amede
2000   "Bridges and Barricades: Rethinking Polemics and Intransigence in the Campaign against Female Circumcision." In *Global Critical Race Feminism: A Reader,* ed. A. K. Wing. New York: New York University Press.
Okin, Susan Moller
1999   *Is Multiculturalism Bad for Women?* Princeton: Princeton University Press.
Olivera Bustamante, Mercedes
1979   "Sobre la explotación y opresión de las mujeres acasilladas en Chiapas." *Cuadernos Agrarios* 9:43–55.
1994   "Aguascalientes y el movimiento social de las mujeres chiapanecas." In *A propósito de la insurgencia en Chiapas,* ed. Silvia Soriano Solis. Mexico City: Asociación para el Desarrollo de la Investigación Científica y Humanística.
1995   "Práctica feminista en el Movimiento Zapatista de Liberación Nacional." In *Chiapas y las mujeres, qué?* ed. Rosa Rojas, 2:168–184. Mexico City: Correa Feminista.
1989   "Sobre la explotación y la opresión de las mujeres acasilladas en Chiapas." *Cuadernos Agrarios* (9):30–48.
2004   "Sobre las profundidades del mandar obedeciendo." In *Tejiendo historias: Tierra, género y poder en Chiapas,* ed. Maya Lorena Pérez Ruiz. Mexico City: UNAM.

Olivera, Mercedes, and Roberto Ramírez Méndez
2001   "Poder e identidades de etnia y género en el estado de Chiapas." In *Identidades indígenas y género,* ed. M. Olivera. San Cristóbal de las Casas: CONACYT/UNACH.

Otzoy, Irma
Forthcoming   "Indigenous Human Rights in the Maya Region: Global Politics, Moral Engagements and Cultural Contentions." In *Human Rights in the Maya Region: Global Politics, Moral Engagements, and Cultural Contentions,* ed. Shannon Speed, Xochitl Leyva Solano, and Pedro Pitarch. Durham, NC: Duke University Press.

Page Pliego, Jaime T.
2000   "Medicina indígena: Interrelación y globalización." In *II Encuentro Indígena de las Américas: Memoria 1999, 19–21 abril, Chiapas, México.* San Cristóbal de las Casas: Sna Jtz'ibajom.

Palacios, Guillermo
1999   "Lectura, identidad campesina y nación: El proyecto sociocultural de El Maestro Rural en inicios de los años treinta." In *Bajo el signo del estado,* ed. José Eduardo Zárate Hernández, 35–53. Zamora: El Colegio de Michoacán.

Palomo, Nellys
n.d.   "Tejiendo visibilidad: La presencia de las mujeres indígenas." Unpublished paper.

Palomo, Nellys, Yolanda Castro, and Cristina Orci
1999   "Mujeres indígenas de Chiapas: Nuestros derechos, costumbres y tradiciones." In *Las Alzadas,* 2d ed., ed. Nellys Palomo and Sara Lovera, 65–81. Mexico City: CIMAC/Convergencia Socialista.

Palomo, Nellys, and Sara Lovera, eds.
1999   *Las Alzadas.* 2d ed. Mexico City: CIMAC/Convergencia Socialista.

Paniagua, Alicia
1983   "Chiapas en la coyuntura centroamericana." *Cuadernos Políticos* (38): 36–54.

París Pombo, Maria Dolores
2000   "La mujer, el indio y la patria en el discurso político chiapaneco (1970–1993)." *Desacatos* 4:103–118.

Patricio, María de Jesús
2000   Interview conducted by Maylei Blackwell, April 1. Tape recording. Oral History Interview I (Side A). Conducted at the Segundo Encuentro Nacional de Mujeres Indígenas, Chilpancingo, Guerrero.

Pérez, Emma
1999   *The Decolonial Imaginary: Writing Chicanas into History.* Bloomington: Indiana University Press.

Pérez Castro, Ana Bella
1988   *Entre montañas y cafetales.* Mexico City: UNAM.

Pineda, Francisco
1996   "La guerra de baja intensidad." *Chiapas* (2):173–195.

Postero, Nancy
2001   "Constructing Indigenous Citizens in Multicultural Bolivia." www.
        geocities.com.
*Propuestas de las mujeres indígenas al Congreso Nacional Indígena:
Seminario Legislación y Mujer: Reformas al artículo 4 constitucional.*
1996   Mexico City: SEDEPAC.
Rangel, Georgina
1997   "Vivir entre la guerra." In *Las Alzadas,* ed. Sara Lovera and Nellys
        Palomo. Mexico City: CIMAC/Convergencia Socialista.
Regino, Adelfo
2001   "Negación constitucional." *La Jornada,* April 28.
Robles, Sofía
1999   Interview by Maylei Blackwell, August 31. Tape recording. Oral His-
        tory Interview I (Sides A & B). Conducted at the Offices of Servicios
        de Pueblo Mixe (SER), Oaxaca City, Oaxaca.
Rojas, Rosa
1995   *Chiapas: La paz violenta.* Mexico City: Ediciones La Jornada.
Rojas, Rosa, ed.
1994   *Chiapas y las mujeres, qué?* Vols. 1 and 2. Colección del Dicho al
        Hecho. Mexico City: La Correa Feminista.
Rosaldo, Renato
1997   "Cultural Citizenship, Inequality, and Multiculturalism." In *Latino
        Cultural Citizenship: Claiming Identity, Space, and Rights,* ed. Wil-
        liam V. Flores and Rina Benmayor, 27–38. Boston: Beacon Press.
Rose, Nikolas
1999   *Powers of Freedom: Reframing Political Thought.* Cambridge: Cam-
        bridge University Press.
Rosenbaum, Brenda
1993   *With Our Heads Bowed: The Dynamics of Gender in a Maya Com-
        munity.* Albany: Institute for Mesoamerica Studies, State University of
        New York.
Rovira Sancho, Guiomar
1994   *¡Zapata Vive! La rebelión indígena de Chiapas contada por sus pro-
        tagonistas.* Barcelona: Virus Editorial.
1997   *Mujeres de maíz.* Mexico City: Era.
2001   "Ahora es nuestra hora, la hora de las mujeres indígenas." *Debate
        Feminista* 12(24).
Rowbotham, Sheila
1992   *Women in Movement: Feminism and Social Action.* New York:
        Routledge.
Ruiz Hernández, Margarito
1999   La Asamblea Nacional Indígena Plural por la Autonomía (ANIPA). In
        México: Experiencias de autonomía indígena, ed. Aracely Burguete,
        8–20. Copenhagen: International Working Group on Indigenous Af-
        fairs (IWGIA).

Rus, Diana
1990   *La crisis económica y la mujer indígena: El Caso de San Juan Chamula, Chiapas.* San Cristóbal de las Casas: INAREMAC.

Rus, Jan
1994   "The 'Comunidad Revolucionaria Institucional': Subverting Native Government in Highland Chiapas, 1936–1968." In *Everyday Forms of State Formation: Revolution and the Negotiation of Rule in Modern Mexico,* ed. G. M. Joseph and D. Nugent. Durham, NC: Duke University Press.

Rus, Jan, Rosalva Aída Hernández Castillo, and Shannon Mattiace
2003   *Mayan Lives, Mayan Utopias: The Indigenous Peoples of Chiapas and the Zapatista Rebellion.* Lanham, MD: Rowan & Littlefield.

Sabines, Juan
1980   *Primer Informe de Gobierno.* Tuxtla Gutiérrez: Gobierno del Estado de Chiapas.

San Andrés Accords on Indigenous Rights and Culture
1999   "San Andés Accords on Indigenous Rights and Culture." Trans. Lynn Stephen and Jonathan Fox. *Cultural Survival Quarterly* 12(1): 33–38.

Sánchez, Consuelo
2003   "Identidad, género y autonomía: Las mujeres indígenas en el debate." *Memoria,* no. 174:12–18.

Sánchez Nestor, Martha
2001   "Ya las mujeres quieren todo(s)." *Cuadernos Feministas* 3(15):15–17.
2003   "Derechos de la mujer indígena." *Memoria,* no. 174:19–20.

Sandoval Ceres, Tomasa
1999   Interview conducted by Maylei Blackwell, August 22. Tape recording. Oral History Interview I (Sides A & B). Conducted at the Taller Nacional Sobre Mujeres Indígenas en los Procesos Autonómicos, Mexico City.

Sandoval, Chela
1991   "U.S. Third World Feminism: The Theory and Method of Oppositional Consciousness in the Postmodern World." *Genders* 10:1–24.
1998   "Mestizaje as Method: Feminists-of-Color Challenge the Canon." In *Living Chicana Theory,* ed. Carla Trujillo, 352–370. Berkeley, CA: Third Woman Press.
2000   *Methodology of the Oppressed.* Minneapolis: University of Minnesota Press.

Sandoval Ceres, Tomasa
1999   Interview by Maylei Blackwell, August 22. Conducted at the Taller Nacional Sobre Mujeres Indígenas en los Procesos Autonómicos, Mexico City.

Santamaria, Maya
1996   "Two Watershed Encounters for Indigneous Women in Mexico." *Abya Yala News* 10(1):6–7.

Sault, Nicole

2001   "Godparenthood Ties among Zapotec Women and the Effects of Prot-
         estant Conversion." In *Holy Saints and Fiery Preachers: The Anthro-
         pology of Protestantism in Mexico and Central America,* ed. James W.
         Dow and Alan R. Sandstrom, 116–146. Westport, CT: Praeger.

Sierra, María Teresa

2001   "Human Rights, Gender and Ethnicity: Legal Claims and Anthropo-
         logical Challenges in Mexico." *POLAR* 23(2):76–92.

2002   "The Challenge to Diversity in Mexico: Human Rights, Gender, and
         Ethnicity." Working Paper no. 49. Max Planck Institute for Social An-
         thropology, Halle, Germany.

Smith, Neil

1992   "Geography, Difference and the Politics of Scale." In *Postmodern-
         ism and the Social Sciences,* ed. Joe Dherty, Elspeth Graham and Mo
         Malek, 57–79. New York: St. Martin's Press.

Speed, Shannon

2002   "Global Discourses on the Local Terrain: Human Rights and Indig-
         enous Identity in Chiapas." *Cultural Dynamics* 14(2):205–228.

2003a   "Dangerous Discourses: Human Rights and Multiculturalism in Mex-
         ico." Paper presented at the annual meeting of the American Anthro-
         pological Association, November, Chicago.

2003b   "Indigenous Women and Gendered Resistance in the Wake of Acteal."
         In *Women of Chiapas: Making History in Times of Struggle and Hope,*
         ed. Christine Kovic and Christine Eber, 47–65. New York: Routledge.

2004   "Lucha por la tierra, globalización e identidad: La etnohistoria y et-
         nopresente de Nicolás Ruiz." In *Tejiendo historias: Tierra, género y
         poder en Chiapas,* ed. Maya Lorena Pérez, 91–118. Mexico City: In-
         stituto Nacional de Antropología e Historia (INAH).

2005   "Dangerous Discourses: Human Rights and Multiculturalism in
         Mexico." POLAR 28(1):29–51. Special issue, ed. Shannon Speed and
         Teresa Sierra.

Speed, Shannon, and Alvaro Reyes

2002   "In Our Own Defense: Globalization, Rights and Resistance in Chi-
         apas." POLAR 25(1):69–89.

2005   "Rights, Resistance, and Radical Alternatives: The Red de Defensores
         Comunitarios and Zapatismo in Chiapas." *Humboldt Journal of So-
         cial Relations* 29(1):47–82.

Spivak, Gayatri

1988   "Can the Subaltern Speak?" In *Marxism and the Interpretation of
         Cultures,* ed. Cary Nelson and Lawrence Grossberg, 271–315. Ur-
         bana: University of Illinois Press.

Staheli, Lynn A.

1994   "Empowering Political Struggle: Spaces and Scales of Resistance." *Po-
         litical Geography* 13(5):387–391.

Stavenhagen, Rodolfo

1968   *Ensayos sobre las clases sociales en México.* Mexico City: Editorial
         Nuestro Tiempo.

Stephen, Lynn

1989   "Popular Feminism in Mexico." *Z Magazine* 2(December): 102–106.

1991   *Zapotec Women.* Austin: University of Texas Press.

1997a   "Redefined Nationalism in Building a Movement for Indigenous Autonomy in Southern Mexico." *Journal of American Anthropology* 3(1): 72–101.

1997b   *Women and Social Movements in Latin America: Power from Below.* Austin: University of Texas Press.

1998a   "Género y democracia: Lecciones de Chiapas." In *Género y cultura en América Latina, cultura y participación política,* vol. 1, ed. María Luisa Tarrés, 311–334. Mexico City: Colegio de México.

1998b   *Mujeres zapotecas.* Oaxaca: Instituto Oaxaqueño de las Culturas.

2000   "The Construction of Indigenous Suspects: Militarization and the Gendered and Ethnic Dynamics of Human Rights Abuses in Southern Mexico." *American Ethnologist* 26(4): 822–842.

2002   *¡Zapata Lives! Histories and Cultural Politics in Southern Mexico.* Berkeley: University of California Press.

2005   *Zapotec Women: Gender, Class, and Ethnicity in Globalized Oaxaca.* Durham, NC: Duke University Press.

Swynegedouw, Eric

1997   "Excluding the Other: The Production of Scale and Scaled Politics." In *Geographies of Economies,* ed. Roger Lee and Jane Wills, 167–176. London: Arnold.

Taylor, Charles

1994   "The Politics of Recognition." In *Charles Taylor: Multiculturalism,* ed. Amy Gutmann, 25–73. Princeton: Princeton University Press.

Tiburcio, Hermalinda

2000   Interview by Maylei Blackwell, March 31. Tape recording. Conducted at the Segundo Encuentro Nacional de Mujeres Indígenas, Chilpancingo, Guerrero.

Toledo Tello, Sonia

1986   "El papel de la cultura en el proceso de subordinación de las mujeres indígenas de Chiapas." In *Anuario del Centro de Estudios Indígenas,* 73–87. Tuxtla Gutiérrez: Centro de Estudios Indígenas, UNACH.

2002   *Fincas, poder y cultura en Simojovel, Chiapas.* Mexico City: PROIMMSE/UNAM-IEI/UNACH.

Touraine, Alan

1987   *Actores sociales y sistemas políticas en América Latina.* Santiago: PREALC.

Trinh, T. Min-ha

1988   *Woman, Native, Other: Writing Postcoloniality and Feminism.* Bloomington: Indiana University Press.

Tuñón, Esperanza

1997   *Mujeres en escena: De la tramoya al protagonismo (1982–1994).* Mexico City: Programa de Estudios de Género.

Tuñón Pablos, Esperanza, Martha Rojas Wiesner, and
Georgina Sánchez Ramírez.
1998   *Las mujeres del estado de Chiapas: Diagnóstico sociodemográfico de
        las mujeres de Chiapas, 1990–1997.* San Cristóbal de las Casas: Pro-
        grama Estatal de la Mujer de Chiapas/UNICEF/El Colegio de la Fron-
        tera Sur.
Turbicio, Hermalinda
2000   Interview by Maylei Blackwell, March 31. Tape recording. Oral His-
        tory Interview I (Side A). Conducted at the Segundo Encuentro Nacio-
        nal de Mujeres Indígenas, Chilpancingo, Guerrero.
Ulin, Robert C.
1995   "Invention and Representation as Cultural Capital." *American An-
        thropologist* 97(3):519–527.
Van Cott, Donna Lee
1998   "Roads to Beijing: Reflections from Inside the Process." In *Roads to
        Beijing: Fourth World Conference on Women in Latin America and the
        Caribbean.* Lima: Ediciones Flora Tristán; Santafé de Bogotá: UNICEF;
        Quito: UNIFEM.
2000a   *The Friendly Liquidation of the Past: The Politics of Diversity in Latin
        America.* Pittsburgh: University of Pittsburgh Press.
2000b   "Constitutional Reform and Ethnic Rights in Latin America." *Parlia-
        mentary Affairs* 53:41–54.
Vargas, Virginia
1999   Interview by Maylei Blackwell, December 8. Tape recording. Oral His-
        tory Interview I (Sides A & B). Conducted in Santa Cruz, California.
Vera Herrera, Ramón
1998   "La construcción del Congreso Nacional Indígena." In *Acuerdos de
        San Andrés,* ed. Luis Hernández Navarro and Ramón Vera Herrera,
        33–48. Mexico City: Era.
Villa, Rufina
2000   Interview by Maylei Blackwell, April 1. Tape recording. Oral History
        Interview I (Side A). Conducted at the Segundo Encuentro Nacional
        de Mujeres Indígenas, Chilpancingo, Guerrero.
Villafuerte, Daniel, et al.
1999   *La tierra en Chiapas: Viejos problemas nuevos.* Mexico City:
        UNICACH/Plaza Valadez Editores.
Villoro, Luis
[1950] 1984   *Los grandes momentos del indigenismo en México.* Mexico
        City: Ediciones de la Casa Chata 9, CIESAS.
Wade, Peter
1997   *Race and Ethnicity in Latin America.* Chicago: Pluto Press.
Warren, Kay B., and Jean E. Jackson
2002   *Indigenous Movements, Self-Representation, and the State in Latin
        America.* Austin: University of Texas Press.
Washinawatok, Ingrid
1998   "International Emergence: Twenty-one Years at the United Nations.
        New York Law Review 3(1):41–57.

Wasserstrom, Robert
1983   *Class and Society in Central Chiapas*. Berkeley: University of California Press.
Wieringa, S.
1994   "Women's Interests and Empowerment: Gender Planning Reconsidered." *Development and Change* 25:829–848.
Womack, John, Jr., ed.
1999   *Rebellion in Chiapas: An Historical Reader*. New York: New Press.
Young, Iris Marion
1990   *Justice and the Politics of Difference*. Princeton, NJ: Princeton University Press.
2000   *La justicia y la política de la diferencia*. Madrid: Ediciones Cátedra/Universidad de Valencia/Instituto de la Mujer.
ZNET
2003   "Chiapas Watch. Words at Oventik, Comandanta Esther." August 12. www.zmag.org/content/showarticle.cfm?SectionID=8&ItemID=4038. Accessed December 15, 2005.

INDEX

abortion, 40, 60, 61, 74n.17
Abya Yala, 153n.16
Acteal massacre, xxix, xxx, 111, 112, 114n.7, 182, 201n.7
action-investigation, 74n.13
activist research, 49
adultery, 70
Advisory Commission (Comisión Promotora), 151n.10
Afro-American movement, 66
Agrarian Revolutionary Law, xv, xviin.5
agriculture, 11, 87, See also coffee production
Agustín, Begoña de, 73n.9
alcohol and alcoholism, 13, 90–91, 92, 189, 199, 200, 226, 228–229
Alianza Nacional Campesina Independiente "Emiliano Zapata" (ANCIEZ), xi, xii
alimony and child support, 70
Alvarez, Luis H., 25
Álvarez, Sonia E., 39, 149
Ana María, Major, 83–84
ANCIEZ (Alianza Nacional Campesina Independiente "Emiliano Zapata"), xi, xii
ANIPA (Asamblea Nacional Indígena Plural por la Autonomía/National Plural Indigenous Assembly for

Autonomy), 34, 118, 126, 128–130, 133, 134, 151n.8, 185
anthropology: and activist research, 49; feminist anthropology, 48–49, 64, 65–66; of indigenous women in Mexico, 42–43
anti-poverty programs, 138, 171, 180–181, See also poverty
ARIC-Union of Uniones (ARIC-UU), x–xi, 162
Arizpe, Lourdes, 65
artisans, 78, 87, 102
Asamblea Nacional Indígena Plural por la Autonomía (National Plural Indigenous Assembly for Autonomy, ANIPA), 34, 118, 126, 128–130, 133, 134, 151n.8, 185
assimilation. See mestizaje
autonomous municipalities and regions, xiv, xv, 45, 112, 113, 136–137, 176
Autonomous Pluriethnic Regions (RAPs), 129–130
Autonomous University of Chiapas (Universidad Autónoma de Chiapas, UNACH), 62
autonomy: ANIPA's proposal for Autonomous Pluriethnic Regions (RAPs), 129–130; identity, rights, and, 183–186; indigenous

Council of Indigenous Women,
CONAMI), 115, 118, 122–123,
126, 131–133, 135, 137–139,
141, 142, 149–150, 151–
152n.12, 154n.28, 185
Coordinadora Nacional de Mujeres
Indígenas (National Council of
Indigenous Women, CNMI), 50,
58, 63–64, 68, 73n.11, 115, 130,
136, 141, 149, 152n.12, 185
Coordinadora Nacional Plan de
Ayala (Plan de Ayala National
Council, CNPA), 77
COPLAMAR (National Social Security Institute, General Council of
the National Plan for Deprived
Zones and Marginalized Groups),
101
cortacabezas (headhunters), 194–195
Costa Rica, 73n.9
Cuba, 43
cultural/ethnic citizenship, 36–39
culture and tradition. *See* tradition
and culture
curanderos, 179, 198, *See also* health
services

Dagnino, Evelina, 39
David, Comandante, 151n.10
De la Peña, Guillermo, 36
De los Santos, Marcelino Isidro,
152n.13
death: *cortacabezas* (headhunters)
stories, 194–195; of dissident
peasants, 110, 137; of indigenous
women, 76, 81, 110, 178; infant
mortality, 76, 178; maternal
mortality, 76, 178; poverty deaths,
76, 84, 178
Declaración del Sol, 143
differential consciousness, 145–146,
153–154n.25
Diocesan Council of Women (Coordinadora Diocesana de Mujeres,
CODIMUJ), 60, 78, 101, 182,
185

Dircio, Limni Irazema, 135–136
domestic violence: and adultery, 70;
against dissident women, 43, 90–
91; against indigenous women,
3, 9, 13, 43, 52, 70, 91, 92, 136,
228–229; and alcoholism, 90–91,
92, 189, 228–229; feminist fight
against, 61, 63, 64; legislation
on, 70; penalties for, 40; prevention of, 132, 200; and Zapatismo,
90–91
doxa, 92–93

earthquake in Mexico City, 40
Eber, Christine, 43, 162, 166
ecclesiastical base communities
(comunidades eclesiales de base,
CEBs), 69, 78, 120
Echeverría, Luis, 101
Eckstein, Susan, 36
Ecological Green Party (Partido
Verde Ecologista de México), 157
Ecuador, 46, 48, 141, 143, 152n.15,
153n.19, 153n.24
education: of indigenous peoples,
10; of indigenous women, 3, 8–9,
10, 28, 60, 82, 83, 87, 108, 182,
191–192; nursery and preschool
education, 87; technical schools
for women, 87; and Women's
Solidarity Action Team, 73n.10;
and Zapatismo, 83; Zapatista
movement's demand for, 47
Ehler, Tracy, 65
ejidatario, 163, 174n.1, 175n.3
ejidos: in Chiapas, 99; definition
of, 174n.1; formation of *ejidos*,
x, 174n.1; and governance of
Tojola'bal communities, xvi, 158,
159–160, 162–166, 172, 174–
175n.3; and indigenous peoples,
12, 189; and indigenous women,
45, 163–166, 174–175n.3;
meaning of, xvin.2; NAFTA and
dismantling of, 148
El Salvador, 43, 73n.9

promotoras de salud (lay health workers), 194
RAPs (Autonomous Pluriethnic Regions), 129–130
Red de Investigación Participativa (Participative Investigation Network), 74n.13
Red Nacional de Asesoras y Promotoras Rurales (National Network of Rural Advocates and Advisors), 73n.8, 73n.11
refugees, 63, 73n.9, 78, 98, 111, 182, 225
reproductive rights. *See* birth control; childbearing; sterilization
rights. *See* human rights; Women's Revolutionary Law (Ley Revolucionaria de Mujeres)
Robles, Sofía, 123, 133, 142, 143
Rodríguez Brandao, Carlos, 74n.13
Rojas, Rosa, 221n.4
romerias (pilgrimages), 159
Rosaldo, Renato, 36
Rosalinda, Comandanta, 199
Rousseau, Jean-Jacques, 39
Rovira, Guiomar, 43, 162
Rowbotham, Sheila, 72n.5
Ruiz, Cristina, 169–170
Ruiz, Marcelina, 170
Ruiz, Bishop Samuel, x, 100, 182
Rus, Jan, 159
Rushin, Kate, 57–58, 154n.29
Ruz, Mario Humberto, 159

salaries. *See* wages for women
Salinas de Gortari, Carlos, xii
San Andrés Accords on Indigenous Rights and Culture, xiii–xiv, xv, 30, 34, 37, 104, 107, 127–131, 140, 148, 151n.6, 218
San Cristóbal Center for Ecology and Health (Centro de Capacitación para la Ecologia y Salud de San Cristóbal, CCESC), 78
Sánchez, Consuelo, 186
Sánchez, Marta, 136

Sanchez, Martha, 133
Sánchez Nestor, Martha, 185
Sandoval, Chela, 145, 153–154n.25, 184
scale: definition of, 116; organizing by indigenous women and politics of scale, 115–150, 154n.28; politics of, 115–118
SEDEPAC, 140
self-determination principle, 80
Seminar on Reforms to Article 4 of the Constitution, 126
Seminar on the Legislation and Women, Article 4 of the Constitution, 140
SER (Servicios del Pueblo Mixe), 123, 152n.12
Servicios del Pueblo Mixe (SER), 123, 152n.12
sexual assault. *See* rape
Sierra, Gloria, 73n.9
Sikkink, Kathryn, 148–149
social movements. *See* new social movements
social rights, 34–36
Spanish language. *See* language
Speed, Shannon, ix–xvi, 33–54, 162, 203–221
Spivak, Gayatri, 208
Staheli, Lynn, 116
State Convention of Chiapanecan Women (Convención Estatal de Mujeres Chiapanecas), 68–69, 120–121
Stephen, Lynn M., ix–xvi, 33–54, 157–175
sterilization, 135, 138, 193
Susana, Comandanta, 31–32

TABAMEX (Mexican Tobacco Institute), 101
Teotitlán del Valle, Oaxaca, 166–173
Tiburcio, Hermalinda, 123–124, 125, 136–138
tierras recuperadas ("recovered" lands), 181–182